THE ART OF HENRI-MATISSE

BOOKS WRITTEN BY STAFF MEMBERS OF THE BARNES FOUNDATION

THE ART IN PAINTING
Albert C. Barnes

THE AESTHETIC EXPERIENCE
Laurence Buermeyer

AN APPROACH TO ART
Mary Mullen

ART AND EDUCATION
Dewey, Barnes, Buermeyer, Mullen, de Mazia

ART AS EXPERIENCE
John Dewey

PRIMITIVE NEGRO SCULPTURE
Paul Guillaume and Thomas Munro

THE FRENCH PRIMITIVES AND THEIR FORMS
Albert C. Barnes and Violette de Mazia

THE ART OF RENOIR
Albert C. Barnes and Violette de Mazia

THE ART OF HENRI-MATISSE
Albert C. Barnes and Violette de Mazia

THE ART OF CÉZANNE
Albert C. Barnes and Violette de Mazia

Henri - Matisse

THE ART OF
HENRI-MATISSE

BY

ALBERT C. BARNES

AND

VIOLETTE DE MAZIA

ONE HUNDRED AND
FIFTY-ONE ILLUSTRATIONS

Published by

THE BARNES FOUNDATION PRESS

MERION, PENNA.

Library of Congress Catalog Card Number: 60–8271

Printed in the United States of America
By William J. Dornan
Collingdale, Pennsylvania

PREFACE

FOR more than twenty years representative paintings of Matisse's have hung in the collection of the Barnes Foundation side by side with examples of the great traditions of plastic art, past and present. In the systematic study of these traditions which has gone on during these years, it has therefore been possible to relate Matisse's work to that of his antecedents and contemporaries. The general principles of method underlying our study, and their application to painting, were first published in 1925 in *The Art in Painting;* further application, primarily to a more restricted field, was made in *The French Primitives and Their Forms,* published in 1931. In the present volume the same method is employed in a comprehensive investigation of Matisse's place in the general traditions of painting, and his distinctive purposes and achievements as an artist. Although Matisse is also a sculptor of distinction, a study of his work in that field is obviously beyond the scope of the present treatise.

Our study has been strictly objective, made in the presence of Matisse's pictures and of the other works of art upon which he drew. After the book was well under way there was held in 1931 the Matisse Exhibition at Paris, in which for six weeks were shown about one hundred and fifty pictures illustrating nearly every phase and period of his career. During the entire exhibition we made it our daily occupation to study and make notes on the pictures, and were able to compile a mass of material which has greatly extended the scope of our inquiry and the range of our illustrations. These data we have endeavored to put in such a form as to simplify the study of Matisse's work and warrant a judgment of its value.

The book is divided into two parts, the text proper, in which an account is given of the general characteristics of Matisse's work, and an appendix, containing detailed analyses of particular pictures. In these analyses the attempt is made both to render concrete the conceptions of method and æsthetic principles already stated in the text, and to cover all the important types of Matisse's painting.

For coöperation in preparing the manuscript for publication, the authors acknowledge their indebtedness to N. E. Mullen, Mary Mullen, L. V. Geiger, and Laurence Buermeyer. Grateful acknowledgment is also due to Madame Georges Duthuit and to Mr. Georges Keller for their painstaking services in procuring numerous photographs and considerable information useful in preparing the section in the Appendix entitled "Data on Works of Art Mentioned."

ALBERT C. BARNES.

VIOLETTE DE MAZIA.

MERION, PA., January, 1933.

CONTENTS

CONTENTS

APPENDIX

LIST OF ILLUSTRATIONS*

Henri-Matisse (photograph) . . . . *Frontispiece*

* Numbers in brackets after titles refer to numbers in "Data on Works of Art
Mentioned" (Appendix, page 431), and are used also as identification under each
illustration.

PAGE

Matisse—Paintings (Continued)

LIST OF ILLUSTRATIONS

THE ART OF HENRI-MATISSE

CHAPTER I

INTRODUCTION

OUR method of approach to the study of Matisse's work begins, as must any intelligible account of the rôle of art in experience, with the axiom of psychology that all we do depends ultimately upon our instincts. Although in the process of satisfying our instinctive desires we take many steps to which we have no instinctive prompting, as when a man earns money to allay the fear of poverty, or to provide for the gratification of his ambitions, no such steps would be taken if eventual instinctive satisfaction were not in prospect. Another way of saying the same thing is that all our activities are directed toward experiences good in themselves, the value of which is inherent, intrinsic, independent of any ulterior purpose that they may serve. In our more massive and profound satisfactions there is gratification of a number of instincts: triumph in a contest means confirmed confidence in ourselves; it also means the ending of a threat to our security, the abolition of an obstacle to our other desires, and a possibly indefinite number of other experiences of direct emotional value. In proportion as anyone's character becomes thoroughly organized his purposes enlist the driving force of many separate instinctive wants, and his personality as a whole comes to be involved in all that he does. His satisfactions become richer and fuller, they coöperate with each other instead of conflicting, and come to inhabit a world increasingly coherent and harmonious.

One of the pervasive features of this world is art. The theory that art satisfies a separate instinct, that there is distinct æsthetic emotion, has long since been abandoned. Æsthetic quality, it has been shown, is something which all properly integrated activity shares, not an isolated experience but an aspect of all experiences in which instinctive satisfactions are intelligently blended. What is commonly known as fine art, however, differs from the ordinary expression of instinct in that it does

I

not instigate us to any overt action. We respond to a work of art, to a picture or symphony, not by doing something, but by participating in the experience of the artist himself, seeing and feeling the world as he saw and felt it. This participation is not to be had for the asking; it involves effort, the solution of problems as real as those of actual life, and is as little to be solved by untutored spontaneity as the problems of managing a corporation or practicing medicine. There is a far-reaching parallel between the labor of the artist in acquiring his distinctive vision, and that of the observer who succeeds in sharing it.

The psychological basis of this fact will be apparent if we introduce the conception of "interest." The usual associations of "instinct" suggest something wayward and transient; but no such implication attaches to the "instinct" as conceived by science, since instincts, in a developed personality, are always organized in interests. An interest is objective: it is a concern, and an abiding concern, with something which is real independently of us, and which may be a person or a community, or a cause such as the advancement of science or democracy. Feelings which do not thus take us outside ourselves into something objective, and keep our attention fixed upon it, are unstable and trivial, they are a welter of emotion which may justly be stigmatized as sentimental. Unless our attitude toward the object which calls forth an impulse is permanent and is made a means of orienting our activity and systematizing our perceptions, our feeling for the object is nothing more than a mood, exhilarating perhaps but unseeing and undiscerning, and any supposed enthusiasm on our part actually amounts to mere intoxication and gush.

This necessity for sustained active attention and methodical study exists equally as regards our practical and "personal" interests and our interest in art. We consider unreal any alleged interest in a person or cause which does not lead to understanding and active consideration; similarly, interest in art which leads to no persistent effort to see and understand is either pretense or self-deception. This is true both of the artist and of the observer of art. No man becomes either an artist or a connoisseur merely by having violent emotions about musical forms, about dramatic situations, or about visible things. The artist not only feels, he makes systematic endeavor to assimilate, grasp, comprehend, what other artists have done in interpreting our common world, and with the help of their interpretation to see what no one else has yet seen. Just as little can anyone desirous of understanding art enter into its spirit without a similar endeavor to acquire the eyes of the artist and to use them to rediscover what the artist has discerned. A painter, in other words, has made an experiment and a discovery. He invites us to make the experiment for ourselves and to share the discovery if we can. No one really interested will decline the invitation or shirk the effort needed to make the experiment. But effort there is, and without it the discovery will never be made.

Preliminary to our investigation of Matisse, we shall indicate a method for making the experiment of learning to see, which is common to artist and observer. How indispensable such a method is, is only too apparent from the abortive issue of most attempts at criticism of art. Critics constantly confuse extraneous associations and gusts of irrelevant emotion with insight into artistic realities; they do so either from indolence or from the lack of any method for discerning the objective qualities which make a painting an authentic work of art. Interest, as we have seen, is genuine only when it is guided by intelligence to sharpen and organize its perceptions; without this it is dissipated in futile sentimentalism; and the application of such intelligence *is* method. Mastery of method is as integral a part of any real interest in art as is mastery of anatomy and physiology in the interest in curing disease, or mastery of financial principles in banking.

CHAPTER II

METHOD

THE close relation between method and art will become clearer if we consider in some detail the *psychology of perception*. At every moment of our lives we are in the presence of some existing material state of affairs, some environment, to the nature of which our sensations bear testimony. This is so true as to approach platitude; but its truth may easily obscure another fact no less salient, that the present existence of which we are aware is never the total material state of affairs, but only a part of it. The sum of our sensations at any given moment includes, let us say, the pressure of our clothes against our bodies, the sounds of traffic passing in the street outside, the murmur of a voice in the next room, a host of obscure organic sensations in our bodies, and so on indefinitely. We cannot be aware of them all, and if we could it would be folly to attempt it, since what many of them testify to is irrelevant to our immediate purposes and hence meaningless. The situation in which we find ourselves, in the only pregnant sense of the word, is no more than a part of our total material environment. On the other hand, it is also something not at the moment existing at all: it has a past and a future, it includes elements remote in space and time, of which no present sensations inform us. The events most acutely in our consciousness may be happening a hundred miles away; they, or their results, may not actually impinge on our senses for weeks or months, but they may be so vastly more important to us than the happenings in our vicinity that our actual bodily actions may be like movements in a dream. Even when our attention is definitely focused upon what is physically here and now, the sense of our awareness is never exhausted by the sensations we get from it. What we have learned about it in the past and what we expect from it in the future, its promise or threat, are so

4

closely interwoven with what is physically present in it, that the two are inextricably blended in our feeling, and can only be distinguished by analysis. All awareness, all perception, in a word, contains both sensation and meaning, so fused that often we can no more separate them than we can when looking at a play, to use William James's example, draw a sharp line between actual physical objects and objects skilfully painted on the back-drop of a stage setting. At every instant we are aware of a set of qualities immediately present, and another set not present in the same way, but integrally connected with the first and constituting the remote aspects of the situation of which we are conscious.

Here again the conception of interest is enlightening. Which of the indefinitely numerous candidates for our attention shall be successful, which element of the here-and-now shall enter our awareness, and which of their indefinitely numerous objective connections shall emerge into our consciousness as meaning, depends upon our interests. We spoke above of our organic sensations as ordinarily escaping analysis, but for an invalid they do not: they are symptoms, and symptoms by definition demand attention. Furthermore, not only does the type of sensations and of meanings vary with interest, but the fulness and coherence of each vary with the degree of development in the interest. If the invalid is also a physician, he is aware not only of his organic sensations, but of variations in his pulse, in his color, in the sound of his heart-beats; and what enables him to be aware of them is a greater number and more precisely articulated system of meanings.

All general types of interest induce corresponding general types of sensitiveness. A physician knows how to detect signs which mean health or disease, a detective or prosecuting attorney, signs which mean innocence or guilt. Sometimes the physical signs—stammering, or flushed cheeks—may be the same, but they are set in a different context of meanings, and prompt to different courses of action. No meaning is ever immediately guaranteed to be valid; when suggested it calls for confirmation, and this, which requires the possession of other meanings —a knowledge of further connections of what is suggested—

brings on in turn fresh observations. Seeing the flushed face, the physician takes the patient's blood pressure, the detective questions the suspect about his actions the evening before. The system of meanings, in other words, not only sharpens our eyes for what is present here and now, it indicates what we are to look for further.

The interests, and the meanings corresponding to them, which have thus far been taken as examples, are alike in this, that they are all practical. The patient is to be cured if possible, the suspect is to be released if certainly innocent, held for trial if probably guilty. In contrast to the foregoing, our æsthetic interests are not in things or events as signs of other things or events, but in things valuable in their own right. Flushed cheeks are no longer symptomatic of anything: the artist is not concerned with what is going to happen, or ought to happen, to his subject, and neither is the observer of the painting. In so far as any one of us is freed from practical necessities and obligations, or has energy to spare in the midst of practical concerns, he is able to discard preoccupations with cause and effect, with signs and things signified, and to look for aspects in the world which bespeak our attention in their own right. This does not mean, as has been erroneously supposed, that art is a relapse into mere feeling, that, as some of the ill-advised defenders of impressionism asserted, the artist's eye is "the eye that can only *see*," i.e., receive visual impressions. Development of the æsthetic interest requires development of a set of meanings no less elaborate and closely interknit than the meanings which confer proficiency in practical life or science. These meanings are no less serviceable in sharpening one's eye for fresh impressions of actual things in the world, than in acting as hypotheses to guide to new fields of observations. Like scientific conceptions, they are means of organization, organization of the impressions received at any single moment, and relation of those impressions to others past and future.

Art, of course, is no more the object of any single interest than is the world of practical affairs. Interest in the world of men and society is the natural basis of literature: the novelist and dramatist elaborate and organize the meanings which in some degree, though fitfully and unsystematically, engage the attention of everyone. Out of the tangled web of human relationships they select the comic, ironic, pathetic, tragic, or dramatic skeins, and by a judicious selection of circumstance and incident reweave them into a new fabric. Which of these characteristics shall predominate, give essential quality to the work, depends not only upon the writer's general literary interest, but upon the interests built up by the totality of his particular experiences, by which his individual personality is moulded. To attempt to do anything, without this selection, emphasis, "composition," is not only to court but to insure failure; events just as they happen could not be put in a newspaper, could not even be described, since naming anything is itself a process of selection. Similarly, painting extracts from the chaos of visual impressions those that will embody such meanings as color-contrast, modeling by light and shadow, linear pattern, composition in space, no one of which is more than vaguely perceptible to any one whose eye has not been opened to plastic qualities and relationships. How these qualities and relations are united, which of the visible aspects of things are emphasized and in what manner, depends again upon the personality of the artist, that is, upon his experience and individual interests.

The foregoing may be summed up if we say that what we call the color of a mind, the quality of a personality—trivial, weighty, frivolous, dignified, shallow, profound, mean or noble —depends upon the total organization of the interests, the funded meanings, which make it up. Meanings, interests, habits, are, indeed, but other names for one thing considered from varying points of view: they represent the effects of circumstance on character, the interaction between the organism and the environment in which each is continually modified by the other.

In the preceding paragraphs we have described perception as it occurs ideally, with that constant interaction between immediate experience and intelligible organization of meaning which constitutes reason or intelligence. Neither in life nor in art, unhappily, does the interaction always proceed successfully. There is constant change both in our environment and in ourselves; and in a perfectly adjusted individual, in a completely malleable environment, the changes in the individual would interlock perfectly with those in the environment. Every change in the world would be noted and appropriately interpreted; the ensuing reaction would fit into and direct existing natural processes to an auspicious conclusion. However, our responsiveness is never perfect, and nature is always in some measure refractory. We overlook, misinterpret; the coöperation we expect from external forces is not forthcoming. Often, no serious damage is done, if we see wrongly at first we can look again, and things obdurate in the beginning finally yield; but the problem may be insoluble for us, and then begins that isolation between the self and its world which blinds and exiles the self, and renders the world permanently untractable.

Everyone, without exception, suffers from this liability in so far as his sensibilities are not attuned to subject-matter of a particular sort. Gifts and abilities are specific, and so is sensitiveness: ready perception of mathematical relations may be accompanied by incapacity to grasp the nuances of meanings in words; extremely acute discrimination of musical quality may go with utter indifference to pictorial quality. Everyone's mind has blind spots, regions in which perception, if not impossible, is so laborious that a thorough organization of meanings, and a fine discrimination of sensations, could not be attained. The question here, however, is not of inborn limitations, but of acquired: of blindness due to premature hardening of meanings, mechanization of response. In the presence of change which baffles us, we may either postpone the solution of the problem until another time, returning to it anew at intervals; or we may solve it by fiat, using a meaning as a pigeonhole in which to file it away, and refusing to recognize the qualities in it which would forbid such a disposal. The use of meanings to dispose of facts, to distrust and deny them, is a sign of intelligence become congealed, and is accompanied by incapacity for any but routine perceptions. As our minds lose their openness and flexibility, as they grow hard, our world loses its freshness and novelty, and grows drab and monotonous.

This blight of premature senility may fall upon either the observer or the artist. Not only do we all tend to withdraw from aspects of the world in which we have never found or have lost interest, but the less open-minded among us may view with hostility unfamiliar aspects of those things which do engage our attention. This hostility is what is meant by academicism. Academicism in the observer or critic takes the form of disliking the novel, the unstereotyped; in the artist, of refusing to profit by the discoveries of other artists or traditions than those with which he is familiar. Doubtless it is true, from the point of view of physical nature, that in the artist's world "there is nothing new under the sun." Clouds, sea, hill and meadow have not changed since painting began. But the artist's environment, that which demands response from him, includes art itself, and such events as the discovery of Negro sculpture and Oriental art by European painters, or the rediscovery of El Greco, may profoundly change the situation in which he finds himself. Inability to recognize such discoveries, to assimilate whatever in them may be germane to his own purpose, or detect in them suggestions for the enlargement of his purposes, is a sign of artistic paralysis. The paralysis may be only partial, as when a writer, retaining his technical proficiency and even his hospitality to new suggestions which are relatively superficial, seeks refuge in a world which as a whole is dead and gone. Such are our neo-classicists and neo-mediævalists in literature. Or the absence of plastic originality, the arrest in plastic growth, may take the form of an excursion into the outré, exotic or bizarre, as in Ryder or Turner. This is not to deny that the exotic and bizarre may furnish suitable motifs for a living art—we shall see abundantly in the chapters to come that they may—but if they become a refuge instead of a mine for new material, their use is an indication of failing powers. The artist who, lacking any fresh plastic insight, seeks to lend a factitious novelty to his work by resort to fantastic or literary-mystical subject-matter— Böcklin and Davies are examples—is like the man who lives a life of meaningless routine and seeks to embellish it by unlimited phantasy-building in his spare hours, or to lend it color by eccentricities in dress, speech or manner.

We may sum up the foregoing by saying that all perception depends upon meanings, by which alone we are enabled to seize upon and organize the significant qualities in the world. The aggregate of the meanings in our possession, organized and available for interpretative use, is another expression for "intelligence," and the generalized statement of the way intelligence is applied is also the definition of method. Without intelligence, i.e., the application of relevant meanings, our perceptions can never lay hold of objective qualities in the things perceived, and unless there is such discovery of objective reality there is no "experience," in the true sense of the word: there is at most a drift of sensation which means nothing and which is incapable of organization and retention as a basis for subsequent experience. Experience and method are thus correlative. Just as we can perceive nothing without method, so a method, abstractly stated, unused in application, is without significance. Education in art means a constant interaction between method and actual perception, by which perceptions are enlightened and intelligence is given concreteness. We do not, in other words, see pictures as works of art except with the aid of a method of plastic insight. What many, perhaps most, people imagine to be an experience of plastic art is simply identification of subject-matter, since of course everyone possesses the method of seeing actual material objects and events as they affect our practical life. This is the most elementary of errors, that of looking at paintings as though they were illustrations or documents; it is implied in the definition of art as imitation; and unfortunately it is not confined to the tyro but is found also in art-criticism which comes from high places and has the authority of influential names.

The first necessity for a valid method is then to define the quality which makes a picture a work of art. A detailed definition of this will be given in the chapter on Plastic Form and Design;* it may be anticipated here by saying that plastic form

*See p. 14.

is the painter's personal vision of what the visible world reveals to him: the ensemble of qualities of color, light, line and space which makes any thing or situation significant, arranged in a unified form in accordance with a definite design, that is, purpose. Without reference to design, without understanding what an artist is driving at, we cannot hope to understand any painting. Art is vision or insight, but insight is always personal, it is something which no camera could conceivably possess; and to grasp it we must enter into the personality of the artist and place ourselves in his point of view. The fact that vision is always *of* something explains the objective quality of art, its reference to something which is necessarily perceptible to an observer who shares the artist's vision; the fact that it is personal explains the necessity of grasping specific purpose or design, by which the painter's individuality expresses itself.

Design is of course only the beginning of the story: the design must be executed, and if it is irrelevant to plastic quality it cannot be convincingly executed. Pictures merely narrative are condemned from the start by this criterion: what they attempt to show cannot be shown on canvas, since narrative involves events past and to come, and these events are incapable of embodiment in the picture itself. The interest in these events, furthermore, whether practical or emotional, has no plastic equivalent. But design may fail of adequate execution also through insufficient command of the plastic means, which amounts to inability to envisage objects in terms of *all* their qualities. The necessity for an integrated form corresponds to the necessity, noted in the first section of this chapter, for the integration of interests in a true personality. To see things in terms of light only, or of line only, or of color only, with perfunctory and unconvincing realization of their other aspects, is to fall into melodrama and unreality quite as much as does the writer who portrays his characters as heroes or villains, saints or beasts.

Recognition of these facts enables us to define further the error known as academicism. Design, since it is personal, means a unique correlation of the plastic means: understanding of it enables us to perceive in what manner and degree each of them needs to be employed. Academicism, however, is an attempt to set up a definite rule for the isolated employment of each of them, and so to judge a painting as though it were a mechanical exercise, not a manifestation of personality. Such a rule, invaluable for those who wish to judge without understanding or insight, is completely destructive to all æsthetic appreciation: in art, mechanism means death.

Art, as we have seen, is vision; it is the ability to perceive values which in their entirety have been perceived by nobody else. But though they have been perceived in their entirety by nobody else, it does not follow that nobody has had any inkling of them. All ways of seeing are acquired in the first place by utilization of the vision of others. This is what is meant by saying that all great artists work in a tradition. A tradition is simply a way of seeing that has been shared by a line of painters, each of whom, after mastering what his predecessors had to show him, has gone on to see something new for himself. Absolute originality is an impossibility: no one can lift himself by his own boot-straps. The test of the genuine artist is that he uses the vision of others as a means to more penetrating vision of his own. Employing, in other words, what others have done, he selects from their work the elements appropriate to his individual design, modifies them, and blends them in a form which is his personal contribution to art. The academician, in contrast, is not the master of others' vision but the slave: having no individual insight, he cannot select intelligently and modify sensitively but must follow blindly. When he is an eclectic who draws upon a variety of traditions, what he takes from one source remains unrelated to what he takes from another: his work corresponds to the contents of a rag-bag, to a crazy-quilt, not to a continuously designed and woven fabric. We can now see why academicism also consists of over-accentuation of some special feature or some single plastic element. Unity, which is essential to plastic form as to all æsthetic effects, depends upon an integration of traditional elements *through* integration of the plastic means, and neither integration is possible without the other. If a painter has not the eye to see how the element which comes from one tradition is to be merged with that coming from another, neither can he see how to blend the color, the light, the line and the space by which such merging is necessarily accomplished.

Any method by which pictures can be studied intelligently must take cognizance of all these considerations. Fixing upon *design* as the central element, the determining factor in every painting, it must consider the possible types of design which may be attempted, and analyze the specific designs discovered in representative schools and individual artists. In subordination to this design the component parts of the completed picture, the color, light, line and space, as well as the technical devices by which each of the plastic elements is rendered, must be exhibited in their mutual relationship. Apart from such interrelation and subordination, the function of, for example, the light in a particular picture can no more be understood than could the function of a part in a complicated machine by one who did not know its purpose. A critic who ignores design is in the position of one who wonders why an automobile has a carbureter and magneto instead of, like a locomotive, a firebox and boiler.

Next, the sources of a painter's form must be sought in the work of his predecessors, and the degree of creative transformation and unification be assessed. The result of the whole analysis must be objective, verifiable by other observers. This is not to say that the verification can be made by anyone, as can the reading of a thermometer or the hands of a clock. The objectivity is not that of simple sensation: it is closer to that which we discover in an argument, an organization of premises from which a conclusion follows. Since personality enters, absolute uniformity is not to be hoped for, but what is merely arbitrary and irrational in the personal factor may be reduced toward the vanishing-point. The situation is precisely the same as in intellectual matters: although an argument may appear convincing to one man, unconvincing to another, the area of agreement is vastly extended as men grow in intelligence. So to extend the area of agreement among intelligent and sensitive observers of art is the purpose of the method herein explained and applied.

CHAPTER III

PLASTIC FORM AND DESIGN

THE conception of plastic form is fundamental to all discussion of painting as a distinct art. Plastic form may be defined as an integration of the plastic means in which the artist embodies his unique perception of what to him is significant and moving in the world about him. These means are color, space, line and light. Considered as a physical object, a painting is a set of areas of color which intersect to form lines and are varied in tone to give the effect of light and shadow. Necessarily the expanse of the canvas yields two dimensions and the third dimension is added by indications of perspective, modeling, and other incidental means. Variations in light and shadow add to depicted masses the characteristic of solidity. This separation of the different means, however, is, in all successful art, a matter of discrimination and not of literal physical isolation; each of the plastic means is capable of modifying and uniting with all the others—a union without which the unity essential to art is impossible. What determines their interrelation is the principle of design, the purpose in accordance with which the artist uses line, light, color and space to construct his work. Since, finally, there can be no art which is not individual and creative, the authenticity of a painter's æsthetic achievement can be judged only in the light of his personal use and modification of the traditions of painting. When the integration of the plastic means is successfully executed, the picture achieves reality; when it is one-sided or mechanical, conviction is lost and the painting becomes academic and unreal.

Color may have an intrinsic sensuous appeal by virtue of richness, variety or glow, but this is much less important in a painting than the effect due to color-relations. The painter's sense for color-relations appears in color-contrasts, color-harmonies and color-organization in general: unless these relations are fitting, the immediate appeal of a single color may de-

14

tract from instead of enhance the value of the form as a whole. Conversely, and this is preëminently true of Matisse, colors which in isolation will appear strident and unpleasant may, by their reciprocal action, enter into a union which is appealing. The more important functions of color, however, depend less upon immediate color-relationships than upon the coördination of color with the other plastic means. Its most obvious relationship is to light, which is indeed a direct modification of it. Modeling directly results from the continuous gradations of light and shadow, but the participation of color may be more integral when it is used structurally—that is, when color is so completely integrated in the actual solidity of objects that it does not seem merely to be applied to the surface but to be the material out of which the objects are actually made up. Again, color and light may be united in atmospheric effects by which unity is given to the form through the pervasive presence of a glow or mist. **Light,** when accentuated more than its correlate, color, may also be used to unify a picture either by providing a focal point of high illumination or by a distribution in alternation with shadow over the canvas to yield an independent light-pattern. Modification of light, parallel to that of color, is also an ingredient of drawing at its best.

Line, though it is often by inferior artists conceived independently of color and light, is fully convincing only when used in conjunction with these. If made the sole instrument of drawing, line may be of illustrative, photographic or decorative significance but it fails in fulness of expression and, therefore, lacks plastic reality. Considered by itself, it is the most obvious instrument of conveying perception of actual objects in the real world; but even illustration, to have a legitimate place in plastic form, requires a departure from literal imitation: the painter must select and render those linear aspects of things which make the object what, for him, it essentially *is*. Line may be either a clear-cut demarcation between areas of color or it may be an area of transition with a neutral tone into which the adjacent colors overflow. The most complete utilization of color usually appears in drawing of the latter type, and involves variation in color in accordance with every change in line. When line is sharp and clean-cut and the areas of color are completely separated from each other, the drawing entails loss of full plastic value.

The fourth of the fundamental plastic means is **space**. In two-dimensional composition, objects are arranged to right and left and above and below each other; in space-composition, they become also masses related to each other by depth of spatial intervals. In both types there may be either a single focal point with reference to which the subsidiary masses are placed, or no single object may be conceived as focal, and unification be achieved by direct relationship of the various masses to each other. The composition, like the other plastic factors, is at its best when the space-relationships are enhanced, or even constituted, by the coöperation of all the plastic means. An area of color, for example, a spot of illuminated sky, may serve compositionally as a mass by balancing an actual object in another part of the picture. Drawing, too, may be not drawing merely of a single object but of the picture as a whole: the line or color in the drawing of one object may be continued by the line or color of an adjacent object; or instead of merely continuing, the elements of drawing may contrast with one another, or rhythmically duplicate one another, and thus serve diverse functions in achieving variety and unity in the painting as a whole. Both immediate color-relations and areas of glow or mist may further knit together the masses of the composition as may also even a single pervasive color.

For any understanding of plastic form, the conception of **design** is basic. The plastic quality of a painting can no more be perceived by one who does not grasp its design than the bearing of an argument by one ignorant of the thesis to be proved. Just as the plot of a book embodies the writer's purpose, the painter's design may be regarded as the integrating plan of the picture, the principle by which all its detail is connected and ordered. Design fixes the degree to which each of the plastic elements is employed and the degree of simplification or departure from literal realism. Into it enter two factors: first, the personal vision of the artist, his capacity to see a certain set of aspects and relationships in his subject-matter and, second, the subject-matter itself. *What* is to be shown, in other words, determines the manner of the showing, and although it is of course impossible to correlate the two precisely, a particular type of subject-matter may involve relative emphasis upon any one of the plastic means and subordination of the others. Such subordination does not impair plastic reality provided that what is subordinated is conceived with sufficient fulness and executed with sufficient skill to attain its own appropriate degree of conviction. Drawing, for example, unless it is executed by all the plastic means and not by line only, is inadequate even as mere illustration. Again, if any aspect not central to the design is emphasized, it stands out as a jarring note and to that extent destroys plastic reality.

Design is of two sorts, "expressive" and "decorative." Expressive design aims to reveal the artist's individual grasp of what is essential in his subject-matter. Decorative design aims at immediate charm in the work of art and is not intended to convey any interpretation of the deeper aspects of things. As we found in discussing the separate plastic means, this distinction in authentic art is one of aspects and not of things. If either expression or decoration is present to the complete exclusion of the other, it is at the expense of plastic fulness and, therefore, of reality. A design embodying merely a perception of essentials is too abstract, intellectual and remote; a design merely decorative loses conviction by complete divorce from the real world and is æsthetically on the same level as a fabric or a rug. It is by expressive design that a sense of the deep human values of experience is conveyed. In decoration the value resides in satisfaction of our need to perceive abundantly and freely.

Not only is it essential that both the expressive and decorative aspects of design be present but their union must be an organic one, not a mere addition of the decoration to a form which is, in essentials, complete without it. Unless expressive design is conceived decoratively also from the start, the form resulting when the design is executed will fall apart, the decoration appear as mere embellishment, a kind of cheap finery. None the less, though these two types of design cannot be isolated, either one of them may be relatively emphasized. In painting of the very first rank both the expressive and the decorative qualities of the subject-matter are utilized to the maximum extent. But in many very great painters we can perceive a relatively greater interest in either one of them. In Renoir, for example, the decorative aspect is more prominent than in Cézanne, with the result that of the two Renoir has the greater charm, Cézanne the greater power. In painting of less than the first rank there is no organic union of these types of design, and the plastic reality of the picture is correspondingly lowered. However, provided always that the realization of the subsidiary aspect is adequate to the painter's purpose, the essential artistic quality of the form remains. A painting which is frankly decorative may give a relatively superficial version of what is depicted. Bad art appears only when a painting which pretends to be expressive resorts to decoration to conceal lack of fundamental plastic insight. In such paintings we seem to be looking at a cosmetic.

In Matisse the indisputable primacy in design goes to decoration. He is, however, a real and great artist and there is therefore in his work a uniform and successful execution of as much essential reality as is needed to give his forms standing in the real world. His design, at its best, shows a precise coördination of all the plastic means, and their execution is perfectly adapted to whatever decorative purpose animates the picture in question. Because of his wide experience with all the traditions of painting he is able to borrow from the most diverse sources, and because of his artistic integrity these borrowings are always judicious, neither merely imitative nor speciously plastered upon the surface of his forms. His intelligence is shown by the fact that, lacking a command of the profounder sources of inspiration, he selects subjects which call only for the means which are completely within his power. In the chapters which follow, the foregoing principles will be applied to a detailed study of his work.

CHAPTER IV

THE PSYCHOLOGY OF MATISSE

IF an intimate and constant interaction with the environment is a condition of vivid experience and the necessary qualification of an artist, then Matisse's claim to artistic status is indisputable. A man who is fully alive finds himself in a state of constant change, in an environment also constantly changing. These changes interact: a man who brings to his perceptions an always shifting set of interpretative meanings finds that identical objects no longer yield the same experiences; conversely, the effects of previous perceptions change the observer. Matisse's insatiable interest in perceiving in ever-fresh forms the familiar features of the world about him, coupled with his own activities modifying that world and thus giving him something new to see almost from moment to moment, account for the vast variety of perceptions which he has embodied in his paintings. It is this constantly renewed interest which enables him to paint substantially the same subject-matter many times over, each time in a new plastic version, with such a degree of variation that the different versions are never repetitious, always fresh, always original. To this interest in perpetually renewing his perceptions is added an avid intellectual curiosity, which makes him explore all the traditions of art of all periods; this in turn gives him new resources for enriching and varying his perceptions, for carrying out the experiment, the adventure, which is art. Matisse, in a word, has vitality, he has an open and flexible mind, great erudition, adventurousness of spirit; these, combined with unflagging interest in the contemporary scene, in all the artistic manifestations of his time, and with an admirable command of his medium, enable him to paint fluently and exuberantly, reflecting in his work the myriad forms visible to one who is both a living animal and an accomplished scholar.

Yet for all his ready responsiveness, Matisse's reactions

are primarily intellectual. Rarely if ever does he seem driven by passion, compelled to an utterance which he is powerless to restrain. Though free from affectation, he lacks the spontaneity of Renoir or Soutine or, in another sense, of Cézanne: his métier is to contrive, calculate, plan deliberately, to be judicious, conscious of his purpose and tenacious in following it, but never emotionally carried away by it. This temper of mind may have disadvantages but certainly it has advantages. By keeping clearly in mind what he intends and what is necessary for its execution, he is able to weigh the adaptability to his individual form of everything that other painters have done; he has thus an extraordinary repertoire of traditional effects and technical devices at his command, all of them assimilated and, by their skilful adaptation and union, freed from the taint of eclecticism. His intelligence is further manifested in his unfailing recognition of what he can and what he cannot do, and his avoidance of everything beyond his powers: his interests are primarily decorative, and he attempts little or no revelation of profound human values or of the more significant plastic qualities.

Matisse has an extraordinary feeling for the picturesque and a positive genius for organization. These gifts, controlled by his robust intellect, give him an inventiveness which, under the spur of his vitality, of his insatiable curiosity about the contemporary scene, and with the aid of his encyclopedic knowledge of all the plastic traditions, yields a wealth of decorative forms unparalleled in range in the whole history of painting. The fact is intelligible enough when we consider that he has drawn upon nearly all his predecessors and most of his contemporaries for contributions, but the full measure of his versatility can only be appreciated in the light of the detailed discussion to follow.

CHAPTER V

DECORATION AND DECORATIVE DESIGN

MATISSE, as we have seen, is by temperament primarily interested in the decorative aspects of things, and by training, by his great erudition, admirably equipped to give to this interest a rich and widely varied expression. We have also seen that this bent and practice involves a sacrifice of the more profound interpretative values, both human and plastic, characteristic of the greatest artists; and in our final estimate of Matisse's position in the hierarchy of art we shall endeavor to indicate exactly how far this deficiency detracts from the value of his work. In the chapters on his use of the various plastic means and traditions of painting, we shall see how the decorative possibilities of each of these is taken advantage of; the topic of the present chapter is the general principles of decorative design and their application to Matisse's painting.

The psychological basis of the appeal of decoration is our general need to perceive abundantly, easily and agreeably, quite apart from all interpretation of the thing perceived. The bright color of flowers and sunsets, the deep blue of the sea, flecked with foam and edged at the shore with lines of breakers, are instances of natural phenomena which immediately meet this need, which possess intrinsic decorative quality. In what are called the decorative arts the principle involved is isolated and presented in a relatively pure form. Silver, china, jewelry, rugs, wall-paper, tapestry, furniture, may have both rich sensuous quality and appealing pattern. The appeal is genuine and legitimate, yet the examples suggest at once the æsthetic limitation of *mere* decoration. No one would think of Chippendale or Gobelin as artists of the same order and standing as Titian or Rembrandt. There are a whole world of values in painting which are absent from any rug, however richly and sensitively designed, and no vividness of color or charm of pattern can make up for the absence of the recognizable things we all know, live among, and feel deeply about. Both plastically and human-

21

ly, decoration is inferior to what, in the chapter on Plastic Form and Design, we have called expressive form, a contention which is confirmed when we consider wholly non-representative painting, the cubistic pictures of Braque and Picasso, for example, in which plastic design is reduced to little more than pattern.

Of course, in all the greatest art, expression and decoration are united so intimately that only by an effort of abstraction can they be distinguished. In the great Venetians, and in Velásquez, El Greco, Rembrandt, Renoir and Cézanne, everything— color, light, line and space—contributes to an insight into important and moving aspects of the world and also directly charms and delights us. If either aspect becomes isolated or over-emphasized, there is proportionate loss of power and conviction. No eye to essentials can redeem what is altogether bleak, barren, repulsive to the senses; and mere pattern, from which every interpretative quality has been banished, is so devoid of meaning that it becomes cloying. Lack of decorative effect diminishes expressive effect also; and at the extremes, in painting which lacks either aspect altogether, æsthetic value has evaporated. It is true, however, that there may be a relative emphasis upon one or the other aspect without detriment to the value of the work. In Renoir, as we have already noted, the decorative aspect is more in evidence than in Cézanne; in Cézanne the very diminution of embellishment is essential to his greater austerity and power.

Matisse, to repeat, is primarily interested in decoration, but this is by no means to say that his work is without expressive force. The subject-matter of practically all his work is clearly recognizable and genuinely interpreted; only, it is interpreted primarily in those aspects which are in themselves naturally ornamental. It is the picturesque aspects of things which he brings out, and he chooses as subject-matter objects, scenes, settings, which readily lend themselves to such treatment.* Decorative

*E.g., colorful Oriental costumes; exotic objects and settings, such as rugs, braseros, aiguières, mashrabiyyas; light, bright, vivid, delicately colored flowers in colorful and patterned vases; bright sunny landscapes of Corsica and the French littoral; brightly illuminated interiors; patterned draperies, wall-papers, screens, balcony-railings, etc.

elaboration often involves extreme distortion, and the character of the distortion is significant : in Cézanne it serves to emphasize the solidity of the objects and their presence in extremely convincing space; in Matisse it usually flattens out both the objects and the spaces, and thereby presents a version of them more suited for inclusion in some such decorative design as that of a tapestry or poster. We may say in general that while Matisse, except on rare occasions, discards precise realism altogether, he retains sufficient expressive form to keep his objects definitely in the real world, and then proceeds to an adventure in drawing out and elaborating decorative possibilities—an adventure which has given us the richest and most varied array in decorative forms to be found in the work of any painter not interested also in the deeper forms of expression.

Without an understanding of Matisse's essential interests and purposes no appreciation of his form is possible, and absence of such understanding has led many critics to stigmatize his work as freakish, anarchic, the sign of mere idiosyncrasy, or a sensational counterfeit of art. It does have a bizarre quality, but this, far from being due to any breach with the traditions or to feeble command of his medium, is essential to his design, it testifies to his mastery of just the effects which he needs for his purposes. All his distortions are incidental to his decorative design : his procedure is always orderly, intelligent and resourceful, and the audacity that academicians feel and dislike indicates not eccentricity but vitality.

We have already noted the meaning of design : the purpose, plan or "plot" in accordance with which a painter orders the visible expression of his reaction to the world about him. In it everything in his personality plays a part, his intellect, his knowledge, his initiative, his whole equipment of powers, and the residue left by all his experience. The first essential to design is unity, order. A work of art, like a situation in life, is satisfactory æsthetically if it has a structure, if its parts hang together successfully; if, in a word, it is a real whole and not a mere collection or conglomeration. Just as an argument embraces assumptions, observations and general principles chosen and assembled to lend conviction to the conclusion which forms its thesis or *demonstrandum,* so in a work of art every element, color, line, space, and light, must be adjusted to one another and to the design as a whole. In this total set of relationships none can be altered without damage to unity and so to æsthetic effect. In the chapter on Plastic Form and Design we have already noted this general principle; the present problem is to point out the particular uses of the plastic elements and traditions, the distortions and emphases, by which Matisse achieves his own personal type of decorative design.

Here as everywhere the two general principles of design are rhythm and contrast. Rhythm involves repetition, which may embrace all the plastic elements: a color in one part of the painting may find an echo in another part, and so also of line, or sharp contrast of light and shadow, or the order of masses in space. Or the design as a whole may be repeated on a smaller scale in some particular area or areas of the picture; this constitutes one of the most effective types of design. When the repetition is accompanied by difference, and the element repeated is set in a context of other qualities widely disparate, rhythm acquires the added effect of contrast; more generally, contrast heightens the effect of variety. The æsthetic requirement is not only for unity, but for unity in diversity, since monotonous sameness is as uninteresting as chaos. In Matisse's designs the rhythms and contrasts serve to convey drama; not, as with Tintoretto and El Greco, expressive plastic drama of action in the subject, but drama primarily in the plastic means in the interest of immediate embellishment.

Matisse's work is never haphazard, it is the solution of a problem clearly conceived and solved to a large extent by conscious intellectual processes. In the treatment of subjects with intrinsic ornamental appeal, the distortions are fewer and less radical than with an object which is ordinarily of interest for its independently real or human qualities—a face or figure, for example. Sometimes these methods are original with Matisse, sometimes they are taken from the traditions; but in either case they are judicious, combined in a new context, and used skilfully to bring out the precise aspects which have decorative significance.

We shall now consider very briefly, as a preliminary to subsequent chapters, the way in which Matisse's decorative designs oblige him to handle color, line, light and space, though
these are so interfused in the unity of his general form that
his use of them cannot be kept sharply distinct. One general
plastic problem, for example, is that of unifying such details
in the background as draperies, screens, wall-paper, or arabesques formed by trees, with such objects in the foreground
as figures or still-life; this usually, though not always, involves a relative flattening of all the objects and a notable diminution in the number of planes. These distortions of space and
modeling are constantly accompanied by corresponding distortions of color and line. Line, instead of being simply contour,
the meeting-place of areas of color, is frequently a colored
band; color, which in hue is often a complete departure from
the natural color of the object depicted—flesh, for instance,
or the foliage of trees—is very generally applied in compartments. As we shall see in greater detail in the chapter on Color,
Matisse rarely uses either color-chords* or structural color: the
convincing solidity which the latter contributes to an object
would usually clash with Matisse's decorative purpose. The
basis of the greater number of his effects is color, but color in
its ornamental aspects. We find in him, therefore, hues which
are exotic, bizarre, striking, but which, when taken in isolation, are often harsh and unpleasing. The relations of these
colors, both to each other and to the other plastic elements, constitute the most important single factor in the total decorative
value as well as in the unification of the design. Sometimes the
background and foreground taken together form an ensemble
of contrasting color-areas from which solidity and three-dimensional quality are almost entirely banished (56).† Occa-

---

*A "color-chord" is a small area in which two or more juxtaposed colors
overflow into each other: for example, red and an adjacent blue with reciprocal interpenetration constitute a "color-chord."

†This number and all similar documentation by numerals, throughout the
text, refer to the works of art which are listed in the Appendix under "Data
on Works of Art Mentioned." Matisse's paintings bear the numerals from
1 to 176 inclusive; his black-and-white work is numbered from 200 to 223
inclusive. Numerals beginning with 300 refer to works by other artists, as
specified in the list in the Appendix on page 431.

sionally, foreground and background are treated as two large areas contrasting in color and in degree of accentuation of pattern, with spatial intervals reduced to such a point that foreground and background are virtually parts of a single plane (148, 154). Or instead of unification of this sort, there may be rhythmic duplication, in the background, of color, line, shape and technique which make up the principal objects in the foreground (10, 48, 110, 120, 123, 131); vice versa, units accentuated in the background may be rhythmically echoed in the foreground (56, 154). When this is done, not only is there close resemblance, or even identity, between the duplicated units, but all of them fit into a pattern extending throughout the picture.

For the sake of unity and decoration, Matisse plays fast and loose with spatial relations not only between foreground and background as a whole, but between the objects in each, or between their constituent planes. In a general composition with more than usually well-realized order in deep space, one area may consist of an accentuated patchwork of colors in planes set very close together (14). In pictures of the odalisque type the contrasting figure and background may be unified by similarity in the manner of their distortion (152), or else figure and objects may be distributed equally in foreground and background and executed with equal degree of simplification or clarity of detail; the violence thus done to realism is amply justified by the richness of the new decorative ensemble (172).

The foregoing examples, naturally, are illustrative and not exhaustive: Matisse's methods of unifying design could be fully described only by a detailed account of every one of his pictures. He never repeats a design in its entirety, and with every variation of purpose there is significant variation in the ways and means of its execution. For his themes he draws upon the whole range of experience which his exuberant and many-sided interests have made real for him—nearly everything concerning life and persons genuinely alive—and the execution of his purposes is aided, though never controlled, by a repertoire of devices taken from every field of plastic art. His audacity makes his effects, with their extreme distortions and apparent disregard of precedent, shocking to the conventional observer, but the shock is transformed into a thrill of pleasure when one grasps his decorative purpose, and his intelligent adaptation to it of all the great traditions. Matisse's work makes no break with the past; it is engendered by noble ancestors and its appeal is to fundamental human interests; but to share with Matisse the adventurous expedition into new realms of experience we must share his alertness to new sensations and new forms, his sensitiveness to the picturesque, his feeling for vivid colors and novel patterns. We must share with him also—a matter requiring study and analysis—his knowledge of the history of painting, his capacity for comprehensive, intelligent planning, his grasp of the possibilities of plastic decorative organization. Such a study is the subject of this book.

We have seen the ubiquity of decorative forms in Matisse's paintings. The precise manner of their integration with expressive forms will become clearer if we consider the source of their appeal. We shall find that frequently an object which to a superficial view appears perilously close to mere pattern, has an appeal to wider instincts, memories, experiences, not explicitly recalled but present in the background of our minds and actively operating there to enhance the expressive force of the total form. With this we come to the subject of Transferred Values.

Summary

Though by no means devoid of expressive quality, Matisse's pictures are in the main primarily decorative, intended to emphasize the immediately pleasing aspects of the world. The ornamental, the picturesque, not the humanly moving or the intensely real, are what we can hope to find in him. This decorative interest determines his choice of subject-matter, which is nearly always something colorful and highly patterned, and his treatment of it by means which best serve to emphasize these aspects. By a natural and inevitable development, which is obviously the result of a conscious, intellectual plan, Matisse uses these materials for purposes which are distinctively his, sensitively adjusting each of the plastic means, and the relevant practices of widely varied traditions of art, to bring out the decorative possibilities of all that he treats. His manner of treatment necessarily involves frequent and sometimes extreme departures from literal realism: objects have a color often totally different from that which they have in the real world; their outlines are either simplified or elaborated into arabesques and patterns radically novel; the line itself is frequently quite other than the natural outline of the object represented, it is not merely a contour, but also a band of color, enclosing a color-compartment; volumes are flattened, planes are reduced in number, and deep space is often converted almost entirely into what seems like the flat surface of a screen. The reason for each distortion is decorative: the unnatural colors are better for the purpose than any literal reproduction could be, the lines make up a more rhythmic ensemble, and the coalescence of foreground and background knits together more closely for decorative purposes the various areas of the canvas. More specifically, Matisse's decoration generally tends toward the bizarre and exotic, so that realism would be a positive disadvantage, while colors and shapes rarely found in nature, as well as forms taken from Oriental art, heighten the decorative effect to the point of strangeness. Another manifestation of the dominance of the decorative motifs is that Matisse departs from naturalism in varying degree: an object already ornamental in itself is much less modified than, for example, human flesh or the contour of an arm or leg. Yet connection with actuality is preserved by the retention of sufficient expressive form to insure that the object portrayed will be recognizable.

One of his typical plastic problems is that of unifying foreground masses with the setting or background in a decorative ensemble. This treatment of foreground and background may follow any one of a number of methods. Taken together these two parts of the picture may form a series of contrasting color-areas; or each may constitute a relatively independent homogeneous color-area, contrasting in hue and in degree of accentuation of pattern, with differences in degree of spatial depth. Or they may be brought into relation by rhythmic repetition of themes of every sort. Sometimes the natural spatial relationships in several objects may be differently distorted, with relative flatness in one part of the design, relatively deep space in another: the objects in the foreground may even have more of the indistinctness usually characteristic of distance than those in the background. The number of his expedients for combining unity with diversity is legion: it illustrates an audacious yet intelligent employment of encyclopedic plastic erudition.

CHAPTER VI

TRANSFERRED VALUES

HUMAN beings always and necessarily interpret the present, the given, in terms of the past. The fact is a truism as regards intellectual apprehension: we understand anything only in so far as we identify it, place it in a context of familiar meanings; but what is not so generally realized is that this intellectual apprehension is accompanied by an imaginative or metaphorical extension of meaning which imports into the experience of the here and now at least a part of the emotional aura, the heat and glow, of our past sensations and feelings. Sometimes, especially when the importunity of practical necessities is relaxed and the situation is propitious to flights of fancy, as on a steamer passing within sight of land off the coast of the Riviera, material objects may attract to themselves swarms of images, and serve as the figures in fantastic dramas. Fleecy clouds sailing over the sky often remind us of animals, persons, buildings; as they move and change we may interpret their movement and change according to our fancy, and weave narratives about them. A portion of the cloud may detach itself and remind us of the spire or façade of a cathedral; or, starting from faint or vague resemblances, we may see in it an elephant's trunk, a shining silver river, or the broad surface of a cliff. Or it may be a living figure moving in stately grace to the melody of a minuet which our memory has cherished for years. Reveries of this sort are only the extreme development of a tendency to figurative perception which is present in all persons at all times. We say of a man that he is adamant, or soft, or a fox, and the emotional quality conveyed by the figure of speech, no less than our purely intellectual estimate, pervades and determines our attitude toward him. We feel in a Cézanne the qualities of a solidly constructed building; a Renoir picture of a girl recalls a rose in a garden on a morning in June. In short, there is scarcely an object or situation in life, or in art—the mirror of life—not fraught with emotional associations for which its objective qualities give no demonstrable ground.

Often the recall is not of memories and feelings as separate and distinguishable psychological facts, but of what Santayana calls the "hushed reverberations" of the original experience: vague thrills, obscure likings and dislikings, a sense of importance or triviality, of which we can no more bring to mind the basis than we can explicitly state the evidence which underlies many of our most fundamental beliefs. As with intellectual beliefs, there are in our minds in solution a vast number of emotional attitudes, feelings ready to be reëxcited when the proper stimulus arrives, and more than anything else it is these forms, this residue of experience, which, deeper, fuller and richer than in the mind of the ordinary man, constitute the artist's capital. What is called the magic of the artist resides in his ability to transfer these values from one field of experience to another, to attach them to the objects of our common life, and by his imaginative insight make these objects poignant and momentous. Far from being the exotic flower which "practical" people look at askance, art is an essential and vital part of life in that it reveals the meaning, the universal significance and emotional import of innumerable facts and experiences which without it would be flat and commonplace.

The ability to make this revelation Matisse has in high degree, and through it he attains to a form genuinely expressive as well as decorative. Though he does not, to repeat, illuminate for us the qualities of things which evoke the deeper human feelings, he does bathe his world with the glamour of the joyfully picturesque, of freshness and an eager *joie de vivre,* as well as of the exotic and the bizarre. This is vastly more than mere pattern, it is the expression of a truly personal vision. Matisse's vision is always colorful—not only in the literal sense of the word, but in the figurative, as when we speak of a colorful scene or personality.

We shall now consider the ways in which Matisse accomplishes this transfer of values. In general, they consist largely of giving to a picture, whatever the literal character of its subject-matter, the effect of a bouquet of flowers (19), a poster (56), a piece of cretonne (140), an Oriental rug (166), a Persian tile (175), a mosaic (10), a tapestry (154), or even a map (23), since the effect of many maps is directly ornamental. When the subject-matter is less decorative in itself, when it is ostensibly an interior, a landscape or a portrait, the degree of distortion required for the transfer of value is greater than when it is a flowerpiece or a still-life, though in the detailed use of the plastic means there is always extensive distortion: no still-life by Vermeer or Chardin ever looked like a Matisse. So also does Cézanne transfer values by distortion, and the fact that his values are very different, that he introduces by ordered spatial relations and structural color the massive immobility of a fortress or a mountain into a plate of fruit, ought not to blind us to the identity of the principle involved.

The devices, as well as many of the actual effects, employed by Matisse in the realization of this phase of his decorative design, are largely Oriental in origin. Frequently a still-life or an interior scene immediately suggests a piece of **tapestry,** and the suggestion is borne out when we examine the design as a whole (148, 154). The fabric seems to be hung from the top of the canvas and to cover the whole of its surface, over which extend ornamental motifs common in tapestry, though there may be no precise imitation of detail. The upper part, which corresponds to the background, seems heavy; the lower part, more lightly painted, with its representative objects less solid and in more delicate colors, seems like a less weighty drapery joined to the section above. The decorative emphasis is thus shifted to the upper part, a shift conducive to the tapestry-effect but inconsistent with a naturalistic rendering of the subject-matter, and inconsistent also with anything like a precise imitation of tapestry-effects. There is a real union of values, without any obvious and facile short-cut to either.

Another effect which Matisse often superimposes upon practically every variety of subject-matter is that of the **poster** (56, 141, 156, 167). This generally involves a composition of color-compartments, in which are interwoven objects, figures and ornamental background in an appropriate version of spatial relations, with the most ruthless sacrifice of every sort of realism. In no other single type of pictures does Matisse bring to bear so great a variety of color, patterns, and technical devices in the interest of diverse decorative effects. Attributes of objects which even decorative artists treat with considerable fidelity to realism are radically altered; these, and the familiar embellishments of Oriental art, are here carried to new and greater decorative heights. When the pigment is thinner, the solidity of the objects correspondingly diminished, and the floral decorations more numerous, these poster-effects assume the quality of cretonne or chintz (140). When the composite color-pattern is basically one of few large simplified bands, the suggestion may be that of a flag (34). Occasionally he overshoots the mark and insufficient expressive form is kept to assure plastic reality (38); the decorative ensemble may sink to the level of a chromo (158, 174); it may be merely a color-pattern (59); or attempted effects analogous to the specious *papier-collé* treatment of the cubists may result in failure of the patches of color to enter integrally into the design (165). On the whole, however, some of the most successful and characteristic of his pictures are to be found in this poster-group (31, 34, 50, 51, 56, 131, 141, 175).

A number of specific motifs occur so often in Matisse that they require more extended description and illustration. One of these is the **rosette,** of which the most familiar example is to be found in flowers. The intrinsic appeal of a flower is no more due to its color than to its pattern, which generally consists of a central area from which petals radiate. The added charm of a bouquet of flowers resides not only in the increased mass and variety of color, but also in the diversity in the patterns of the single flowers; in a well-organized bouquet the flowers are usually arranged in a pattern which repeats, as regards focus and radiations, the form of the single flower. Flowers are a conspicuous instance of natural objects with intrinsic decorative quality; arranged in bouquets they acquire a higher degree of unity in multiplicity; they carry the associated values of the out-of-doors, of spring and summer, of budding life. The rosette-pattern characteristic of them, the hub-and-spoke arrangement common to species so diverse as the hollyhock, daisy, zinnia, buttercup, wild rose, marigold and pansy, forms the bridge over which Matisse constantly makes the abstract values of flowers and similarly shaped objects, such as conventionalized stars, or even fireworks, pass to totally different types of subject-matter. A very large number of his decorative paintings are composed in accordance with the rosette-pattern. Sometimes this so dominates the composition that the picture is first perceived as a glorified wheel, or star or flower, and the motif is repeated on a smaller scale in the detail of the painting, in the ornamented draperies, the shape of particular objects, and so on (106, 108, 131, 134, 143, 152). At other times it is relatively blurred, and close observation is needed to discover it in the general arrangement or placing of the masses (105). Another type of it appears when bits of bright color are surrounded by small irregular spots of bare canvas to make up a sparkling unit which resembles a sunburst (56, 70, 77).

Matisse obtains variety in the use of the rosette-pattern by making it sometimes striking, sometimes subtle, either by the introduction of other themes, or by using different plastic means as the instrument of its execution. In one picture the composition may have no suggestion of radiating masses, but the rosette-pattern may appear in the background, and in such incidental objects as flowers, rug and candelabra (144). In another, the motif may occur in a wall-paper in the background, in brush strokes of contrasting color in a dress, and in the converging lines of perspective on the floor (156). In still another composition, actual flowers and decorative motifs in the draperies make up a definite rosette-pattern related to a similar but irregular pattern radiating from the point where a corner of a table meets the background (154). The pattern of brush strokes which constitutes a blouse, a veil, a tablecloth, a bouquet of flowers may be united in each unit in a series of vague rosettes (148). Again, the effect of a hand against a palm tree seen through a window may resemble a sunflower, and between this unit and a decorated drapery, a curtain, and wall-paper there may be varying degrees of similarity (125). In another picture the whole composition is conceived as a petaled flower: a central jar of roses, a woman's head, a fruit-dish, a jewel-casket, each is part of the hub-and-spoke arrangement, and the light, delicate, pastel color-scheme is a further indication that the painting belongs primarily to the realm of flowers (131). The actual presence of flowers as well as of numerous floral decorations here unquestionably facilitates apprehension of the transferred value, but the aid is not illegitimate: apart from all direct indications of the subject-matter Matisse has embodied in the form as a whole the essence of our perceptual and emotional reaction to flowers.

In the picture last mentioned, the rosette-pattern is a mere incidental in a form which is also expressive at a high level of plastic conviction. The activity of the rosette extends to practically all phases, expressive and decorative, of the painting. Not only does it dominate the composition as a whole, but within this comprehensive organization other rosettes play the part of volumes in space, of volumes in planes, and of flat areas compactly set in space, to each of which the rosette-pattern itself adds its distinctive decorative and transferred values. The pattern is auxiliary to expressive effects produced by all the plastic means: the movement of volumes and planes in space, the unification of the composition by color, the structural inclusion of planes in masses, are all plastically more important than the mere pattern, so that the picture represents a genuine synthesis of expression and decoration.

Another source of transferred values employed by Matisse is to be found in **tiles,** Persian, Syrian, Spanish and Turkish. Rarely, however, does the tile-motif dominate the picture as a whole; it usually appears in a small area and is so vividly realized there as to give the effect of a hard, bright solidity. These areas are varied in size, thickness of paint, degree of illumination and choice of ornamental detail to give the effect not only of actual tiles but at times also of a stone wall or multicolored mosaic. Several such effects may appear in a single picture, the tiled floor of which may seem to be actually made of the material of tile, and the background of stone (175).

Again, the foreground of a landscape may be a set of color-patches resembling Persian tiles, with variety obtained by different thicknesses of paint, which make the tilelike units uneven in surface (8). Variations in technique result in emphasis upon either the solidity or the surface-quality of Oriental tiles: the effect of porcelain may be communicated to a flowered cretonne (33) or a blouse (116), or the weight, solidity and general appearance of tile to a wall-paper (79, 81, 145).

In the majority of Oriental tiles of the fifteenth, sixteenth and seventeenth centuries, as well as in a number of Persian textiles, the decorative motifs appear relatively detached from the background and seemingly projected forward. Matisse occasionally duplicates both the effect of the tile as a whole and this detachment of decorative motif. The entire composition of a picture may resemble a heavy Persian tapestry or a slab of tile, the floral ornaments of which are so widely separated from their setting that they function as volumes in space (154). A similar effect confined to one or two areas of the painting gives to drapery or wall-paper the solidity and ornamental character of tile (33, 104, 154). Quite often by brighter and more daring colors, more vividly contrasting and placed in more clearly distinct compartments, Matisse unites the general tile-effect with that of a poster (175).

Matisse's use of the general effect in question always involves considerable departure from the original, and the feeling of the tile is preserved without anything approaching literal imitation: the actual surface is dull instead of glossy and the color-scheme is brighter and fuller of contrasts; the floral or geometric motifs are looser, less like stenciled patterns, and they enter into a general linear pattern extending to other parts of the picture. The tile-effect, when thoroughly incorporated in the form, adds much to the drama and bizarreness of the design.

Another device constantly employed by Matisse is a widely varied pattern of **stripes and bands**. This pattern does not correspond to the essential nature of anything so immediately moving as flowers, but it is what fixes and holds our attention in innumerable things intimately connected with our everyday

life, such as clothing, tablecloths, draperies, wall-paper, buildings, flags, banners, furniture and many objects in nature. In the
things themselves the appeal of the linear pattern is enhanced
when color is added, and it goes without saying that Matisse
pushes this enhancement far beyond anything found in the
realm of material things. In by far the majority of his paintings this stripe-and-band motif appears, either dominating the
design or playing an important rôle in it. When applied, as it
continually is, to subject-matter not itself striped and banded,
it often involves extreme and far-reaching distortion; but
whether the subject painted is a landscape (101), a nude (29)
or a still-life (20), recognizable identity is preserved—not in
spite of but by means of the bands—and the emerging creation
has adequate specific quality of the subject-matter, a wealth of
new decorative aspects and forms, and the transferred value
of diverse things which in the past have conferred moving
force upon the stripe-and-band pattern.

The whole composition in many of his paintings consists of
a series of stripes or bands so organized as to give to the matter of each painting the value of other individual experiences:
broad areas of color, divided into stripes, may make a still-life
look like a banner (53); alternate stripes of bare canvas and
vermillion, lilac, buff, cerise and blue may lend to a background the effect of a bright, gay flag (148). In another composition division of colored areas by lines makes the colors
themselves function chiefly as stripes, pervading and dominating the design in which a figure, rendered by a broad contour of dark color and by long areas of related light and shadow,
constitutes an essentially single arabesque-shaped band (167).
Bands which make up a composition as a whole may also serve
special purposes in its component parts; for example, objects
are often drawn and modeled by contrast of strips of color,
which may further serve to render space and, by their pattern,
increase its charm (14). By changes in tone and quantity of
pigment, in vividness of color-contrast, or in degree of linear
continuity in the strips, Matisse succeeds in transferring values
from the most diverse sources, from mosaics, tiles, gowns,
upholstery, as well as from various great traditions of painting.

The conception of the background as a series of stripes and bands is not uncommon in the traditions generally,* though extension of this pattern as dominating note to the foreground is Oriental,† not Occidental. Matisse not only habitually makes this extension (49, 61), but in his treatment of space, he is able by bands of color to achieve the effect of deep distance when his design requires it, to bring background and foreground into organic relationship, and to attain numerous effects characteristic of the traditions but rarely or never rendered by similar means in the art of the West. Matisse is not the first Occidental artist to achieve space-effects by means of bands of color :‡ what is novel is the great increase in his hands in the number and plastic effects of the colored stripes. Sometimes a band of black about two inches wide gives an effect of depth as in Titian or Rembrandt (150, 167). Elsewhere, a broad vertical band representing a figure (117) or part of a shutter (16, 22, 103) at the extreme side of the picture, functions as the foremost plane in the composition and thus sets the other objects and areas in an ordered series of receding planes. Bright as well as dark colors become capable of giving the idea of distance : a band of blue, for example, in contact with three decorated and arched bands of vermillion, carries the eye back into space and incidentally heightens both the appeal of the pattern and the dramatic color-contrast (158). A total linear pattern of bright and dark stripes often extends rhythmically throughout the picture and weaves together all its parts (64, 90, 145).

Matisse varies his bands in innumerable ways—in their color, their width, their shape, the direction in which they lie on the canvas—and the combination of these types of variation yields an inexhaustible wealth of expressive and decorative forms. Color, bright, exotic and powerfully contrasting, is as always the chief agent in these effects, but no plastic element is neglected. The devices, with corresponding differences in effect, are too diverse for any systematic classification ; one frequently used is a series of bands of bright colors which, related to

*E.g., 413, 421, 423, 439.   †E.g., 362, 367, 369, 379, 382.
‡E.g., 355, 422, 425.

strips of still brighter ones, make up the total background (108, 148, 150, 174). Usually, not more than two or three of these bands are of uniform color, and the rest of the stripes are ornamented with floral or geometric motifs.

At times, these stripes and decorated bands become a field for the exploitation of daring contrasts within a gamut of colors so bright and unusual as almost to overwhelm the senses; the complexity of background is increased by greater variety in number and width of the stripes, and by their alternation with checkerboard or triangular areas functioning as bands (174). The total effect is then that of a bright, multicolored flag or banner, decorated with striking and bizarre patterns. Another flag-effect results from the interaction of a few broad bands of deep color forming the landscape-setting to a full-sized figure (34). In other instances, the background of stripes or bands is organized to represent a section of a room including such features as panelled wall, drapery, screen, balcony, shutter, window with vista; the decorative value of the whole is enhanced by arabesque-motifs or geometric linear patterns (51, 61, 73, 84, 90, 91, 98, 108, 109, 125, 136, 140, 141, 156, 157). This combination of complex and bizarre patterns of lines and striped areas, organically related to other linear patterns, usually less complex, in other parts of the picture, yields very striking color-pattern compositions. In this aggregation of usually bright and exotic colors, one or more of the stripes or bands is occasionally of an uninteresting dull tone which, by its effects in contrasts and relations, functions as successfully in the color-pattern as do the bright tones (141). An underlying pattern of bands sometimes appears in a background-drapery in which the same color is maintained through the bands except for its slightly darker tone at the points of division (163). In this case the bands in the background are an echo of a more pronounced pattern of stripes in the modeling and drawing of the main objects in the foreground.

The striped or banded background is rarely a merely decorative setting: it is also a very active element in bringing about the equilibrium of decorative and expressive values. Its major function, however, is practically always to serve as a vehicle by which is conveyed an extensive range of plastic values, especially those of space, color, volumes and planes, distinctive of many great traditions of painting. This is true likewise of the function of the stripes or bands in other parts of the picture. Whatever their degree of accentuation, and whether they emphasize only certain objects in the background and are relatively absent in the foreground, or vice versa, they serve a well-defined purpose in the particular design. That design may embody also technical devices which Matisse has taken from various traditions and used constructively to make a personal interpretation both of the traditions and of experience in the everyday world.

We have now completed our account of the general principles of decorative design as these apply to Matisse, as well as our survey of some of the main devices by which he effects transfers of value as well as organizes purely decorative forms. Such a discussion and survey are of course only a preliminary to tracing in detail his use of the traditions of painting and of the several plastic means in the execution of his designs. To that we next proceed.

SUMMARY

If an object has been part of an experience having emotional value, another object resembling the first may subsequently attract to itself at least a part of the original emotion. Such values we have termed "transferred values": they often exist even when there is no conscious recall of the original experience. They are ubiquitous in Matisse's pictures, and do much to confer upon them expressive as well as decorative value. These transferred values add a colorful, lyric charm to his pictures of even the most commonplace objects or situations. The transfer is accomplished through radical distortions, though never so radical as to prevent identification, and least radical when the object approximates that from which the value was drawn. Both the general method and many of the specific effects involved are largely from Oriental sources.

One general type of design is that which draws its value from the quality of a piece of tapestry, though without any precise imitation. It depends upon an extensive employment of ornamental motifs throughout the whole picture in which, occasionally, a shift of emphasis is made to the upper part, with violence to naturalism but with great decorative enhancement. Another type is the poster-effect, usually in a composition of color-compartments interwoven with ornamental details, with high degree of distortion. Thinner pigment, diminution of solidity, and greater abundance of floral motifs transform these poster-forms into designs resembling cretonne.

In addition to these types of design Matisse has another set of devices which specifically contribute to the transfer of values. One of these is the rosette-pattern, by which the effect of flowers, wheels or conventionalized stars is secured. This hub-and-spoke motif, usually involving richly diversified line and color, sometimes forms the groundwork of the form as a whole, and is also repeated in various parts of the picture; on other occasions it is less obvious, or is confined to an area here or there. Representation of actual flowers, patterns of brush strokes, choice of color and light pigment to suggest flowers, are instances of Matisse's versatility with this device. At his best, he combines this rosette-pattern with a general plastic organization of color-relationships and composition of masses in space to achieve a high degree of expressive as well as decorative conviction.

Tiles also serve Matisse as a source for transferred values, though this motif is almost always incidental rather than dominant. The effect depends upon choice of ornamental detail, and almost always results in a relatively hard surface-quality like that of porcelain, mosaic or stone. Often the hardness is communicated to materials not naturally hard, such as fabrics and wall-papers. The tile-effects are never literally imitative, and the manner of their use is very varied; frequently they are combined with the poster-effect.

Another device of the same general sort, which by transference yields the values distilled out of a great range of experience, is the stripes and bands that may make a portrait, a still-life or an interior scene look like a flag or banner. Stripes and bands appear everywhere in the important and interesting things in nature, and in Matisse their natural appeal is increased by greatly enhanced colorfulness and by decorative elaboration of their constituents. In varying degree of importance they are used in nearly all his paintings, often with subject-matter requiring extreme distortion to admit of their application, but always with increase in decorative and transferred value. They are varied in every imaginable way—in size, shape, position, degree of ornamentation with interior motifs, and in alternation with checkerboard or triangular areas. The motif may be also the means to every sort of plastic function, to drawing, modeling, and space-composition.

In the traditions of Western art there are anticipations of this use of stripes and bands, but in Matisse's hands, as in those of the Japanese, it becomes a means of organizing foreground as well as background, and its plastic uses are much more diversified than in any of his European forerunners. In the realization of the various effects of stripes and bands the chief agent, as usual, is color in daring and original contrasts. Light, line and space also play novel, unexpected and enormously varied rôles but, except in rare instances, their use conforms perfectly with the general decorative purpose and involves no loss of plastic unity. Form of this sort is genuinely expressive, not only of the essentials of the situation, but of the artist himself, of his intellect, his personality, his peculiar and exceedingly great capacity for creative reorganization of the materials of experience in a very personal and highly decorative design.

CHAPTER VII

CREATIVE USE OF TRADITIONS

EXPERIENCE is the source of every work of art—experience as a fund of material from which the artist, eliminating what is irrelevant, selects, emphasizes and reorganizes the phases which interest him, and creates out of them a characteristic personal form. Matisse necessarily follows this rule; but the material upon which he draws for his forms consists, more largely than with most painters of his high rank, of the traditions of plastic art. These traditions serve him, along with things actually seen about him, as his point of departure, and so successfully does he merge the diverse elements which he takes from the traditions into a fresh, individual, personal form of his own that the derivations from other painters may be considered less as influences than as material which he lays under contribution for his individual purposes. Particular phases of particular pictures, the feeling of Renoir's delicacy, for example, or Cézanne's volumes in space, or the decorative motifs of the Japanese or Persians, have been stripped to bare essentials, and reworked in a novel version to form combining elements which nowhere else are encountered together. Not only details of form are thus employed, but technical devices also, and his adaptation and application of these to his own individual ends shows his originality in creating a distinctive style. He invariably sets the plastic quality of derived forms in a context of qualities other than those of the prototype, in ways that prove his extraordinary originality, ingenuity and resourcefulness. His pictures are not only interpretations of objects, they contain also a re-vision of other painters' interpretations, thoroughly infused with Matisse's own spirit.

Like all the painters of our day, Matisse naturally and inevitably made extensive use of the common stock of plastic resources handed down in the traditions of Western Europe. It is obviously impossible to catalogue and describe exhaustively his borrowings from the great schools of painting but a few of

43

the more notable will be indicated. He is of course indebted to the Venetians as is every painter who works primarily and systematically with color. Color is the fundamental organizing principle in practically all Matisse's work, though, as we have seen, it is the decorative value of color which chiefly engages his attention. His work does not specifically resemble the Venetians': his detailed use of color in the rendering of light, line and space, as well as in its immediate effects and relationships, owes less to the Venetians themselves than to subsequent artists who developed and modified their tradition. His space, for example, in so far as derived from the Venetians shows modifications by Manet (90), Cézanne (33), Daumier (11) and Courbet (14); his drawing and modeling come largely through Cézanne (20) and Manet (66), and also occasionally through Delacroix (11) and Daumier (11). In the surface-quality of his painting, though specific resemblances do not appear, there is sometimes a strongly pronounced Venetian feeling in his versions of Daumier and Cézanne (11, 33, 34, 85). His occasionally sharp contrasts of light and dark accompanied by heaviness of paint and drawing (44, 46, 76) have a Spanish flavor independent of the more obvious Spanish influence that reached him through Manet. At times, in his portraiture, there is a Spanish feeling which seems to come at least partly through Courbet (68). The intime feeling of interior scenes, associated with the Dutch genre painters of the seventeenth century, as well as certain of their technical practices, recur intermittently in Matisse's work, but usually in a form closer to that of those French artists—Chardin, Renoir and Cézanne—who were also indebted to the Dutch (125, 128, 135, 150, 155). The great sources of immediate influence are impressionism, post-impressionism and the Orientals.

MATISSE AND IMPRESSIONISM

While Matisse never painted an entire picture in the complete impressionistic manner, his work is never entirely free from the mark of impressionism. "The major features of the impressionistic technique are as follows. (a) Application of spots of pure color side by side in all parts of the canvas. (b) Obvious brushwork in the application of color.   (c) Variation in size of the spots of color and in size and perceptibility of the brush strokes. (d) Use of light in connection with color in three ways: first, as a sort of focus upon which the light is concentrated in order to bring out the glow of the color; second, as a general illumination by which the canvas is flooded with sunlight; third, by such a distribution of this colored light all over the canvas that a homogeneous color-mass replaces the literal representation of perspective theretofore employed by painters."* These practices —brush strokes, general lighting, and well-lighted individual pure tones—Matisse found suitable to the construction of his own forms, after modifications adapted to his primarily decorative purposes.

Brush strokes, his most frequent and persistent impressionistic device, are practically never of the juxtaposed complementary colors of the impressionists, and their use in modeling by hatchings of color is subsidiary to their function as pattern in a general decorative ensemble. The short, either straight or curlicue, brush strokes of Monet, Sisley and others, when used by Matisse, show less contrast of color in the individual strokes and a more vivid contrast between the total areas of color patterned by the brush strokes (138). Moreover, the color-scheme in which they function in Matisse bears no resemblance to Monet's or Sisley's except in those rare pictures in which the light, fresh and delicate tones of the impressionists are selected as a theme for a characteristic Matisse experiment in color-variations (138, 146).

Matisse adheres perhaps more closely to the impressionistic technique in his landscapes than in his figures or interior scenes. The changes he makes in it are directed to specific purposes in each case, as when a small area of brush strokes closely resembling the impressionists' achieves an effect of contrast with adjacent areas of uniform color or bare canvas (26, 31, 141). In general, however, the new and distinctive effects in Matisse's adaptations of the impressionistic technique are due less to the brush strokes themselves than to their organization in areas that

*A. C. Barnes, "The Art in Painting," Harcourt, Brace & Co., 1928 (First Edition, Barnes Foundation Press, 1925), p. 317.

function actively as broad units in the entire color-pattern.

Matisse occasionally resorts to the pointillists' brushwork of dots or short dabs of color and obtains in limited areas effects not unlike those of Seurat, Cross or Signac (10, 111, 127). Here also the dots or strokes are adapted to more complex decorative purposes. His dots are less mechanical, their color is more exotic than the usual pointillist complementary colors, and the units so treated are set in a context of more varied traditional practices.

Typical impressionistic methods of using **light** are also adapted by Matisse in numerous ways. Even a single picture may present one or more of the following features originated or adapted by the impressionists: a flood of sunlight over the whole picture (31); a focal concentration of it (50); an accentuated pattern of light (7, 137); a use of light as one of the principal compositional means (31); a fusion of light with color in a homogeneous unit embracing the entire painting (26, 29, 88); effects of light obtained by areas of bare canvas (26, 88); emphasis of highlights by means of impasto (21, 33, 114), and enrichment of modeling by colored shadows (29, 40, 42). Although Matisse's early work leans heavily upon the impressionists, the total effect is different chiefly because his brighter tones and more vivid color-contrasts make the light more dramatic as pattern (7), more luminous as a general suffusion (19, 21), and more often distributed over large areas (31, 48, 51). In his later work the impressionistic lighting is greatly reduced, and extensive draft is made upon other traditions;* none the less, even his later results would not have been possible but for the impressionists.

Matisse's **color,** *per se,* owes little to the impressionists, except in the few paintings, already noted, in which his purpose was obviously in substance the same as theirs (138, 146). His habitual adaptation of their various devices which affect color —colored shadows and colored light, brush strokes and broadened, simplified drawing—together with the selection of a palette of bright, contrasting, pure colors, testify to the enduring influence that impressionistic color-effects had upon him;

*See chapter on Light, pp. 138–140.

but, except in his earliest work, in those rare paintings in which notes of actual impressionistic color occur (12), the influence is generally pervasive and subsidiary. The delicate tones of Monet, Sisley and Renoir, while constantly reappearing in his late work, especially in landscape, become constituents of radically different and novel color-ensembles (110, 138, 146): he adds exotic and often weird shades, and vivid color-contrasts and compositional color-relations essentially non-impressionistic. Again, the impressionistic colors may be dominated by hues derived from other traditions, from Gauguin (41), Cézanne (101) or the Orientals (84, 108); or they may themselves be one of the means by which he modifies other traditional derivations to create color-organizations of his own (72).

Matisse's borrowings from the impressionists, thus far enumerated, are general and are taken from that tradition as a whole. But it is to Manet that he owes more than to any of the other impressionists, and the influence has persisted from the beginning of Matisse's career up to the present. The familiar long and broad brush stroke of Manet plays an important part in Matisse's work of all periods (21, 36, 40, 100, 103, 113, 114, 123, 126, 128, 132). Sometimes these brush strokes actively contribute, as in Manet himself, to expressiveness of drawing (102, 132); more generally, they are adapted to new purposes; for example, more isolated than in Manet, they become primarily decorative (103, 112, 114, 126); combined with Cézanne-like hatchings of color, they acquire a specific function in a patterned type of modeling (21, 33, 42, 85, 155); diminished in perceptibility, they merge more completely with the pattern of color-areas to which they lend subtle internal variations (77, 92, 94); used in different sets of colors, they aid in unifying the contrasts (84); utilized with dramatic contrast between the color of the juxtaposed strokes, they carry out the exotic and dramatic character of the design (42); they may function also as linear factors in a complex pattern of color (21, 42). In short, they are adapted and modified to yield the widest variety of plastic effects.

The most significant and prominent derivations from Manet are simplification of drawing, flattening of volume, and luminous quality of color, all of which characteristics rank perhaps as the most important and influential of Manet's contributions to the traditions. These derivations are used so constantly and as the nucleus of so much reorganization of the other traditions as to be among the most fundamental factors in Matisse's form.* From Manet come also the plastic utilization of areas and spots of bare canvas† (35, 88, 114); the employment of certain colors in particular relationships, more especially deep black related to tan (36, 66, 92, 102); the patterned depiction of eyes‡ (71); the occasional relative isolation of the light and dark colors in modeling§ (103); and the continuity of the background and immediate foreground in a single color-plane which forms a sheetlike setting to the principal masses (51, 57, 66).

In Matisse all these borrowings undergo radical reorganization, of which we shall indicate briefly the more important types. Elimination of detail approaches the point of extreme generalization and the broadened units combine in a specific type of color-pattern (76, 114, 123, 132); the execution is usually less heavy, more delicate (84, 98); brush strokes become less perceptible in the modeling (94) and the broader areas are often circumscribed by linear contours as in Cézanne and the Byzantines (42, 51, 66, 69–70–71); there is a more abundant use of bare canvas (36) in larger areas (19, 35) and with greater compositional activity (98, 103); the luminous quality is usually more superficial, not so deeply structural (53, 107, 136); the black becomes more assertive and dramatic because of its contrast with lighter and brighter colors (69–70–71, 81, 135); the occasional emphasis upon black-and-white effects is accompanied by heavy drawing and increased pigment and gives a form nearer to the original Spanish type from which Manet derived (76); the relative isolation of light and dark is less a factor in modeling than, as in the Byzantines, an element in a decorative pattern (56, 103); eyes take on traits characteristic of the Egypto-Roman and Byzantine tra-

*See chapter on Drawing, pp. 81–82, 83, 87, 88.
†But see also p. 64.   ‡See chapter on Portraiture, p. 181.
§A typical example in Manet: the right hand in "Boy with the Fife," Louvre.

ditions (42, 69–70–71). In addition Matisse introduces bright, exotic and more definitely patterned colors, by which the ensemble of the Manet motifs is endowed with a new value primarily decorative (108a, 121, 131, 171). There are also instances in which an entire theme taken from Manet, with characteristic color-scheme, drawing, technique and treatment of background, is employed as a basis for variations which, although they bring the work definitely into Matisse's own style, leave Manet's unmistakable flavor clearly perceptible (66). Occasionally, Matisse shows that he can draw as expressively as Manet and in a practically identical manner (100, 102, 114); such *tours de force*, however, are often indulged in by the best of artists for their own amusement and with no intention to plagiarize.

From the foregoing survey it is clear that Matisse has never used any complete phase of the impressionist tradition, or that tradition as a whole. Moreover, the influence of the tradition has usually been not direct, but through the post-impressionists.

<h2 style="text-align:center">MATISSE AND POST-IMPRESSIONISM</h2>

In addition to the post-impressionists' modifications of the impressionists' practices, Matisse adapts constantly the more distinctively post-impressionistic forms of Cézanne, Renoir,* Gauguin and van Gogh.

Matisse's debt to **Gauguin** is revealed in the broad areas of rose, green, blue and orange which, in pictures of his recurring intermittently in practically all periods, appear with a tonal quality almost identical with Gauguin's (41, 48, 53, 168, 173).† Gauguin's quasi-arabesque color-pattern also reappears in Matisse, but with many new traits (31, 168),‡ of which the most notable is the greatly heightened effect of movement (31). His modifications of the Gauguin colors include a surface-quality more like that of Cézanne and Daumier (53);

---

*Renoir is included among the post-impressionists because, even though at certain stages of his career he painted typical impressionist pictures, by far the most important and individual of his work is as remote from impressionism as are the mature achievements of Cézanne.

†Cf., e.g., 53 with 440.   ‡Cf., e.g., 168 with 442.

greater accentuation of light in spots and better general illumination yielding more nuances within the broad areas (41); a more vivid, exotic and daring context of other colors (53); more dramatic contrasts (41); and more extensive and varied use of bare canvas (41). In addition to these modifications directly affecting the colors and their relationships, Matisse's execution is lighter (168) and his technique less monotonous (41, 168). The Gauguin notes, placed in contexts reminiscent of other traditions—e.g., Cézanne's composition (173), Byzantine pattern (48), Chinese arabesques (168)—are so organically related to these other elements that they become integral parts of Matisse's own form.

In much of Matisse's early work the prevalence of thick impasto and ribbonlike brush strokes recalls **van Gogh,** but the brush strokes are shorter, more varied in size and direction, less uniformly distributed over the canvas as a unifying agent, and, particularly in his later work, less loaded with pigment. The thickness of Matisse's impasto is less monotonous, its appearance is often more nearly that of mosaics, and areas patterned with thick brush strokes are often juxtaposed to smoothly painted sections. In all cases, the context and the total set of plastic relationships are entirely different from van Gogh's (5, 21, 48, 110).

Matisse's utilization of the forms of **Renoir** is particularly noticeable in the light, delicate Nice type of pictures. The derivations consist of the gentle, light and delicate drawing* (109, 115, 140, 146), the color-ensemble (109, 151), and the thin washes of paint which give water-color effects (95, 109, 140, 148, 151). Occasionally, his drawing has the expressiveness and vividness upon which depend the intentness and reality of Renoir's figures (135, 138); sometimes, too, as in Renoir, modeling is achieved by scarcely perceptible color-hatchings which tend to flow into each other (123, 136, 150). Fluidity, grace and daintiness are also obtained at times by transparent washes like Renoir's; Matisse uses the wash on loose flowing contours (still-life in 152), and very frequently with pervasive lavender tones to depict the delicate surface and

*See chapter on Drawing, pp. 83, 85, 90.

texture of flesh (144, 148). Each of these features is appropriately modified and given a distinctive setting. The light and delicate color-scheme may be related to the striking black-and-white contrasts that recall Manet (135), or to a context of traits taken from the Chinese (115), or from both Cézanne and the seventeenth-century Dutch genre painters (150). However, in spite of these creative additions to the elements borrowed from Renoir, Matisse loses more of Renoir's color-effects than he is able to assimilate and retain. Not only is the sensuous quality of the color different but it lacks Renoir's rich color-chords; moreover, his surfaces remain comparatively arid, and, most important of all, the less organic function of color in modeling deprives it of the warmth, expressiveness and structural conviction of Renoir's.

Of all the post-impressionist influences upon Matisse, that of **Cézanne** is the most fundamental, persistent, pervasive and important. It extends to his work of all periods, and its adaptations are always controlled by the dominating decorative purpose. Cézanne's compositional arrangements of subject-matter are very frequently used by Matisse (20, 26, 33, 53, 85, 101, 173), though his less organic color and more decorative line, light and space result in ensembles primarily decorative in comparison with Cézanne's massive and deeply expressive form.

Matisse's common method of modeling by hatchings and planes of color is very close to that of Cézanne, but simplification of the planes and diminution of their number, combined with less structural color, make his objects less round, less solid and less weighty (20, 33). When a thick impasto lends a sculpturesque quality to the objects, the effect is due more to the thickness of the actual paint than to real modeling such as Cézanne's by means of the color-values of the planes (21). Occasionally, the hatchings and planes, rendered with relatively thin pigment, are modified by elements of drawing taken from Manet and Renoir (150). In another adaptation of Cézanne's modeling the planes are relatively isolated areas of light and shadow, little more than units in a decorative pattern (103).

In all of these modifications of Cézanne's method of modeling it is apparent that Matisse does not strive to reach the degree of weight, mass and solidity which Cézanne attained by piling the hatches of color on top of each other. He reduces the number of hatchings as well as their perceptibility, makes the color brighter and emphasizes the contrast between the tones of the individual hatches. Objects thus modeled become primarily a series of colored areas, elements in a decorative pattern, rather than solid objects constructed of color and functioning as volumes in space as in Cézanne. In other words, Matisse makes the degree of solidity of his objects commensurate in plastic value with the color-units, linear patterns, patches of colored light and brush strokes, all of which are treated in harmony with an all-embracing decorative design.

The purpose of Matisse's diminished solidity is clearly seen upon examination, in individual pictures, of the widely different degrees of three-dimensional quality and the variations in execution by planes and hatchings. For example, a jug in a still-life may be as solid and three-dimensional as in a Cézanne, and in consequence form a dramatic contrast with adjacent flat planes of color (173). Modeling by planes may be modified by long, broad brush strokes which simulate the effect of hatchings (33, 85); the planes may be so arranged as to become part of the active linear element of a complex decorative design (42); or they may also be used in conjunction with mosaiclike patches of color (21).

Many of these pictures are only slightly reminiscent of Cézanne; this is due partly to reduced pigment and especially to the usual introduction of simplified drawing akin to Manet's. When heavy pigment is used, the effect of Cézanne-like color-planes outweighs that of the Manet simplification (20, 33); when the quantity of pigment is reduced the Manet effect prevails, and the planes of color are visible only upon close inspection (121). Whether Cézanne's or Manet's influence prevails, the color-ensemble is totally unlike that of either source, and the specific character of the design obviously guides Matisse's choice between the two derivations.

Linear contours in Matisse are sometimes reminiscent of Cézanne's but they function less in modeling than as elements in linear patterns and color-contrasts (7, 20, 23, 26, 33, 34, 45). The line itself when used in modeling is often more ragged than Cézanne's and its decorative emphasis is less reminiscent of him than of the Byzantines.

Examination of the compartmental pattern, made up of patches of color and light, common to both Cézanne and Matisse, reveals more differences than similarities.* Matisse's patches are less numerous and he makes more frequent use of broad areas; nevertheless, his pictures are more obviously a patchwork because of his more vivid color-contrasts and the more pronounced linear character of his drawing. These patches are, primarily, shaped color-areas which function chiefly as constituents of a total pattern; in Cézanne they are, first of all, planes of structural color that build up solid volumes. To say this is to say again that the decorative function is paramount in Matisse and subsidiary in Cézanne.

In Cézanne's still-lifes one or more objects are frequently placed above the table or plate, as if suspended in space without support; thus is established a novel dynamic spatial relationship between the unsupported object and those resting on the table or plate.† Matisse also makes use of this effect of levitation but for purposes different from Cézanne's, as, for instance, when dramatic spatial contrast depends upon a large expanse of subtly-rendered unoccupied space thrown into relief by an accentuated interval between a chair and a figure seated, but unsupported (57). In another composition a bunch of flowers is levitated, obviously to fit into a spatial version of Matisse's oft-repeated merging of objects and background in a decorative ensemble (152). Still another distortion of spatial relations strongly reminiscent of Cézanne occurs when floral decorations of a screen are detached from their background and made to function as volumes moving either forward or backward in space (150‡).

Drawing of tree-trunks by two or three parallel broad strips of color, a favorite practice of Cézanne, is the foundation upon which are based Matisse's more decorative tree-trunks executed in strips of brighter and more daring color, more vividly

*Cf., e.g., 26 and 101 with 408.   †See 414.   ‡Cf. 412.

contrasted and relatively deficient in solid structural quality (26, 41).* Here, as usual in Matisse's work, the strips of color are rhythmic duplications of numerous other line- and color-elements.

Cézanne's color-scheme, even with modifications, rarely appears in Matisse and when it does the color, less weighty and structural, is more uniformly applied, has none of the juicy texture of Cézanne's color, and is inferior in richness of the color-units (101, 161). Matisse's occasional simulation of Cézanne's surface-quality is attained by subtle merging of light with color to produce nuances of various intermingled tones; in these cases, Matisse's color is sometimes structural to a considerable degree and quite near in tone to his predecessor (33, 85); at other times the general appearance of the surface is like Cézanne's but the color remains relatively superficial (34, 161); in still other cases Cézanne's surface is tempered with a Daumier effect but the result lacks the depth and solidity of either of its prototypes (53, 58, 76). Even in those of Matisse's early paintings which strongly suggest the immature work of Cézanne, the appreciable plastic difference between the two is due to Matisse's primarily decorative interests (11).

A review of Matisse's manifold borrowings from the impressionists and post-impressionists shows no attempt to reproduce any of the original forms. The selected elements are materially modified and so adapted to individual decorative designs that they generally lose their original plastic rôle and become integral parts of a new entity. The two most important, significant and active factors in this new form are the patterned organization and the bright, exotic, daring, and sometimes gaudy, color which is inextricably tied up in the characteristic and inimitable Matisse form.

Matisse and the Oriental Traditions

Features of Oriental art play a more important part in Matisse's work than do his derivations from the impressionists

*Cf. 410.

and post-impressionists. Many of the general characteristics of his designs have their origin in Oriental art as a whole, and specific traits of the Japanese, Chinese, Persian, Byzantine and Egyptian* traditions reappear in his paintings of all periods.

GENERAL ORIENTAL FEATURES IN MATISSE

The preponderant decorative interest of the Orientals explains the fitness of their forms for Matisse's purposes. The outstanding feature of his work is unquestionably the strange, exotic colors presented in daring, bizarre combinations and patterns. These colors and tones, their relationships and combinations, and even their framework of pattern, as well as the technical execution in color and pattern, are most often based upon features in Japanese prints, Byzantine mosaics, Persian tiles and miniatures, and various types of Oriental textiles. The patchwork type of color-composition common to all these forms of Oriental art reappears in Matisse; that is, he rarely uses the tonal gradations of the Florentines and Venetians, and while he does use the small vibrant color-units of the impressionists and the color-modulations of the post-impressionists, these traits occur less extensively than the broad areas of contrasting color which, as in Oriental art, organize the picture in a composition of color-compartments. Mainly through this means Matisse converts Cézanne-like patches of color into an accentuated decorative feature of his design (56); the result is more like the Orientals than like Cézanne, and while the characteristics of each source are perceptible they are fused in the new form. Oriental too are the lavender-toned colors so pervasive in Matisse's color-schemes, and, as in the prototypes, the manner of their application and their relationships with daring and strange colors determine the exotic and bizarre character of the ensemble.†

The Oriental methods of sacrificing realism to decoration

*According to the distinguished authority, Laurence Binyon, Byzantine art is best described as "East-Christian" (personal communication). But for the sake of convenience the Byzantine and Egyptian traditions are termed here Oriental even though "Oriental" is now generally used as equivalent to "Asiatic" art.

†Cf., e.g., 339 and 361 with Matisse's Nice pictures.

are utilized by Matisse to obtain some of his most striking effects. One of these methods consists in flattening out three-
dimensional objects so that they function as compactly-wedged
broad planes rather than as volumes; some of the planes are
relatively uniform, others decorated with arabesques or floral
motifs. This practice, so pervasive in Oriental art and especially characteristic of Persian miniatures* and Japanese
prints,† had a widespread influence on all subsequent decorative art. It has been utilized by Degas‡ and Gauguin,§ but most
of all by Matisse. In him, the procedure, modified in detail and
reinforced by contextual associations derived from other traditions, produces a greater variety of individual decorative ensembles (35, 64, 131, 141).

Another Oriental practice developed by Matisse with innumerable ingenious variations consists in blending all elements
of the picture—foreground, figures, objects, background—
into a single, all-inclusive decorative surface. In the Orientals,
as in Matisse's most characteristic work, foreground and background have often the same degree of prominence, regardless
of their widely divergent realistic, representative or illustrative value. The obvious purpose is to construct an organization
of the whole picture in terms of the rhythmic arrangement of
the linear, spatial, light- and color-components (25, 36, 64,
148, 154). This type of decorative design is found in early
Egyptian fabrics,¶ Byzantine mosaics,** Chinese frescoes,††
Persian miniatures‡‡ and textiles,§§ in Japanese prints,¶¶ and,
indeed, in practically all forms of Oriental art. An adaptation of the same principle by the impressionists, though with
less sacrifice of realism, makes the whole canvas a homogeneous
mass of colored light which emphasizes the vibration of variegated colors under direct sunlight. Matisse's adaptation of it is
the source of so many new and striking effects that the subject will be dealt with more fully in the chapter on Composition.***

Oriental again in origin is Matisse's general accentuation of

*E.g., 338, 339, 340.   †E.g., 378.   ‡E.g., 396, 398.   §E.g., 441, 442.
¶E.g., 310, 311.   **E.g., 322.   ††E.g., 330.   ‡‡E.g., 338, 346, 347.
§§E.g., 342.   ¶¶E.g., 365, 371.   ***See pp. 156–157, 158.

linear drawing to yield patterns. His lines may be broad strips of color, either uneven, as in the Byzantine mosaics to obtain patches of color (21), or continuously solid as in Egypto-Roman portraits to draw analogous types of patterned faces (42). Occasionally also, his linear rhythms have a fluidity suggestive of the Chinese and Japanese (31).

Matisse frequently obtains the effect of the cartouche, the oblong area of script so common in many forms of Oriental art. As in the originals, he relates rhythmically the shape, color and pattern of internal motifs in the cartouche-like unit with the shapes, colors and decorative motifs elsewhere in the composition. This effect of the patterned oblong cartouche appears frequently in the bands in many of Matisse's designs (109, 124, 128, 129, 134, 139, 141, 157, 158). Sometimes, the decorative effect of the script alone is used in a generalized form and adorns irregularly shaped areas—a piece of lace on a chair, a wall-paper—with small conventionalized floral units or vaguely indicated patterns (95, 151).

Aside from the more purely plastic devices of the Orientals, Matisse shows his fondness for the subject-matter of Oriental life by reproducing their type of persons, poses and costumes, and such of their household articles as the brasero, aiguière, rugs and mashrabiyya. The inevitable adventitious illustrative associations are usually incidental to the plastic effects provided by Oriental colors, lines, patterns, organized in many original and distinctive decorative ensembles (69, 70, 108, 134, 144, 151, 154, 167, 174).

MATISSE AND THE JAPANESE TRADITION

The principal and most direct Oriental influence upon Matisse seems to have been that of Japanese prints. Two circumstances probably explain this influence: first, Matisse is by nature a decorator and a colorist with a predilection for strange colors and bizarre combinations; second, at the beginning of his career, Japanese prints, screens and fans were the vogue in France, and had been drawn upon by many of the most important artists of the nineteenth century for decorative elements which became firmly embedded in the impressionist and post-impressionist traditions. Actual Japanese prints and fans are frequently reproduced in the work of Manet,* Whistler,† van Gogh,‡ and many others; and decorative features charac-teristic of the Japanese abound in Degas and Gauguin, and occur, though less frequently, in Renoir, Cézanne and their con-temporaries. This was a genuine assimilation of the funda-mental plastic principles of the Oriental tradition; it swung the pendulum away from Courbet and his antecedents and in-troduced the Oriental element into the art of the era established by the painters of about 1870. It was into this congenial en-vironment that Matisse was born, and it was to the Oriental strain that his own psychological temperament most naturally responded. An estimate of the value of his achievements in this field may be best undertaken by a brief consideration of the characteristics of Japanese prints, some of which they share with other forms of Oriental art, and of the debt owed them by the important painters of the late nineteenth century.

Among the outstanding features of Japanese prints are the following: highly decorative design; vivid contrasts of bright and light colors; extensive use of black in lines and in areas; contrast of colored and blank areas; patchwork organization of color-areas; simplified drawing; miniature-quality; fine, continuous, clean-cut linear contour; linear arabesques; water-color quality of color; profusion of decorative motifs.

The degree of Japanese influence in the work of the paint-ers of 1870 and later is an index of each man's general inter-est and of his creative ability. In Whistler, for example, the Japanese elements stand out as eclectic devices and specious decoration.§ Degas, a much greater artist, owes to the Japa-nese the quality of his arabesques and much of the decorative character of his linear elements;¶ minor influences from the same source are perceptible in his compositional grouping, in the pose of his figures, and in his selection of subject-matter.** In most of Manet's work the predominance of Velásquez's and Hals's influences tends to obscure the Japanese character which

*E.g., 391, 393.   †E.g., 395.   ‡E.g., 444.
§E.g., 394, 395.   ¶E.g., 397, 399.   **E.g., 400.

is often pervasive and generalized, but is also specifically apparent in the decorative simplified drawing, in the use of black, in the flat color-areas which help to convert volumes into silhouettes,* and sometimes in the specious resort to actual Japanese objects, such as fans and prints.† Van Gogh at times made the actual reproduction of Japanese prints fit well into his decorative design,‡ and he also made a legitimate plastic use of such Japanese traits as the chirographic linear arabesques,§ the arabesque arrangement of floral decoration in the background¶ and, more pervasively but less frequently, the tones and relations of color.** In Gauguin, the Japanese feeling is more a flavor, and is due to the exotic quality of his color and his quasi-arabesque patterns.†† In Monet, Sisley and Renoir, a Japanese strain is likewise indicated by the frequency of fluid arabesques, decorative lines, and the homogeneity of color in foreground, middle ground and distance, though in them the influences have been so thoroughly assimilated that the Japanese thread is barely perceptible in the general fabric.

More than any of the foregoing, Matisse, because of his intense interest in bold decoration and exotic color, responded naturally and inevitably to the influence of Japanese prints. None of the Japanese characteristics is reproduced literally but many are unmistakably recognizable as ingredients in a new form. The influence is apparent in his work of all stages but more constantly, and as a leaven to more numerous and more complex and varied decorative ideas, in his later work. The identifying marks of the influence are found in the daring contrasts between exotic colors, the prevalence of linear patterns and the decorative treatment of space and composition.

Many characteristics of Matisse's **color** separate him from the impressionists and ally him to the Japanese. His color is less solid, more on the surface than the impressionists', it is brighter and more vivid, it lacks the fluidity of tone that makes color-chords, it is set in more positive and vivid contrasts, and it appears in bolder and more definite patterns. The Japanese strain in his color comes occasionally from the light delicate

*E.g., 392.   †E.g., 391, 393.   ‡E.g., 444.   §E.g., 445.
¶E.g., 446.   **E.g., 445, 446.   ††E.g., 442, 443.

tones of the early prints* but more frequently from the later type with gaudy colors, so popular in Paris toward the end of the nineteenth century. The color-relationships in both the early and late prints are repeated by Matisse in color-ensembles sometimes very close to the originals. Point by point comparison between a late print† and a painting by Matisse (157) shows that both are compositions of color-compartments characterized by daring contrasts between exotic colors and by the prevalence of bands, stripes and arabesques. More specifically, almost identical tones of blue, green, lavender-coral, yellow, tan, gray, rose and brown enter into similar relationships in each; Matisse's thin washes of paint almost reproduce the tonal lightness and delicacy of the print; the screen in the painting, divided into sections to give the effect of paneling, is not unlike the banded background of the print. With all these points of similarity, however, in their totality the two are completely distinguished: the colors are used in different proportions in each, and the principal tone in the Matisse is a lavender-rose, in the print, a bright green. Similar parallels between paintings by Matisse and Japanese prints which have close resemblances in detail but equally significant differences in total form could be multiplied almost indefinitely.‡

Besides the color-tones and relations which Matisse takes from Japanese prints, he incorporates in his form several other of their distinctive characteristics. As in Japanese prints, areas of dull color with arid surface are frequently introduced in an ensemble dominated by bright and vivid colors without diminishing the appeal of the color-effect as a whole (136, 141, 158).§ Areas of either solid or attenuated black, and effects of dramatic black-and-white contrast occur both in Matisse and the Japanese prints, and in both they are focal in the rhythmic organization of the picture. In the prints the black areas are either flat and uniform or striated with fine, closely-paralleled curves of lighter tone; in Matisse their execution is practically always in the manner of Manet, as is sometimes too their rich

*358.   †E.g., 370.
‡Cf., e.g., 36 with 375; 162 with 366, 367, 374; Nice color-scheme with 361, 379.
§Cf., e.g., 367.

and luminous tone-quality.* Notwithstanding all these points of resemblance, the color-ensembles of Matisse acquire an identity of their own by changes in the quality of the color and in the manner of its application. His color is usually brighter and more animated because of the sensuous quality of the pigment; color-areas are made less bleak by their internal lighting and brushwork; contrasts are more vivid, and color-patterns bolder and more striking. The difference in color-effect is due also in part to the thicker pigment in Matisse's paintings and to his accentuated spots of sunlight alternating with the relatively broad areas of light that are common to both forms.

Another constant feature of Japanese prints is the accentuated **linear pattern** formed by contour-lines which define color-compartments. In the adaptation of this feature, Matisse uses broader and heavier lines, he reduces their number and degree of continuity and varies their character even in a single picture (70†). This greater variety of line is especially noticeable in the faces, which the Japanese usually draw with the same thin continuous line as that used in the rest of the composition. The nearest effect to this Japanese use of line is found in Matisse's engravings (221, 222), lithographs (209) and pen-and-ink drawings (216).

The decorative **arabesques** of Japanese prints made by patterns of lines in draperies, by floral decorations, by shape and movement of color-areas, by pose of figures, also reappear in Matisse's paintings, but they are fewer in number and their linear contour is less precisely defined. As in the prints, however, the arabesques are organized in rhythmic patterns very frequently contrasted and interrelated both with other arabesques and with more static angular motifs such as directly vertical, oblique or horizontal bands and stripes.‡

The ubiquitous **bands and stripes** in Japanese prints give rise to a great variety of decorative patterns, as they do also in Matisse's work, and by very similar ways and means.§ In

*Cf., e.g., 69–70–71 with 360, 366, 372, 376; 93 with 377; 140 with 380.
†Cf., e.g., 372.
‡Cf., e.g., 64 with 369; 49 with 368; 46 with 363; 157 with 379.
§See chapter on Transferred Values, pp. 36–40.

both forms we find, for example, a background-setting consisting of a series of narrow stripes adjacent to broader bands
ornamented with motifs which suggest medallions or flags
(174*) ; a set of vertical bands contrasted with horizontal and
oblique stripes (90,† 156‡) ; a long vertical band at one extreme side of the composition playing an emphatic rôle in the
organization of the pattern and of the space-relations (22,
158)§ ; or curvilinear floral motifs on bands effecting very
decorative contrasts of color and pattern (64, 143, 144).¶ The
bands in the prints may represent sections of a room, or
they may be areas of bright color bearing Japanese script and
suspended in space, isolated in representative value from the
rest of the subject-matter but very active in the pattern. Matisse varies the procedure by converting more numerous actual
objects (20, 61), figures (29, 69–70–71, 91, 109), draperies
(90), landscapes (111), into bands, or by decorating them
with larger and more loosely drawn motifs (64, 134, 144). When
these bands are decorated with superposed patterns, the motifs
are sometimes Japanese in effect (64, 134) ; sometimes they hark
back to a Persian rug or tile (81, 124, 144). Neither the Persian
quality nor Matisse's floral-shaped motifs made by irregular
dabs of color, which supplant the script of the prints, alter the
basically Japanese influence.

The Japanese origin is equally obvious in Matisse's decorative treatment of shutters, windows, mirrors, pictures on walls
(49, 80, 86, 90, 92, 128),** and in his manifold compositional
and decorative use of screen, door and balcony (73, 81, 91,
119, 157).†† His practice of juxtaposing a series of areas, each
decorated with a different type of angular, rosette- or arabesque-
pattern contrasting in color and size, is less specifically Japanese because it occurs with equal frequency in Persian miniatures and Chinese painting (141, 162).‡‡ His treatment of
space is at various times near to three types of space-composition clearly discernible in Japanese prints, viz., (a) perspective in the foreground, rendered by means of a series of parallel

*Cf., e.g., 368.　　　　　†Cf., e.g., 369, 373, 383.　　　‡Cf., e.g., 380.
§Cf., e.g., 364, 369, 381.　¶Cf., e.g., 380.　　　　　　　**Cf., e.g., 369, 374.
††Cf., e.g., 379, 381, 383.　‡‡Cf., e.g., 333, 347, 370.

oblique lines which increase the bizarre pattern of the composition (79, 156);* (b) organization of the perspective of an
interior in three planes which come to a meeting point in the
far background, and form a sort of inverted pyramid of space
in which the compositional units are arranged (156);† (c)
roominess in the spacing of figures and objects in an interior,
and compactness of the planes in decorative objects in the
background, resulting in an effective contrast in the total space-
composition (156).†

Matisse's **drawing** of figures also recalls at times that in
Japanese prints in the graceful fluid pose of head and body
(158),‡ occasionally in the large oval outline of face with
comparatively small features (93), and in the general use of
a single type of facial expression in different figures (47, 143,
148, 152, 153, 156, 160, 162). He avoids literal duplication of
the Japanese face by substituting for its characteristic fine and
usually continuous lines, a set of looser, broader, more varied
and interrupted lines, and a more pronounced pattern of features into which enter elements taken from the Egypto-Roman,
Byzantine and Manet traditions.§ Similarly, his drawing of trees
is often Japanese in its decorative linear curves (26, 31, 41),
or in its union of angular-curvilinear patterns and softly-shaded
bloblike color-areas which have undulating edges (72, 133).¶
The general drawing of the trees, either in curvilinear patterns
or in broad areas, is much looser in Matisse than in the prints,
and the technique is generally derived from the impressionists
and post-impressionists. Occasionally, too, Matisse obtains by
scraped paint a surface-quality of pigment quite similar to the
dry, smooth-grained effect in the Japanese prints (89**).

Matisse's utilization of these Japanese features, numerous as
they are, is genuinely creative: they are generalized and so
thoroughly incorporated in his own form that they rarely reappear unaltered. In fact, this generalization and assimilation
of the Japanese influence is so complete that a trained observer
could look at scores of Matisses without conscious reference
to Japanese prints. The miniature-quality of the prints is lack-

ing, Matisse's drawing is broader and looser, and much of what is most significant and distinctive in his work has no counterpart in the Japanese. In other words, the new effects secured are not at all limited by Japanese forms.

MATISSE AND THE CHINESE TRADITION

The Chinese influences in Matisse's work reside as a rule in his accentuation of the Chinese elements already present in Japanese prints and in modern European painting. In fact, a number of the Japanese elements just noted are modified in Matisse by being tempered with qualities more typically Chinese. For instance, his arabesques and curvilinear patterns are less clean-cut than in the Japanese and tend toward the diffuseness of the Chinese (26, 94, 123, 133, 168). His application of paint sometimes simulates the fluid Chinese washes of color, and so alters the Japanese character of tones and of color-relationships as to increase the looseness of contour in the patterns of color-areas (26, 36).

Matisse's borrowings from Manet include a number of traits originally Chinese and restored by Matisse to a form more nearly their original. Areas uncovered by paint, for example, serve numerous similar plastic functions in Manet, the Chinese and Matisse, but they are less frequent and less decoratively eloquent in Manet. The use of broad and definitely-shaped brush strokes in conjunction with bare areas is almost as frequent in Chinese painting of the Ming dynasty* as in Manet or Matisse. The brush strokes of the Chinese, wider even than those of Manet and less loaded with pigment, make the drawing appear broader, and more simplified, fluid, diffuse and delicately executed. Matisse's drawing of similar type is usually a combination of elements taken from both the Chinese and Manet, and the effect is midway between the two in diffuseness and delicacy (26, 123). Extreme simplification of objects so that their shape and volume are represented by contour-lines with little or no aid of color or shadow—sometimes a feature of Manet's drawing—is often found in Matisse's

*E.g., 331.

also (98, 140), and is quite common in early Chinese work.* His occasional use of a color-scheme tending to a dark mono-tone effect, in conjunction with diffuse contour of the areas, is also Chinese in general feeling (77).

Matisse's derivations from Cézanne are also sometimes tem-pered with influences probably Chinese in origin. A landscape, for instance, with linear elements accentuated and a color-scheme and technical execution based upon Cézanne's is sug-gestive of the Chinese in its large expanses of diffuse color (78). Similarly some of his modifications of Cézanne's well-marked color-planes may impart a diffuseness reminiscent of Ming landscapes (26). Often too, when Matisse incorporates in his pictures the charm and delicacy of Renoir, the drawing becomes more diffuse than Renoir's, the paint is thinner, and the total effect recalls Chinese water-colors (151).

Elements taken more directly from the Chinese than those just enumerated are found in Matisse's arabesques, linear con-tours and "islands" of colored light. The fluid serpentine qual-ity of the linear arabesques that dominate so many of his litho-graphs (202) and pen-and-ink drawings (200) is an outstand-ing characteristic of Chinese work.† A comparison between the interlacing arabesques of trees in some of Matisse's paint-ings (32) and those in "Musa Basho" by Ko-Shihhuang (Ka-shiko)‡ confirms the probability of the Chinese derivation. Perhaps of like origin are his linear contours accentuated by uneven thickness and sometimes broken in continuity by diminution of tone or by small portions of blank canvas (50, 94). This feature in Chinese art is especially common in con-tour of faces and edges and folds of garments.§

In Chinese painting, color, line and light are often integrated in irregularly shaped areas which seem to float in free space, detached from the surface of the substance which they repre-sent. These areas, which may conveniently be termed "islands," interrelated with arabesque-formations and accentuated linear contours, are mainly responsible for the characteristic decora-tive quality of ancient Chinese painting and drawing. Matisse avails himself of the decorative value of these islands by modi-

*E.g., 335.   †Cf., e.g., 200 with 336.   ‡332.   §E.g., 334.

fying their components in various ways to make them fit into new and individual designs (26, 36).*

Whatever his method of obtaining Chinese effects, his variations from the original technique may be seen in one or more of the following respects: less diffuse and less loosely flowing washes of color; positive and emphatic color-pattern which overbalances the floating vaporous quality of Chinese patterns; and diffuse drawing accomplished by adaptations of Manet's method. In any case, the Chinese motifs in Matisse are so organically related to features taken from other traditions, or are executed with such marked differences that they are submerged in the totality of his form.

MATISSE AND THE PERSIAN TRADITION

Except in his treatment of space, Matisse owes to the Persians few traits not common to Oriental art in general. He adopts the Persian depiction of space by contiguous planes that carry distance to the top of the picture instead of directly back, but attains a new effect by increasing the activity of the planes in the color-pattern, sometimes in step- or accordion-like formation (64), sometimes as a patterned screenlike background setting off the main part of the subject-matter (19). Space thus treated gives to realistic objects and purely ornamental motifs an equal decorative value in the ensemble. Often in Matisse, as in Persian miniatures, figures and objects function more essentially as areas of color in a pattern than they do in their realistic or representative aspects (19, 56).

Persian tiles also are drawn upon by Matisse for decorative effects: the resemblance is perceptible in areas which have a surface-quality and ornamental motifs strongly suggestive of the tiles. Particularly in his later work these areas frequently serve as one of the bands or stripes in decorative backgrounds (79, 81, 104, 145). The surface-quality of tile is usually obtained by an area of pigment heavier than that in the rest of the picture; this area has an ivory ground, and upon it appear, in contrasting colors, floral or geometric motifs which resem-

*See also in chapter on Light, pp. 139–140.

ble the decorative patterns common in Persian and Syrian tiles. Areas of this sort, though placed in a great variety of contexts and well merged with the decorative ensemble, are not always free from a suspicion of the mechanical.

As noted in the chapter on Transferred Values, the decorative motifs in Persian tiles and textiles often appear detached from the substance of the fabric and stand out as volumes or planes in space. Matisse adopts this feature and makes it serve a greater variety of decorative purposes than in any of the Oriental arts (15, 33, 154).* Sometimes particular Persian decorative motifs are implanted in compositions more varied in color and more complex in general design than the originals (104, 108);† at other times, decorated units are contrasted with flat areas of uniform color, as is often the case in both Persian and Japanese draperies and garments (42, 64, 141, 216). Frequently Matisse obtains a general Persian effect without Persian technique, as when a suggestion of the color and decorative qualities of the miniatures pervade some of his most characteristic paintings (69, 84, 95, 141). Often, his total design bears a general resemblance to a heavy Persian tapestry or rug (27, 154, 172), or to a large tile (175). Similarly, his color may recall the Persian miniatures, not in specific hues or tints but in such general characteristics as the soft, pastel delicacy of exotic color (134), and the bizarre but harmonious relationship of bright, vivid, delicate color-patches to areas of dull and arid unappealing color (141).

We may now consider how Matisse incorporates the Persian derivations in his own designs. His characteristic drawing— simplified, bold and broadly executed—supplants the light, minute execution, the precise linear drawing and the filigree-patterns of Persian miniatures. Also, his contours, alternately sharp, ragged and diffuse, vary the areas and make them less definitely compartmental. In general, the Persian traits in his pictures are so interwoven with those of the other Oriental traditions and with elements contributed by Matisse himself that they appear as a pervasive quality which cannot always be abstracted and identified in isolation. For instance, ara-

*Cf., e.g., 337, 341.   †Cf., e.g., 343.

besques of light tones superposed on a still more lightly-rendered tablecloth, partake of both Persian and Japanese qualities, and neither the arabesques nor the decorative ensemble can be assigned definitely to either tradition (148). Again, the bright colors in Persian miniatures are rarely so daringly and vividly contrasted as they are in the Japanese and in Matisse.

MATISSE AND THE BYZANTINE AND EGYPTIAN TRADITIONS

Among the forms of Byzantine and Egyptian art that Matisse has adapted in some of his characteristic designs, the most important are Byzantine mosaics and medals, Egyptian textiles and Egypto-Roman paintings. The plastic characteristics of these forms may be divided into three general categories: (a) mosaic effects obtained by spots of color; (b) drawing and modeling by color rendered by irregularly shaped patches, broad lines or bands; (c) linear accentuation of facial features. The importance of these elements in Matisse's work makes necessary a detailed study of the prototypes.

Mosaics owe their characteristic appearance to the broken-up surface resulting from juxtaposition of small pieces of stone. Variations within the technique are responsible for two general effects. (a) Sometimes a broad area of single color is broken up by the irregular pattern made by the contour of the individual stones. Matisse occasionally simulates this effect by breaking up a relatively large area of color with an active pattern of small brush strokes of approximately the same tone (111). (b) More generally the stones are of different color or tone, and their irregular shapes and vivid color-contrasts determine a lively pattern of color-spots. Matisse obtains this effect by distributing small strokes, dabs, or spots of bright and contrasting color sometimes over the entire surface of the painting (10),* sometimes over limited sections in a total design of contrasting broad areas of color (141).

---

*A similar principle prevails in the technique of the pointillists, but it became a mechanical process in Signac and Cross; in the best of Seurat's work, it is subsidiary to larger expressive ends, most notably, space-composition (e.g., 447).

Matisse achieves a number of other mosaic-effects by variation in technique. For example, in mosaics the whole area of a face, figure or drapery is often divided into series of large patches and broad lines or bands of color, each of which, made up of several small stones of approximately the same color, contrasts sharply with the adjacent patches and bands; the reciprocal action of all these elements gives decorative equivalents of shadow, middle tone and highlight. Often the bands are, at least in part of their extent, parallel to each other.* A corresponding effect is obtained in Matisse by the juxtaposed bands or broad stripes of contrasting color which so frequently draw and model his figures and draperies (14, 29, 156). The texture and color of his individual stripes appear more continuous, that is, they are less broken up by internal pattern of brushwork than they are in mosaics by the irregular small stones. As in many mosaics,† the boundary lines are frequently not straight, but often indented like the teeth of a saw (14, 29, 136). Occasionally too, Matisse's modeling of a face by juxtaposed irregular patches of bright color is mosaic-like in composite effect; but his patches are larger, of brighter and more vividly contrasted colors, and their linear contour is less sharply defined (21, 56). Other general differences are due to hatchings of color in the manner of Cézanne and to alternation of the areas broken up or patterned as in the mosaics, with large surfaces of unbroken color (21, 48, 56).‡ When the mosaic-effect is emphasized at the expense of the hatched planes of color, the result is a relative flatness, with three-dimensional quality about equal to that of actual mosaics.§ Still less solidly voluminous, because of the lightness of the pigment, are the islands of color done in a manner combining that of the Chinese, and of Cézanne with that of the mosaicists (101). Quite often in Cézanne's work the hatchings, patches and small planes of color also resemble the broken-up surface of mosaics, but Matisse utilizes more elements of the original mosaic form, he accentuates and extends its specific traits and fits them to his own decorative purposes.¶ His occasional isolation of patches of

*E.g., 318.   †E.g., 319.   ‡Cf., e.g., 313.
§Cf., e.g., 21 with 316.   ¶Cf., e.g., 21 and 56 with 415.

light so that they do not merge with the structure, is a resumption of the practice of the mosaicists as occasionally used by Manet (103). Such patches, and their relations to lines of contrasting color, occur frequently in the early mosaics* and also in the Byzantine panels.† Another characteristic of Byzantine mosaics*—detachment of parts of the body by means of broad lines of contour—is sometimes adopted by Matisse with the effect that breast, abdomen, elbow, ankle are separated from the rest of the body and function as volumes, stripes and bands or other plastic factors (31, 136, 166). A similar effect is obtained in early Hindu‡ and Negro§ sculpture by means of grooves circumscribing the volumes; in Matisse it is achieved by a broad line of color.

A difficulty in precise identification of sources is offered by one of Matisse's devices which is present both in mosaics and in early Egyptian textiles. It consists of multiple linear contours of figures or objects, the contours being in different colors, and those outside wider than the line defining the shape of the object. In other words, the actual line of contour is paralleled by a series of lines different in color and wider, which themselves tend to become areas of color (29, 31, 32). In Matisse these "area-lines," as they may conveniently be termed, are usually more loosely drawn than in mosaics¶ and Egyptian fabrics,** and their contacts with each other are not so continuously linear and clean-cut. But, as in many mosaics, they often enter into the large swinging movement of line and color (31, 32), and sometimes even constitute the compositional motif of a total design (29, 94). His use of all these characteristics, which in the mosaics were the inevitable result of the peculiarities of the medium, illustrates again Matisse's adventurous search for every plastic device suitable for inclusion in his decorative design.

In his work of all periods Matisse draws freely upon the **Egypto-Roman type of face** as it is found in many Byzantine mosaics,†† paintings‡‡ and medals,§§ in Egyptian textiles,¶¶

---

*E.g., 317.   †E.g., 324.   ‡E.g., 312.   §E.g., 327, 328, 329.
¶Cf., e.g., 317.   **Cf., e.g., 306.   ††E.g., 313, 320, 321.   ‡‡E.g., 324.
§§E.g., 325.   ¶¶E.g., 306, 307, 308.

in early Italian painting under Byzantine influence* and, especially, in the Egyptian funeral portraits, usually termed Egypto-
Roman, of the first three centuries of the Christian era.† The
facial features, especially the eyelids, eyebrows and nose, are
depicted by broad, dark and relatively continuous outlines
which form a striking linear pattern dramatically contrasted
with the adjacent areas of lighter or brighter color‡ (21, 42,
48, 64, 69–70–71, 168).

Matisse intensifies this pattern by lines which are broader
and more loaded with color, and occasionally by deeper shadows under the eyes. Most frequently he alters the Egypto-
Roman type of pattern by admixture of a technique and method of drawing akin to Manet's (68, 153). By different degrees of diminution or accentuation in the elements of his
modification, and by varied plastic settings, Matisse obtains
effects which extend from linear patterns as exaggerated as in
Egypto-Roman portraits (48) to a mere suggestion of the
prototype (62a, 103).

MINOR ORIENTAL INFLUENCES

Numerous additional traits are also selected by Matisse from
Oriental sources as relatively minor factors in designs more or
less Oriental in flavor. His occasional continuous thin line of
color, of even width (31), is anticipated in Egyptian frescoes;§
but the greater fluidity and grace in Matisse and the more active contribution of this line to modeling are qualities more
suggestive of early Greek drawing.¶ The blue, rose and lavender in his Nice pictures recall both the tones and relationships
of the delicate color-ensembles of Egyptian polychrome textiles.** Certain other Oriental color-effects are obtained by Matisse in various ways: for example, in one of his paintings, the
border of a vermillion mashrabiyya gives an effect quite similar, in its relations with adjacent color-areas, to that in certain
Egyptian textiles of the fifth and sixth centuries (144††).
Again, the reds and greens of a still-life evoke the feeling of

---

*E.g., 326. †E.g., 304, 305. ‡See illustrations, pp. 234, 235, 256, 257.
§302. ¶Cf., e.g., 300, 301. **E.g., 309. ††Cf., eg., 311.

solidity and color-power communicated by similar colors and relationships in Egyptian textiles of the eighth century (27*). In other compositions, the delicacy and the relationship of pink and blue areas recall the color-effect of an Egypto-Roman panel of the second century,† with the difference that in Matisse the surface of the colors is more animated by light and by spots of bare canvas (90, 132). Again, as in portraits of the Mughal school of miniaturists, Matisse occasionally sets a large-sized figure rendered in broad color-areas against a uniform background of neutral tone (69‡). Finally, the surface-quality of his paint—dry, dull, arid, unappealing—is much like that of the Rajput school of the seventeenth century and of Indian miniatures in general,§ and the raucous quality of many of his individual colors recalls that of Armenian miniatures (136¶).

Matisse and His Contemporaries

Matisse's extraordinary sensitivity to the picturesque, and to the essentials of all forms of art, made him also responsive to influences from important contemporaries. He was one of the first to recognize the individuality and power of ancient Negro sculpture when it was discovered and utilized for new plastic purposes by the artists of Paris at the beginning of the present century. In some of his pictures, pieces of Negro sculpture are depicted as part of the subject-matter (39, 70); in others, their characteristic angularity, rigidity and distortion, and their boxlike units appear pervasively in his individual forms of organization (51, 136, 166, 174). Cubism, a partial derivation of Negro sculpture, is occasionally reflected in simplified distorted drawing, in emphasis upon angular patterns, and in a gamut of dull dark colors arranged in planes (52, 57, 77). A few of his pictures show a modified Modigliani version of Negro sculpture, e.g., heads with column-like neck, slanting eyes, exaggeratedly long nose, and execution partly by areas of scraped canvas (176). At times, his pattern of heavy

*Cf., e.g., 309a.   †303.   ‡Cf., e.g., 351.
§E.g., 349, 350.   ¶Cf., e.g., 352.

dark line which defines contour and also is specifically decorative, gives the stained-glass effect characteristic of Rouault (32, 51, 67). The vague, ill-defined and floating quality of Redon's flowers is also occasionally obtained by Matisse by drawing loosened to such an extent that parts of the flowers seem indistinguishable from cloudlike decorative motifs in the background (30). Sometimes this floating quality appears in one part of a picture the rest of which is heavily painted, and the union of these seemingly discordant elements forms a strikingly dramatic contrast (44).

From whatever tradition or painter Matisse quarries the raw material of his forms, the borrowed element is transformed by his invention, intellectual initiative, sensitive responsiveness to the requirements of plastic unity, into a decorative creation of charm and plastic integrity.

Summary

Like all artists, Matisse derives his material from experience, but with him this material consists in unusually large measure of the traditions of painting. His vast erudition enables him to draw upon practically the whole domain of the plastic arts, and his originality and artistic importance can be realized only in the light of a review of his judicious selection, skilful adaptation and sensitive transformation of elements from the most diverse sources.

The link that binds Matisse to the Venetians is their common use of color as the most important factor in the organization of design; however, their influence reached him almost entirely through other men. Such were painters of the Spanish and Dutch schools, and in more recent times Delacroix, Daumier and Courbet. His chief intermediate sources were the impressionists and post-impressionists. From impressionism he derived his visible brush strokes, often his manner of illumination, and his well-lighted colors, all, however, employed primarily for decorative purposes. His brush strokes serve chiefly to diversify and ornament large areas of color, which replace the small juxtaposed color-patches of the impressionists, or the dots and dabs of the pointillists; and his light is similarly more often distributed over large areas. These broad expanses of lighted color make up a more definite pattern of areas than is usually to be found in the impressionists, and though the color retains the impressionistic brightness, its exotic and often unnatural hues, placed in vivid contrasts, assume new and distinctive compositional functions.

Among the impressionists, Matisse owes perhaps his chief debt to Manet, especially in technique, drawing, luminous quality of paint and general flatness of volumes. He often carries Manet's simplification to the point at which objects, drawn with a minimum number of brush strokes, lose most of their individuality in generalized, quasi-abstract patterns of line and color. Modeling is often so subordinated to the employment of decorative detail that it is scarcely more than incidentally suggested. With Matisse's advancing development the Manet influence is more and more woven into his form, and in ever novel contexts.

The impressionist influence was largely transmitted to Matisse through the post-impressionists, but these painters also exercised an important influence of their own. Gauguin's broad color-areas and his actual colors left their mark upon Matisse, but in the latter they are more varied and the effects enriched by subtler relationships. So also with van Gogh's ribbonlike brush strokes and thick impasto. These are much more discriminatingly employed, interspersed with areas of uniform smooth paint, and their relationships yield an essentially different form. In some of Matisse's pictures the light, delicate drawing recalls Renoir, and so too do his occasional delicate color, thin pigment and light flowing contour. His primarily decorative purpose requires color much less convincingly structural, less richly nuanced, and relatively arid.

The same general decorative purpose controls Matisse's adaptation of the form of Cézanne, to whom, among the post-impressionists, he is chiefly indebted. His constantly accentuated planes and his hatchings of color are largely from this source, though the color is less rich, weighty and organic;

there is similar resemblance in modeling, though Matisse's, because of pervasive flattening and reduction in the number of planes, is less convincing. Usually Cézanne's influence is modified by a simplified drawing like Manet's; sometimes the line itself recalls Cézanne's but functions chiefly as a constituent of pattern; when it is used in modeling the preponderant emphasis upon decoration gives it a Byzantine flavor. Color-compartments in Matisse are larger and more clear-cut than in Cézanne, the contrast in color between them is sharper, and they are chiefly units in a general decorative design. Matisse's objects, like Cézanne's, are sometimes levitated, but less for the sake of spatial organization than to set them in the ornamental pattern of the background, or else to establish a dramatic contrast between varied spatial effects. Matisse's surfaces sometimes approach the richly nuanced mingling of light and color of Cézanne's, but the color, even when it is most structural, is less convincing, and less warm and glowing.

Matisse's chief debt is to the Oriental tradition and is most apparent in his bright and exotic colors related in audacious combinations and in accentuated patterns. These colors, the patterns in which they are arranged, and the general manner of execution, all have Japanese, Persian or Byzantine prototypes. This is notably true of the pervasive lavender in Matisse's color-scheme, and of the organization of color in areas relatively uniform within, but contrasting in hue with adjacent areas. This form of color-patchwork is often fused with Cézanne's to yield a new form, identical with neither, but sharing the primary Oriental decorative function. The same Oriental influence appears in the flattening of objects into a compact series of planes, sometimes with, sometimes without, variation by ornamental motifs, and in the merging of foreground and background in a single surface organized in rhythmic units of color, light and line. Oriental too are the decorated oblong bands recalling the effect of the area of script in Japanese prints, and also the general accentuation of linear drawing to yield patterns. In the latter, the lines may be broad and either uneven or solid, or they may be relatively continuous and flowing, according to the Oriental source drawn upon. Often the actual subject-matter is Oriental but practically always without sacrifice of plastic to illustrative values.

Japanese prints, the most important of these Oriental influences, were especially valuable for Matisse's decorative purposes because of their exotic colors set in vivid contrasts, their accentuated linear patterns, and their decorative space-composition. The actual sensuous quality and comparative superficiality of the color, its lack of the fluidity that yields color-chords, the color-scheme itself, and the use of thin pigment or washes to give an effect of lightness, are further points in common, as are also the inclusion of drab areas in a bright color-design without detriment to the brightness, and the frequent presence of blacks or dark slate grays, often dramatically contrasted with notes of relative whiteness. Matisse secures, however, greater richness and variety by increasing the brightness of the colors, the force of their contrast and the degree of internal illumination, by accentuating the pattern, by decorative brushwork, and by adding to broad areas of light sets of spots of even higher light. His line is broader, heavier and more terse, and the linear arabesques are neither so ubiquitous nor so unbroken, though they often continue to play an important part in the rhythmic organization of the form as a whole. Matisse found in the Japanese many examples for the bands and stripes which are one of his most important decorative features, but in his hands they are notably varied in detail and execution. Apart from many decorative motifs taken from Japanese treatment of particular items of subject-matter, Matisse has also incorporated in his forms elements from the Japanese treatment of space. His drawing of figures shows fewer Japanese traits, but the influence is sometimes there in the fluid rendering of figures and faces, occasionally with actual borrowing of Japanese cast of countenance. His drawing in general is looser than that of the Japanese, it lacks their miniature quality, and the injection into it of elements from other traditions results in a more striking and quite individual pattern. In general, even the features of Matisse's work closest to Japanese originals are modified in some detail of technical execution, rendered by different plastic means, overlaid with other values, and set in a context sufficiently varied to maintain the complete integrity of Matisse's own form.

The aspects of Chinese painting utilized by Matisse are partly of direct source but consist chiefly in modifications of the Japanese, and in details already used by modern European painters and further modified in Matisse's own work. Linear patterns and lines enclosing color-compartments are less clearcut in the Chinese and in Matisse than in the Japanese, and the difference is largely due to the former's application of broad fluid washes of paint, with corresponding modification of tones and relations. The use of areas of bare canvas which Matisse and Manet have in common is also a Chinese practice, as is the use of broad brush strokes; Matisse in this respect is sometimes closer to the Chinese fluidity, simplification and lightness of execution than he is to Manet. A painting by Matisse which follows Cézanne's linear accentuation and well-marked color-planes may be transformed by a pervasive Chinese diffuseness; and similarly Matisse's adaptation of Renoir's delicacy is largely dependent upon the lighter paint and looser drawing suggestive of Chinese water-colors. More directly Chinese in origin are the fluid arabesques, the "islands" of color, and the variations in thickness and fluidity of line. Usually, however, Matisse's more emphatic drawing and color, and his much more vigorous pattern, greatly overbalance the diffuseness of line and vaporousness of color, and the Chinese contributions remain in the background.

Numerous traits common to the Persians and Matisse occur also in Oriental art in general, although he is indebted directly to the Persians for certain specific characteristics, particularly the treatment of space. Space, as represented in Persian miniatures, by a juxtaposition of planes which extends from the bottom to the top of the picture, is frequently adapted by Matisse with increased activity of the planes in the color-pattern, sometimes as a patterned screenlike background or with the appearance of steps or accordion folds. Matisse's contrast between bright and drab areas is probably Persian in origin no less than Japanese, as is the fusion of foreground and background in a single decorative design in which figures and objects are used less representatively than as units in a color-pattern. The feeling of light delicate color and decorative pattern characteristic of Persian miniatures is very frequent in Matisse's work, but pervasively, without obvious similarity in execution. The effect of a total design may be essentially that of a Persian rug or tile, or the resemblance may be confined to a single area which often takes its place in a general pattern of areas, bands or stripes. Detachment of a decorative motif from its background of fabric or substance is common to the Persians and to Matisse, but in this as in other respects the Persian influence is transformed by increased simplification and vigor of drawing in place of filigree tracery, by less precise demarcation of color-areas, and a union with other elements which make impossible its isolation as a distinct strand in Matisse's form.

Byzantine mosaics are at least partly responsible for the breaking up by Matisse of relatively large areas of color into patterns of small brush strokes, sometimes of the same tone, sometimes of varying tones and shapes, corresponding to the stones out of which the mosaics are built up. Mosaics are also one of the sources for his modeling by juxtaposed bands or stripes, with either even or ragged edges. Matisse departs from the mosaic-form in making the color and texture of the lines more continuous. Another point of similarity is the modeling of faces by irregular patches, with consequent increase of decoration and diminution of solidity. When employed by Matisse, this practice is varied by more vivid color and less rigid separation between the patches than in the mosaics. The area-lines found in Matisse have anticipation in both mosaics and Egyptian textiles, but depart from their prototypes in their looser drawing and greater compositional activity.

Minor Oriental borrowings appear in a continuous thin line reminiscent of that in Egyptian frescoes; in the use made of the delicate color-scheme of Egyptian textiles; in patches of light isolated from structure which appear both in mosaics and Byzantine panel pictures; and in adaptation from the Egyptians and Byzantines of the Egypto-Roman type of face, with its striking linear pattern, modified by broader line and more emphatic color-contrasts. Among other Oriental effects is the detachment of parts of the human body, as in mosaics and Hindu sculpture, which Matisse achieves by broad lines of color.

Many of Matisse's angular, rigid decorative linear patterns are close to those of Negro sculpture, both in its original form and in such modern adaptations of it as Modigliani's and the cubists'; to the latter he owes also an arrangement in planes of dull and dark colors, and an additional type of abstract angular pattern. Minor borrowings from other contemporary artists are also judiciously adapted to Matisse's form. Indeed, his utilization of all these ancient and contemporary idioms is legitimately and intelligently fused in his own creative expression.

CHAPTER VIII

DRAWING

A COMMON misconception of drawing is that it consists of the depiction of objects by means of line. Line, however, never stands alone: in a well-organized picture it is related to color, light and space in a totality every element of which modifies every other. Thus interrelated, the plastic means unite in a "drawing out" of the essential quality of an object or situation, and it is only this conjoined function of them all that can appropriately be termed drawing. Drawing thus has two phases: the unification of the means in a whole which has plastic order and reality, and the elucidation, through this whole, of the essential quality in the thing drawn. The two phases are distinguishable but not separable, since what is essential in anything depends upon the observer, and what is essential for one person may be trivial or non-existent for another.

Drawing is thus an aspect of design: it might almost be regarded as design or form in process of coming into being. A figure or object may be said to be "designed," "formed," or "drawn," and the final effect referred to is the same with all three expressions; the word "drawn," however, calls attention to ways and means, to construction out of color, line, light and space. It emphasizes the specific set of devices, plastic factors, by which the essential character of a particular subject is "drawn out." There is no single correct way of drawing anything; but this is only to say that design or form is personal, and personality cannot be standardized or stereotyped.

An account of Matisse's drawing must therefore indicate his selective treatment of subject-matter, his elimination of everything not germane to his major interest in decoration, and his accentuation, elaboration and reorganization of what is relevant to it. This involves, with him as with all the great painters, a selection, not only from material objects and scenes but also from the traditions of painting, of such aspects as are appropriate to the effects intended. All these aspects combine to make drawing an expression of the artist's personality, and to endow it with characteristic identity. Matisse's consistently decorative drawing necessitates distortion of realistic detail: it is simplified, broad, and usually, from the naturalistic point of view, bizarre; but it has great fertility of resources, and its adaptation to complex, highly diversified, and very individual designs is extraordinarily ingenious.

A study of the isolated elements of drawing, that is, line, light, color and space, fails to tell the whole story unless we recognize the harmonious relationships between these elements and the part played by their union in the total design. What an artist brings out or selects, what he slights or omits, and what he supplies imaginatively—the representative, illustrative, abstract or decorative factors in a painting—determines both the individual plastic means and their relationships. Bright colors, for example, patterns of light and line, and spatial rhythms, are factors common to the drawing of both Matisse and Cézanne, but the two differ as to what is drawn out by these means: Matisse's color, light, line and space affect each other differently than Cézanne's and the result is that the two forms, very similar in their components, represent extremely divergent types, the highly decorative and the deeply expressive.

This integration of elements to achieve plastic drawing of distinction and individuality is effected by Matisse in almost as many different ways as there are types of design. A method common in his early work is so to relate pronounced linear patterns to patches of bright rich color, much modulated with light and applied with thick impasto, that the drawing is accomplished mainly by planes of loaded color arranged in compartments (21, 40, 48). The technique is essentially Cézanne's but the form is Matisse's own.* Another type of drawing is the result of an interplay of spots of bare canvas, simplified representative detail, distorted space, contrasts of color, color-areas treated as accentuated bands, and technical devices

*Cf., e.g., 21 with 415.

adapted from both Manet and Cézanne (19, 53, 164). In general, this type of drawing is primarily in color, but emphasis upon any one of its constituents may make it appear as pronouncedly linear, or patchy, or lumpy, or as a volume, or as a unit of space, or as an area of accentuated light. In every instance, the drawing brings out such qualities of the objects as are essential in a decorative organization dominated by color: a figure, for example, retains only the outline and suggestion of a human being, and is primarily a unit of color, light and line in harmonious decorative relationship with other equally unrealistic objects (19, 164).

Types of drawing may be classified according to the extent or degree of simplification, modification and distortion required to bring the artist's raw material, his subject-matter, into harmony with the effect aimed at, the design; also according to the particular simplifications and distortions imposed by the employment of some specific plastic device, such as brush strokes, or by a form of organization, such as composition in color-compartments.

We have already noted, in the chapter on Decoration and Decorative Design, that Matisse usually treats most realistically those objects which are naturally most decorative, flowers and diaphanous fabrics, for example. He accomplishes this not by literal reproduction of detail but by a broad, loose and generalized rendering that draws out such decorative qualities as lightness and delicacy with the fulness of feeling evoked by their counterparts in nature. This essential quality of things naturally decorative is often not only retained but transferred to other objects in the composition which are in themselves less intrinsically ornamental. Thus in a painting of a bouquet placed in a room, the compositional objects—vase, flowers, table, curtain, shutters—all share the lightness and delicacy of natural flowers (140). This is accomplished plastically by a delicate color-scheme with water-color quality of tones and execution, Manet-like simplifications, and loose linear contours consisting chiefly of bare canvas, all factors blending harmoniously in a single effect of floating delicacy and lightness. Matisse's decorative drawing is thus not a flight into mere phantasy, but an extension and generalization of the grace and charm which much of the real world actually possesses.

Occasionally, Matisse's design calls for a relatively higher degree of realism, and figures are then drawn with greater solidity, more representative detail, and more marks of identification than in the usual run of his work (133). At other times, a few well-selected brush strokes, in Manet's simplified style, make the drawing very expressive (102, 114, 123); or a light and delicate execution may aid in conveying the sense of reality and intentness characteristic of Renoir (135, 138). Illustrative value of a high order sometimes appears in effects due partly to association of ideas, as when color, line and light in areas shaped like islands and related to arabesques and linear patterns—common to the Chinese—constitute the plastic foundation for the more or less literal depiction of a Chinese type of face and garments (168).

The most extensive distortion and most complete abandonment of realism is characteristic of those numerous pictures in which values are transferred from objects radically disparate from those ostensibly presented.* The composite effect in these designs may be that of a poster, cretonne, tapestry, flag, mosaic, or tile; in such cases the drawing of each of the objects in the actual subject-matter requires commensurate distortion. Thus do figures and still-life objects become part and parcel of a general decorative design in which they stand on a par with ornamental motifs on wall-paper and draperies. This primarily decorative drawing of objects is varied to accord with the particular effect of the organization as a whole. It may require that figures be simplified, modeling diminished, that lines of contour function chiefly as decoration, or that volumes in space, the incidence of light, and the position of shadows, be grossly distorted from the way they appear in nature. Each of these departures makes its own demands upon the drawing of every object, so that we find different sets of relationships between the elements in each type of drawing.

The foregoing points may be made clearer by reference to two types of composition embodying decorative values trans-

*See chapter on Transferred Values, pp. 30-40.

ferred from one phase of experience to another. In the first, in paintings which convey by their organization the effect of a heavy tapestry or wall-decoration, the drawing establishes approximate compositional equality between figures in the foreground and decorative objects and motifs in the setting (169, 172). In the second, in a decorative space-composition centering around a seated figure, the figure is emphatically three-dimensional and is rendered by a pattern of stripes and bands, but spatial definiteness and patterned quality are continuously diminished in the series of objects receding from the foreground (14).

In addition to differences in types of drawing such as the foregoing, in which the plastic organization is adapted to the communication of some value in large degree dependent upon actually existent things, there are a vast number of types which are directly determined by the preponderant activity of one or another of the plastic means themselves, or by some combination of them, either selected from a single tradition or from several traditions. Matisse often converts substantially the same subject-matter into different designs, largely by means of changes in the complex relationships between the elements of the drawing. A nude in a room, for example, may appear in three different designs, with drawing varied to correspond with the requirements of each. The drawing of the figure in the first (134) is accomplished through the interaction of five separate factors: (a) arabesques common to linear contour, to light-and-shadow, and to folds of drapery; (b) pervasive lavender tone; (c) rosette-like arrangement of lines and areas; (d) modeling by planes of contrasting color; (e) spotted pattern of facial features. These factors are interwoven in a single unit of highly decorative drawing in harmony with the exotic Oriental flavor of the total design. The background of broad color-areas, pervaded with tones of lavender, and decorated with a pattern of colored spots arranged in curvilinear and rosette-motifs, is formed by rhythmic repetition of most of the elements which enter into the drawing of the figure. Thus the way in which the figure is drawn is what makes it an integral part of the design.

The second of this series, in contrast with the first, is notably simple (109). The Renoir-like lightness and delicacy of the
figure is drawn out by means consonant with a design characterized by the same general quality: anatomical detail is reduced, and the rather slight modeling is executed by a few
stripes of delicate flesh-color nuanced with subtle tones of
orange and lilac which function as unaccentuated planes of
transparent color, and are repeated in the pattern and color of
the setting. In other words, the figure and the setting are both
drawn mainly by rhythmic vertical, horizontal and oblique
lines and stripes of subtly-contrasting, light, delicate colors.

The obvious purpose of the third composition of the series
under discussion is to reproduce the fantastically picturesque
effect of objects placed awry in a room 84); consequently,
the drawing, in each of the elements, is so conceived and executed as to bring out, not the literal appearance of what is
drawn, but the abstract character "awryness." A large expanse
of rose-red rug carries the perspective of the floor obliquely
upward instead of directly backward, and the ornamental decorative motif of the rug adds to the strangeness by its unrealistic placing. A like feeling emerges from the objects in the
room, each of which is awry, and from the unnatural relationship of head, leg and foot to the rest of the body. The figure
is related to the setting by being drawn mainly by flat areas
which form a large bizarre arabesque-pattern pervaded by reverberations of the rich rose of the rug.

The foregoing analyses show that whatever the type of
drawing, the constituents unite to give the single æsthetic
effect demanded by the design. Further examples of this con-
cord of drawing and design are offered by several different
types of organization. In a portrait, for example, broad lines
of color, related to patches of exotic and contrasting color,
may draw out the essential quality of a figure, cat, chair and
background and also determine the individuality of the total
organization (48). Again, in a flowerpiece, loose contour and
elimination of representative detail combine with thin washes
of color to draw out the lightness and delicacy characteristic
of both the design and the individual objects of subject-mat-

ter (140). Another picture, characterized by rhythmic repetition of arabesques, maintains similarity of drawing in all its features by broad lines of colored contour so related to patches of color, brush strokes and area-lines that each object has a quasi-arabesque formation (32). Alteration in the proportions of the plastic constituents of these individual units results in the varying degrees of voluminous and patterned quality needed to diversify the design. Again, an organization of exotic tones in roughly geometric shapes is often dominated by a particular color, and these elements of pattern and color enter into the drawing. A nude, for instance, is drawn and modeled by planes of the particularly exotic lavender which pervades the whole composition; the rhythmic duplication of both the lavender and the color-compartment themes unifies the composition and establishes its identity (141).

In all of Matisse's well-realized designs, each object is drawn in harmony with the artist's total purpose, but the method does not necessarily duplicate that of other components of the design; indeed, the methods may actually contrast, and the contrast itself may play an important compositional rôle. A Cézanne type of still-life composition, for example, is converted into a more striking decoration by drawing the tablecloth, plate and fruit by patterns which are contrasted with large expanses of unpatterned exotic color in the buffet and wall (173). A pitcher in this painting, drawn with Cézanne-like solidity, in comparison with the relative flatness of the other objects, makes of the drawing one of the participants in the dramatic contrasts characteristic of the design. In another painting Matisse reworks various features of the drawing of the seventeenth-century Dutch genre painters, of Chardin and of Manet, into an individual design (155). In this, the consistent delicacy of the flowerlike landscape, curtain and bouquet, contrasts as a compositional theme with a second theme of solidity in volume-and-space units, also rendered in delicate colors. The design as a whole recalls more the feelings associated with flowers than the dynamic relationships between solid objects in space. Nevertheless, the space-volume effect is maintained sufficiently to make our feelings swing back and forth pendulum-wise between the lightness and delicacy and the weight and power. This added æsthetic effect is clearly due to the introduction of light, delicate color as a constituent of the drawing of objects functioning primarily as light volumes in space.

The sources of Matisse's drawing are many, but each derivation from traditional forms is creatively adapted to its new context. With these borrowed motifs he does what countless musicians have done with the themes of their predecessors. The Manet-Cézanne type of simplified drawing, for example, is developed as a theme in an organization made up of a Manet color-scheme, the striped modeling of mosaics, and decorative features typical of Japanese prints (92). Another composition, similar in color-scheme to Gauguin's, owes its identity to a thematic development of Cézanne's method of drawing by small patches of color (41). In practically every use of the traditional styles of drawing it is possible to detect the principle in accordance with which Matisse's own design exercises its transforming influence.

The range of Matisse's striking color-pattern compositions requires in turn simplification and accentuation of each of the constituents of drawing. Often color and light remain relatively on the surface of objects and sometimes cover broad expanses with little variation in tone (31, 51, 56). Volumes are frequently flattened into broad color-areas that have only about the same three-dimensional quality as the screens and draperies with which they merge in a total decorative organization (91, 141, 154, 164). Some of his designs require such extreme simplification that the main characteristic of the drawing in some of the units is the broad line of contour around areas of color or bare canvas (92, 98, 140). Facial features may be totally eliminated (123, 132) or reduced to a few irregular dabs of color to give to an area the status of a single unit in the color-pattern (56); or the features may be filled in to make a consistent part of a bold predominantly linear pattern of color (21, 42, 48, 69–70–71). Simplicity of design, manifested in a composition with few broad areas that have only a small number of tonal variations, sometimes requires a corresponding reduction, even to elimination, of the linear details of objects other than faces, as when the folds of a gown are minimized in order to have the area function as a large expanse of color (94).

This elimination of representative detail is carried further than Manet's.* Manet's and Matisse's pictures are both flat, but the plastic significance of their flatness differs: Manet's brings out expression of character in a figure, essential quality of objects, subtlety of space; Matisse's, like his simplification in general, often reduces the main figures and objects of subject-matter to decorative units on a par with those in the setting.† That this decorative emphasis is intentional is shown by the fact that, in a few paintings, his epigrammatic drawing of figures is as expressive as Manet's (102).

Matisse's characteristic economy of means is due to no paucity of resource, and results in no monotony of method or effect. He displays remarkable ingenuity in varying, frequently in the same picture, the emphasis put upon each of the plastic means, so that any one may, in turn or conjointly, dominate the drawing. Practically every traditional method of using each constituent is on occasion utilized by Matisse, always with emphasis and elaboration of its decorative aspects to accord with the nature of the design.

As we should expect, the prime factor in Matisse's drawing is color, in all its aspects of sensuous quality and plastic function. Abandonment of naturalistic consideration makes it possible to use color to elicit from objects not in themselves colorful, luminous, delicate or exotic, any or all of these qualities, and to embody in the objects new and striking relationships, not only between the colors themselves but between the color and the other plastic means. Replacement of naturalistic color by exotic makes the sensuous quality itself a means of drawing out particular decorative phases of subject-matter: this sensuous quality may be bright, vivid, delicate, luminous as well as exotic. The effect is often not the immediate result of the quality of the individual colors, but of their relationships: it arises from conjunction with other colors in ensembles reminiscent of

*Cf., e.g., 100, 113 or 114 with 390.
†Cf., e.g., 97 with 393; and 48 with 387.

pastel (131, 142) or water-color (95, 109, 160), or in patterns of contrasts either dramatic (69–70–71) or subtle (98) or bizarre (56, 167). Aside from, and in addition to, the impact of the color itself upon the senses, the color draws out the substance of objects by its relations to the other elements of drawing, any one of which may be accentuated: light (88), line (31, 50), quality of pigment (104, 109) or its application in brush strokes (21, 114).

An extensive range of different effects are added when patches or broad areas of color participate actively in the drawing, as when the contact of the patches defines contour and shape and thus forms linear patterns without the use of actual lines (22); or when the patches help to draw out the substance of objects and achieve modeling by their contrast of tone (56), by being superposed as hatchings (33), by establishing relations between solid color and linear patterns (104), or by functioning as planes of color related in space (26, 72). Still further, the pattern formed by these areas of color brings out the specific decorative characteristics of the drawing in paintings which convey such effects as those of mosaics (21), poster (141) or cretonne (164). When the color-patches lack vivid contrast or sharp contour they may be of material assistance in a delicate and simplified drawing of faces, figures and objects (109).

Linear contour often contributes much to Matisse's drawing, either as a major element or as a reinforcement to color. Contour defining shape may take the form of a sharp contact of color-areas (22, 48) or of an actual line. This line is often black (51, 69–70–71) but is sometimes merely lighter (141) or darker (109) in tone than the area outlined; it may also be a stripe of contrasting exotic color (31) or even an area of bare canvas, white or tinted (35, 50, 56, 93). Linear contours also aid in drawing the solidity and substance of objects either primarily by their plastic effects* (45, 94, 98) or by their re-

*That is, over and above their function of defining contour, the lines may so enter into relations with each other that they give such plastic values as three-dimensional quality and movement to the area contained between the linear contour, without recourse to color or light-and-shadow to effect modeling.

lations to color and light (7, 31, 51, 69–70–71). The degree of accentuation of linear contour is determined by the nature of the design; for example, it is emphasized in ensembles characterized by extensive linear patterns (80, 90), or by area-lines (29, 31), or by plastic line-drawing (45, 98), or by clean-cut space-composition (51, 57, 90). On other occasions, the sharpness of linear contour is greatly diminished, as when Matisse aims at a Renoir-like effect of lightness and delicacy (109).

The various methods by which linear contours are obtained, and the different purposes served, again illustrate Matisse's ingenuity, his grasp of the traditions and his capacity for organization. In three different designs (21, 42, 48), faces and facial features are defined by different relationships between broad lines of color and patches of color; the result is three different and individual versions of the Egypto-Roman or Byzantine type of head. Other relationships between similar elements of drawing yield effects reminiscent of stained glass or of Rouault (11, 58, 67). The changes wrought in the linear contours are different in each organization and often consist of variations in width and degree of continuity of line, in degree of contrast with adjacent color, and in quality and depth of tone. These variations are observable even within a single picture (11, 21, 31). Additional effects in linear drawing are obtained in the following ways: by scraping the paint to make thin white lines (86); by variations and contrasts of color accentuated by long brush strokes (40); by interrupting the flow of the line with spots of color to yield a mosaic-effect (21); by another breach of continuity, this time by spots of bare canvas or thin washes of color, to recall the diffuse outline and the delicacy of Renoir (109); by a linear juxtaposition of spots of color at close intervals to give the effect of a broad line of color (21).

One of the most striking and individual features of Matisse's designs appears in units formed by contour-lines of color or bare canvas paralleled by one or more lines of color which are so wide as to function as areas or bands of color. These latter, which we have termed *area-lines,* reinforce the outline of objects or figures, increase the three-dimensional quality of the volume, and form planes in space; by these manifold activities the area-lines draw out the essence of the object and greatly enhance its decorative aspects (20, 29, 31, 32, 50). Alteration in the proportion of the different constituents of linear contour changes the aspect of the drawing and gives it a wide reach of compositional functions and effects.

Light makes its contribution to drawing, usually as an enforcement of color. The activity of light as a plastic essential of drawing may be best appreciated by closing the eyes sufficiently to dim the vision of subject-matter in order to make the underlying framework of pattern stand out. This squinting reveals the activity of light in all phases of Matisse's drawing, in linear contour (50, 88), color (31, 72), modeling (14, 66, 108) and space (31, 51, 89). Light may aid in drawing out both the expressive and the decorative values of objects and thus increase the scope of their functions in the design (111, 140). It may be actually drawn by means of lighter tones of the same color (56), by contrasting color (51), by thin washes of color (95), or by bare canvas either in spots (19, 111) or in large areas (7, 29). These types of light are often found combined in the same picture, and by alteration in either the degree of their accentuation or the manner of their execution, Matisse is able to draw out a particular quality of objects with varying degrees of emphasis. Surface and textural quality, for example, may be made particularly luminous (53, 100, 104), or may appear as a superficial sheen (107, 108, 152); light may help to accentuate the three-dimensional feeling of objects (160), or it may aid in the drawing of space either as distance (31) or as an arrangement of compact planes of color and light (64).

Space is an inseparable element of drawing whether the object drawn is a flat ornament upon a rug, or a solid three-dimensional object, such as a tree in a landscape; the difference between the flat object and the rounded volume is as much a matter of space as of modeling. Flat objects may be projected upon a single plane, but for the rendering of solid volumes indications of perspective or deep distance are required. In either case, Matisse's drawing of space is a fusion of line, light and color, any one of which may be accentuated and enter also into a compositional theme of color-compartments, color-contrasts, etc. Consequently, the drawing in its entirety may be executed as much by the color-compartments or contrasts as by space (51). Since the particular type of space selected—accentuated, minimized, realistic, decorative—is determined by the general design, its representation is most often non-naturalistic, and the essential effect of distance is given by means which have greater decorative possibility than those of photographic realism (64, 84, 123). The extremely varied means by which space is rendered, and its many and complex functions in drawing and design, will receive detailed explanation in the chapter on Space.

Technique, i.e., the various modes of execution by which the plastic values of color, light, line and space are realized, has an important intrinsic function as an instrument of expression, a means of drawing out the qualities of things. Technique, to Matisse, is not merely a means to an end; it has a positive value in itself, and in its independent capacity it works hand in hand with the other elements in drawing out both expressive and decorative values. Matisse's brush strokes, for example, may help to form the shape of objects (88, 121) or their internal pattern (134, 136); or to render their solidity (33, 85) or their textural qualities (48, 93, 98, 134); they may also enter into the drawing of both the total design and its component parts to convey a host of different illustrative (102, 123) and transferred values (10, 21, 56, 130). Variations in the brush strokes result in different types of drawing, even in the same picture, by alteration in the length of the strokes (21, 29), quantity of pigment (40), or quality of color (21), or by contrast between the colors in the individual strokes (88), or between the patterns made by the brush strokes and the smoothly painted surface upon which they are superposed (110, 134).

The application of color in thin washes is a technical device used by Matisse for drawing out the fluidity, grace, delicacy and lightness of figures and objects (109, 115, 148, 154, 160). The manner of application, the quality of color and the degree of contrast, as well as the proportion of each of these elements, may all be so varied that new relationships determine shades of difference in drawing. Matisse's washes of color are technically quite similar to Renoir's; but they lack his variety of tones and rich color-chords. Frequently, Matisse's washes simulate areas of bare canvas in pictures in which there are also portions of actual bare canvas, and function compositionally as line, light, color or space (90, 95, 160).

Bare canvas, or whatever painting-surface is used, appears extensively in the early Chinese, in Manet, Cézanne and many other artists; in Matisse it is often the most active single constituent of drawing. It may, even in the same picture, function as contour, space, light, color and volume (36, 49, 50, 77, 111). All of these various purposes are served by the relationships established between the spots of bare canvas and adjacent areas of color. Frequently, areas of bare canvas make up definite linear contour and function in both the decorative and expressive phases of the drawing of volume and space (50, 56, 86, 93). They may participate in the drawing and modeling of such objects as an expanse of ground (29), a road (7, 19), a table (98), a window-sill (90), or a vase (40). They are practically constant features of the drawing of flowers (40, 88, 89) and sometimes do the main part of it through relationships to adjacent color, which make the areas of bare canvas function as space, light and volume (115, 154, 174). At times, a set of these relations gives the same degree of completeness to the flowers as if they were rendered in pigment (140). Sometimes in an interior scene, bare canvas aids in conveying both the specific lightness of flowers and the general pervasive lightness of all the figures and objects (115). This lightness of execution, intrinsic to spots of blank canvas, white or tinted, may pervade the drawing of all the objects (140). Again, it may be contrasted with a slightly more solid type of drawing done with actual pigment (89), and the resulting subtle contrast between degrees of solidity and delicacy in the different objects carries out the general contrast-theme of the organization.

These manifold interrelations of spots of bare canvas with line, light and color in the drawing are frequently the most active factors in unifying a composition and in establishing its distinctive character. A flood of light, for example, is brought to a brightly colored focus in the background of a picture by the union of spots of bare canvas and spots of light pink, yellow and green (50). This vividness is made a feature of the design by rhythmic duplications, in various sections of the picture, of bright colors related to spots of bare canvas. In some of these units, bare canvas forms the complete contour of objects and increases the luminosity of the color-area thus defined; in others, spots of bare canvas interspersed in the dark contours break up the continuity of line and thus add variety to the lines themselves and to their patterns. Brightly colored objects in this same picture obtain a slight three-dimensional solidity by the aid of numerous spots of bare canvas which function as highlights. A similar distribution of spots of bare canvas in the color-areas between objects makes of the spatial intervals units of color and light active in the total composition. Brush strokes varying in length, quantity of pigment, sensuous quality and degree of brightness of color, play an important part in establishing the relationships between the spots of bare canvas and the line, light and color of the painting in question.

The foregoing is an illustration of the activity of a single element, bare canvas, in giving form to drawing; it is as adequate for the artist's purpose as would be an accentuation of any of the other plastic means in another type of design. The illustration enforces our contention that drawing in any accurate sense is always a product of the harmonious interaction of all the plastic factors. A unit so drawn conveys the essential qualities of an object and also serves well-defined and diverse compositional purposes. The purpose may be the rhythmic repetition of a single type of drawing in different parts of the picture (140); or a rhythmic contrast of several styles of drawing (33, 173); or the duplication of plastic elements which, in one part of the picture, may be the essential factor in drawing out the essence of a volume, and in another part primarily *not* a constituent of solidity but of decorative drawing (80). Thus balance, rhythm, variety and unity, through the medium of drawing, are established between all the plastic factors—line, light, color, space—and between decoration and expression. One or more of these plastic factors may incidentally be an active agent also in drawing out the essence of any of the component objects and in establishing the nature of the design. In brief, Matisse's drawing is a flexible, skilfully-handled instrument for selection, emphasis, "drawing out," of the aspects of things which are important in the realization of his individual designs.

SUMMARY

Drawing is not to be understood as merely the use of line. It is the extraction of what for the artist's purpose is the essence of his subject, and is thus a phase of his design, to be realized by fusion of all the plastic means, in whatever proportion the design prescribes. Matisse's characteristic drawing is constituted by his selective elimination of the aspects of things irrelevant to his personal decorative interests, and accentuation of the aspects which are relevant, together with supplementation by elements drawn from the traditions or supplied by his individual experience, with the necessary distortion and neglect of realism. No conception of drawing is accurate that does not recognize the fact that relationship between the elements of drawing is as important in attaining the plastic form as is the character of the individual factors.

Matisse's repertoire of resources for drawing out the decorative aspects of objects is almost inexhaustible, though the primacy of color is a constant feature. Heavy color, planes and pronounced linear contour like Cézanne's, or plastic relations of spots of bare canvas, banded distribution of color and distorted space, together with simplification in the manner of Manet —both methods, in Matisse, result in decorative color-drawing; but variation in emphasis may accentuate the linear, spatial, luminous, or whatever other aspect is best adapted to the decorative phase of the object drawn. This particular style of drawing involves acute distortion; on the other hand, objects naturally decorative are drawn with much more fidelity, not to literal detail, but to the spirit, the emotional quality of the object, and, in certain compositions, this spirit suffuses the whole picture and determines the color-, line-, light- and space-qualities involved. When a design does require substantial realism, Matisse is fully capable of achieving it: solidity of color, convincing representation of objects and actions, with appropriate execution, establish illustrative values on a firm basis. Naturally such drawing preserves more realistic detail and resorts to fewer distortions than do the majority of Matisse's pictures in which direct appeal to the associations of particular objects is absent and transfer of values is relied upon for expressive effect. In designs of the latter sort, figures and material objects are primarily decorative units of color, line, light and space: they are of little more essential plastic import than are ornamental motifs in draperies. It is in paintings such as these that distortion appears at its maximum, with reduced solidity in masses, altered incidence of light and of position and coloring of shadows, flattening of space and abandonment of any close linear representation. In every picture, however, the degree of emphasis upon each of the plastic means, the degree of distortion and also the manner of distortion, depend upon the individual design.

The importance of foreground and background may be equalized, or either one of them emphasized, or the particular quality needed may be heightened in such objects as are less conformable to the transferred value intended. In a number of pictures of the same general subject but with essentially different transferred values, the same object may be rendered with totally different eliminations, emphases, and distortions. The color, as regards specific hues, weight and manner of application, the linear development, the modeling, the spatial arrangement, the relation of all these aspects to background, and the whole character of the background, may be totally different in each picture; yet each set of relationships may be harmonious and successful in conveying a definite effect and transferred value.

Though each element in a particular picture must be drawn in harmony with the total design, this harmony may take the form of a general similarity of conception and execution, or it may take the form of a striking contrast. Loose contour, simplification, and light coloring may give a general effect of delicacy both to the design as a whole and to each of its constituents, or a general arabesque-formation may be echoed in every object by broad colored lines and brush strokes, with a great degree of variety and contrast achieved by difference in emphasis on the various plastic elements in each part.

Matisse's resourcefulness in drawing is shown by his ability to use traditions abundantly and yet personally. For example, in a generally flat, light, delicately or exotically colored design, an object or set of objects relatively solid and placed in deep space, reminiscent of Cézanne or Chardin, may be introduced and furnish an effective note of contrast, but the drawing of the object is sufficiently in Matisse's own manner to preserve the unity of the whole. The borrowing is only akin to that indulged in by great composers, whose treatment of other composers' themes is so far from plagiarism that it is rather an evidence of their capacity for significant variation.

Matisse's drawing, though in general in terms of patterned color, is so varied as to involve wide differences in emphasis upon each of the plastic elements. Color is extensively applied in broad areas and is in the main comparatively superficial, and the same is true of light. This involves as a rule the flattening of objects and their simplification, sometimes to such an extent that they become merely color-areas with vague indication of detail, but often with accentuated contour-lines constituting striking patterns. Only in rare instances has this simplification as its end the emphasis of the essential quality of objects; usually the purpose is decorative adaptation. Freed from the requirements of realism, Matisse is at liberty to expend all his ingenuity upon elaboration of the plastic elements in their decorative functions, with variations of every possible sort.

In designs such as most of Matisse's, in which the drawing is done by color, color-relations, including immediate contrasts, movement and rhythm, determine the use of the other plastic means; i.e., the other elements of drawing, invariably used with resourcefulness and variety, are in sensitive subordination to color. To this end the arrangement of color in patches or broad areas contributes in a high degree: these areas by their intersection form linear patterns, they may function as planes in space, aid in modeling, unite with actual lines of color to convey various transferred values.

Linear contour works very effectively in Matisse's form, either independently or as an adjunct to color. Actual lines, sometimes black, sometimes colored, sometimes bare canvas, have numerous plastic functions, such as that of rendering the quality of depth or solidity, both directly and by their relation to light and color. They are usually emphasized in pictures in which pattern is important in general or as an aid to space-composition, and relatively suppressed when the effect sought is one of lightness and delicacy. They are varied in their relationship to patches or areas of adjacent color by being themselves colored according as resemblance or contrast is desired; they are also varied in their width and continuity by technique. In all these different aspects they serve the most diverse purposes. When paralleled by a narrow band of color, an "area-line," their plastic functions are still further enriched: they define outline more vigorously, and give added volume, spatial depth, rhythm of planes, as well as serving much more effectively as decoration.

Light is a powerful adjunct to all the other means of drawing. However executed, whether by variation in tone, color-contrast, or by patches of canvas bare of paint, it may be used to draw out textural quality, effects of glow, luminosity, sheen, solidity or the essence of the design as an organization of space.

Space—an indispensable element in drawing, whether two-dimensional or three-dimensional—is never in Matisse merely a matter of perspective, but is rendered by color, line and light. Hence whenever occasion arises he is able to integrate spatial relationships with his scheme of color-compartments and obtain the fusion of values necessary for adequate drawing.

The technical devices which Matisse uses in drawing are extremely important both for decorative and for expressive purposes, and often form an essential vehicle for the integration of the color, line, light and space. His brush strokes, varied in length, quantity of pigment, and quality of color, may serve to draw out not only shape but textural quality and solidity; they may contribute to the drawing of the total pattern of the picture as well as of the patterns of the individual parts; they are also a means of achieving contrast with areas smoothly painted. Thin washes of color, of varying shades and modes of application, form another technical practice capable of similar expressive and decorative uses: in general it yields, that is, draws out, such distinctive effects as fluidity, delicacy and grace.

A very important device with Matisse is that of leaving spots or areas of canvas bare of paint. Such areas may exercise any and all of the plastic functions in drawing, though of course in relation to adjacent color. As outlines or as definite areas they contribute directly to the drawing of voluminousness and spaciousness. Used in the drawing of flowers, they yield not only lightness but substance; spread about the canvas, they lend an effect of general lightness and, when alternated with rather heavy pigment, an unobtrusive note of contrast. In their general relation to color, especially by virtue of their contrasts with colors applied in perceptible brush strokes, the areas and spots of bare canvas serve as an aid in drawing, modeling, space-composition, color-and-light pattern and rhythm, and thus heighten all the plastic effects without detriment to their own specifically decorative or expressive quality.

Drawing, in sum, is an effective interaction between all the plastic elements, their coöperation as a flexible instrument for drawing out whatever qualities in a given object or situation are essential for a particular design. Such drawing, as well as conveying essential qualities, maintains æsthetically moving relationships throughout the picture.

CHAPTER IX

COLOR

COLOR makes Matisse's pictures what they are. Matisse himself has said that the æsthetic emotion with which an object inspires him is never fully expressed until the object has been completely reconceived in terms of color. His statement is corroborated by the fact that the paintings of no other artist lose so much of their form in even the most skilful and painstaking photographic reproduction: the tones themselves and the forms and relations resulting from their interplay escape the camera. This, of course, is true of any painting, but in the work of other painters more of the basic form finds its way into the photograph. In other words, the essential difference between Matisse and other artists—the Venetians, or Renoir and Cézanne—in whose work color is also fundamental, is that color in the latter is one of the means to an end, while Matisse's color is more nearly an end in itself.

The very attributes that force Matisse's color upon the spectator's attention are also those which establish its identity as self-expression. We have seen similar colors before but from their occurrence in other contexts we may remember them as raucous, crude, or merely odd; this explains why the average person, when he sees Matisse's paintings for the first time, is shocked by the impact of color upon the senses and bewildered by an onslaught of perceptions and associations that run counter to the conventional ideas of painting as an art. The immediate quality of the color itself is the outstanding feature and that which first shocks the senses as well as the sensibilities. The bright, lively, exotic quality, and the bold and daring contrasts of these vivid colors, are disturbing. The number of actual pigments in Matisse's palette is exceptionally large, and includes, for example, two tones of violet and three of green. The unusual tones and the multiplicity of their relations to each other and to each of the plastic factors, are responsible for the bizarre effects that amaze us in his work.

His designs consist of a succession of bold but harmonious patterns of bright, daring and exotic colors in strikingly dramatic contrasts; in each design it is the particular plastic purpose which the color serves that determines the employment of all the other means. Broad areas of color frequently form the vehicle for drawing which is often greatly simplified and may depart widely from the actual color of the object drawn. These areas, in the form of planes, often render volumes, though naturally the modeling is correspondingly flattened; the contrast of the color-compartments is a potent instrument of drama. In other words, Matisse's use of the plastic means other than color is comprehensible only to one who keeps in mind their rôle as adjuncts to direct color-effects. The present chapter is chiefly an account of the ways, numerous almost beyond computation, in which color-organization is effected and contributed to by the use of light, line and space.

Color-Relations

The decorative effects and the individuality of Matisse's color-organization are due more to the relationships between the colors than to the sensuous quality of the tones themselves. That these relationships determine the individuality of Matisse's design is shown by the fact that he often takes individual colors or even whole color-units from other traditions and obtains with them different and individual effects. In other words, the new relationships are the identifying marks in an array of plastic effects that embrace variety in color- and light-values, in dramatic contrasts, in degree of solidity and in unity of design. Thus we see Matisse transform the Spanish black-and-white color-effect (76), Gauguin's exotic rose, green and blue (48, 168), Manet's black and tan (36, 66, 100), or the vivid color-scheme of Japanese prints (156), into individual forms with relationships quite different from those in the originals. The same principle obtains in those of Matisse's pictures in which colors, in themselves gaudy, raucous, dull, dead and of inferior sensuous quality, enter harmoniously into ensembles unified by extremely subtle relationships. This is effected in two general types of color-organization. In one, the lack of appeal of the individual colors persists in the ensemble; but this sensuous quality is responsible for the very particular character of the striking dramatic color-contrasts which constitute the outstanding feature of the design (166). In the other type, contrast is so secondary and the gaudy and the dull tones enter into such relations with the other colors that they actually contribute to the pleasing sensuous quality of the whole (134, 141).

This skilful blending of colors of unequal sensuous appeal is also an outstanding characteristic of Persian miniatures and Japanese prints. Upon both of these sources, as we have already seen, Matisse drew freely for colors and color-relationships, but the Oriental elements are significantly modified and their compositional range, their plastic function, extended. The tone, for instance, is increased in brightness and endowed with more vitality by fusion with light, and the relationships are established by a different technique. Indeed, the sensuous quality of Matisse's color and his fine feeling for its relationships often make interesting a composition which in other respects is banal (81). The internal vitality of Matisse's color is, in general, due more to the brightness of the tone, the effective merging with light and the directness of technique than to tonal modulations or rich quality of pigment. There are a few exceptions, however, in which deep, rich, juicy, solid surfaces add depth to the color (25, 104).

Color-Contrasts

Contrast is the essence of all drama, and it is striking or subtle in proportion to the degree of disparity between the elements contrasted. It is a constant feature in Matisse at all periods, and is realized chiefly by use of color. His color-drama extends from the extraordinarily daring to the infinitely subtle, in a wide range of effects, whether the color-scheme is dominated by bright or by dark tones. The dramatic contrasts may be between two color-areas varied as regards internal pattern

(148, 154); between broad areas of bright, exotic, relatively uniform color (56); between a three-dimensional solid object with few colors and a flat background with more numerous and brighter colors (134, 143); or between color-areas which function as volumes in the upper part of the picture and more nearly as color-planes in the lower (64). Sometimes striking dramatic effects are accomplished obviously by contrasts of black and white (76), at other times subtly with colors either delicate (109) or bright and exotic (40). Whatever the colors, if the relationships are right, we have the abstract feeling of drama; if, however, they are not right, if drama is secured by mere juxtaposition of bright or exotic colors which do not combine as integral parts of the form, the result is specious and lacks conviction (171).

A study of Matisse's color-contrasts must include their intrinsic effects and their function as means to a great variety of designs. The contrasts may pervade the whole picture and thus be an outstanding feature both of the foreground and background considered separately, and of the two in relation to each other (56, 156). Often the unusual and audacious character of the contrast engrosses the attention, as when areas of ultramarine, coral-pink and orange, impinge upon a large expanse of light green divided by stripes of darker green (173). At the other extreme, a set of subdued color-contrasts may owe their particular dramatic character to accentuated black lines around the areas of color (36, 52, 67). Color-contrast may be emphasized by impasto when the thick pigment is juxtaposed to areas of different color applied thinly (21, 24, 40). Often a sequence of light, bright and delicate colors, subtly contrasted, comes in abrupt contact with one or more areas of positive or dark colors (129), sometimes even a jet black (81, 98). The introduction of exotic and daring colors is frequently the instrument of the contrasts which individualize Matisse's versions of traditional forms (26, 33, 122, 145, 173); when the colors introduced are not exotic and resemble more closely those of the prototype, the individuality of Matisse's transformations is diminished (66) or almost lost (5, 12, 103).

Variation in the sensuous quality of the contrasting colors

provides for great diversity of effects. Thus we find ensembles in which the contrasts are between bright, sensuously pleasing colors and dull, uninteresting ones (144, 166) ; between colors near in tone (94, 109) ; between light and dark colors (51) ; between the color of pigment and that of the bare canvas (7, 19, 25, 40) ; between colors radically different in hue but all bright and vivid (56, 167). Quite often, too, the theme of Matisse's color-organization of a picture is a rhythmic inter-play of two sets of colors so grouped and set against each other that their effect is that of two contrasting color-schemes (95, 104, 108, 128).

The frequency and importance of black in Matisse's color-contrasts direct our attention to the sensuous quality of that color and to the manner of its use. It frequently has the rich, lustrous quality of Velásquez's, Courbet's and Manet's black (51, 52), but this quality is sometimes lost because of the way in which the black is tempered with green, blue or brown. As he drew more and more from the Oriental arts, the composi-tional effects of his varied tones of black became increasingly similar to those in Japanese prints. That is, his black in areas or in lines makes startling dramatic notes by contact with white or with light and bright colors, to which it acts as a foil ; thus it both gives vitality or activity to the pattern and functions as a focus in the color-composition (69–70–71, 81).

The plastic function of color-contrasts, that is, the part they play in the design as a whole, is more significant than the drama of individual contrasts. This larger significance is due to the instrumental use of color-contrasts for practically all plastic purposes and in ways which are as characteristic as the effects. Units of color-contrast, for instance, become active composi-tional factors in the color-ensemble by their rhythmic repeti-tion in various parts of the picture. Sometimes a whole unit made of several colors is duplicated (167, 169) ; at other times, one color of the contrast-unit, repeated in another part of the picture in a different color-context, maintains a rhythmic and unifying relationship with the original unit and also contrib-utes to the complexity of the theme of color-contrasts (56, 69–70–71). Similarly, rhythmic color-contrasts between areas and contour-lines aid materially both in the integration of the total design and in the drama and variety of the color-organization (7, 31). Again, Matisse's rendering of spatial intervals by sharp contrast of color is quite different from that of other great colorists, Renoir and Cézanne, for example, who rely mainly upon modulation of tone for that purpose (31, 42). Equally individual is Matisse's effect of deep distance obtained by contrast between a band of bright color and one of dark color (136, 150). His modeling too is frequently achieved by contrast of colors used in parallel bands (14, 29, 156), in small patches or planes (20, 23, 42, 48), or in spots, lines and irregular daubs (21). A similar instrumental use of color-contrasts in his drawing, linear patterns, illumination and compositional arrangement of masses, is responsible for much of the diversity and individuality of his most important paintings.

COLOR-PATTERN

Color and pattern, the factors most essential to successful decoration, attain their highest value when they are so completely unified as to produce a single effect. It follows as a matter of course that the variations in each, and in the manner and degree of their integration, are an index of the artist's interests and of the degree of activity of the decorative forms in his work. Matisse's primary concern for color and decoration has resulted in a variety of color-patterns probably unequaled in the work of any other painter.

A painting by Matisse which does not owe much of its appeal to an accentuated color-pattern is a rarity. At all stages of his work and whatever the extent of his experiments with colors of strange sensuous quality, his ingenuity has been directed to devising new patterns to harmonize with particular colors. His color and pattern work hand in hand as color-pattern even when, as is usually the case, one or the other of them is emphasized. In the interest of this color-pattern type of organization all the plastic means are extremely active, and every other effect such as three-dimensional solidity, realistic movement of line, and psychological characterization, is subordinated in accordance with the exigencies of each individual design. Volumes in the foreground, for instance, may be stripped of three-dimensional solidity and their drawing so simplified that they lose their identity as masses and function primarily as colored areas, on the same plastic level as ornamental motifs on draperies and flat areas of the background-setting. The result is an increase of dramatic color-contrast and of rhythmic duplication of units, and an organized color-pattern which embraces the entire picture. The composite effect is often more reminiscent of a poster, a cretonne, or a flag, than of the actual subject-matter presented, and only upon second thought do we recognize that objects and figures are rendered with sufficient realism to insure their identification (50, 53, 56, 141, 148, 157, 159).

Broad areas of color, so characteristic of Matisse's pattern, occur also in primitive paintings, in early frescoes, in decorative murals, in the work of the Orientals and in that of many modern artists, including Manet and Gauguin. Matisse draws upon nearly all of these traditions, most heavily upon the Oriental arts, especially Persian and Japanese. His borrowings in each case are points of departure for experiments which have so changed the color of the areas, their relationships and their purpose in the design, that each transformation has a plastic identity of its own. A consideration of the identifying marks of Matisse's broad color-areas is necessary to an understanding of some of his most important paintings. His color-areas are rarely completely uniform. Patches of color which at a distance may appear uniform are varied in surface-effect in a number of ways: by slight modulation of tone resulting from the use of lighter color (31), thinner pigment (95), or from areas of bare canvas (50); by brushwork (48, 56); by linear patterns (46, 64); and, occasionally, by subtle color-chords which merge into a rich composite surface-effect (33). In his early work the effect of breadth in the areas results from a tendency of the brush strokes to merge with each other both in actual texture and in color (7, 10). In all Matisse's work these broad areas serve well-defined purposes by virtue of either their shape or color, or of both. For example, emphasis on the geometric shape may contribute to the boldness of color-patterns (48, 56); curvilinear areas may promote the feeling of movement in a rhythm of color-masses (31); dramatic color-contrast may be made more effective by the contact of relatively uniform expanses of color with areas broken up by brushwork (94) or by ornamental motifs (64, 104); finally, broad areas may function as planes of color which participate actively in the decorative organization of space (31, 141).

Accentuated contour of the broad areas works together with the color-contrasts to effect the **compartmental color-pattern** characteristic of those Matisse compositions in which objects and figures function less as realistic representations than as decorative elements or areas of color. This type of pattern is derived largely from Persian miniatures, Japanese prints, Egyptian textiles, Byzantine panels and mosaics, and the European primitives, but Matisse extends its range beyond that in these sources by greater variation in the components of the pattern. Contrast of color contributes to the individuality of the design in most cases, but at times the underlying framework of the areas may also provide a striking pictorial quality partly or wholly independent of the color-contrasts (51, 52, 69–70–71). The degree of accentuation of either element, that is, of color or pattern, provides for a range of effects in which the predominance of either element may establish the character of the compartmental design as primarily an adventure in dramatic color-contrasts or in bizarre arrangement of shapes. The latter is achieved sometimes by accentuation of black or colored line of demarcation between areas so near in tone that the contrast between their color is subsidiary to the contrast between their size, shape and position (57, 67). Less often the varied geometric shapes of the areas are defined by the direct contact of the flat expanses of color (31, 95, 100). Occasionally, instead of having actual lines of contour, the color-areas are changed in tone where they meet, and the resulting modified color-tone is an additional source of effects: the area of demarcation may be broad or narrow, varied in intensity of tone and in degree of sharpness (109). Another effect, that of dramatic color-contrast, is obtained by an actual line of bright and vivid color introduced between two areas, as, for example, a line of Venetian red between areas of yellowish ivory and brownish slate (22). All these methods of treatment, with accentuation of any one of them, are found frequently in the same composition. The question is merely one of emphasis, so that a compartmental composition may present, as a dominating feature, dramatic color-contrasts between the compartments (56), or geometric shapes with or without actual linear contour (52), or a line of contrasting color separating a few of the patches in a composition in which most of the areas have no linear demarcation (40). This change in detail Matisse exploits very abundantly in designs embodying a host of direct plastic values as well as effects familiar to us in everyday life. These transferred values are often rendered by slight changes in treatment without alteration of the compartmental character; for example, variations in modeling and the treatment of space in a still-life may make the representative objects and the ornamental motifs of draperies appear in slight relief from their settings, and give an effect not unlike that of a heavily embroidered or beaded patchwork quilt (154).

The compositional function of color-compartments is so highly important and significant in Matisse's work that they often determine the character and individuality of a design. His organization of color-compartments involves a radical departure from conventional composition of volumes in space. Frequently he renders volumes and space as patches of color, and composition in deep space is given an equivalent in terms of pattern (26); when realistic depth does appear, it is achieved by manipulation of both the color and the pattern of the color-compartments (72). Elsewhere, the color-compartments, of equal degree of prominence in foreground and background, reduce the difference between these two sections of the picture and emphasize the totality of the composition as a single compartmental pattern (19, 53, 141, 164, 167, 175). In this type of composition the figures, still-life objects, spatial intervals, background units, all become patches of color adapted to a variety of designs or purposes; thus, accentuation of color-contrast and geometric shape yields the poster-effect (141); closely packed planes of color largely supersede deep space and convert a still-life or an interior scene into a highly decorative series of bright, daring, exotic colors arranged in compartments (53, 175). Color-compartments used both for modeling of three-dimensional units in the foreground and, on a larger scale, for rendering the few large areas of the background, may maintain a color-compartment organization even in pictures in which positive space-and-volume composition is one of the dominant features (33, 51, 155). Organization by compartmental color is thus valuable not only for purely decorative purposes and for the transfer of values, but also for conveying a considerable degree of essential realism.

Like all other compositional factors, color-compartments are effective in proportion as they coöperate with all the other constituents—drawing, color-contrasts, linear patterns and the various aspects of light and space—to achieve a unified design. When thus used, color-compartments become an indispensable aid to Matisse's decorative methods of organizing color in a form which is individual as well as genuinely expressive of universal human values.

EXPERIMENTS IN COLOR

A study of a group of Matisse's paintings thrills and excites the senses and mind of a trained observer in much the same way and for the same reasons as does a systematic investigation in science. It feeds the senses with an infinity of new impressions, stimulating the mind to organize them in units which in turn create new excitements as they merge harmoniously in well-organized designs. This interplay of the senses, mind, and matter, constantly and successfully readapted to definitely conceived complex purposes, explains the fascination of scientific experimentation. Investigation in science is successful in proportion to the richness of the experimenter's background, his range of imagination, and that feeling of rightness of relations revealed in what he creates. This means that every successful scientific investigator is also an artist; it means too that the individuality of Matisse's art springs from the same psychological roots which in another environment flower into science. Matisse has often said that each of his paintings is a new experiment, a statement confirmed by the pictures themselves, no two of which, regardless of resemblance in subject-matter, color-scheme or general design, are identical in form.* His experiments are chiefly with color and they cover practically every rôle, especially every decorative rôle, that color can be made to play. All is grist to his mill, and whether he is moved by a landscape, a person's character, a still-life, the dynamic relations of volumes in space, or the characteristics of any great tradition of painting, the outstanding feature of the presentation is always one or more of the manifestations of color: sensuous quality, contrasts, pattern, relationships, each peculiar to Matisse. Under our eyes we see the traditional forms of painting broken up and their elements picked out, transformed, recombined, and united in new adventures that thrill us by what they reveal of the experimenter's imagination and technical resources. That the revelation of an increased decorative quality is achieved at the expense of greater expressive values does not diminish either the thrill generated by our observation of the transformation in process, or the validity of the satisfaction that comes from our perception of a new form speaking in its own right.

The range of Matisse's experiments with color as the main factor in this transformation may be illustrated by a brief study of a few particular examples in which landscape furnishes the subject-matter. A color-scheme in which green, gray, tan and lavender are the dominant tones, is introduced into different traditional types of landscape, with widely varying effects (101, 111, 133, 137, 138, 161). Matisse's transformation by means of this color-scheme may take the form either of variations in the technical treatment of the component color-areas or of the introduction of other colors and color-relationships. A composition, for example, based upon Cézanne's treatment of volumes and upon Théodore Rousseau's use of light, becomes a characteristic Matisse color-organization mainly through the medium of a color—tan tinged with coral—so expanded in

*See chapter on Thematic Variation, pp. 163–175.

area that it engages the attention no less than the green and the gray (161). The same general color-scheme worked into another type of composition with traits characteristic of the impressionists and the Japanese, acquires a new identity as a color-organization by an increased brightness and illumination in the green, and by the introduction of more blue (133). Still another version of this color-scheme is obtained by a predominance of green over the other tones in a composition executed mainly by the impressionists' technique of brush strokes and broken color (138). Again, the lavender, toned to grayish lavender and lavender-tan, and used extensively in a composition reminiscent of Cézanne's familiar rendering of houses and trees, introduces a novel note in both the sensuous quality of the color and the checkerboard pattern of its organization (101). Cézanne's solid three-dimensional quality is emphasized by Matisse in another picture of this same category, so that a relatively high degree of weight and solidity are the outstanding features of the color-scheme (137). In still another picture, very numerous small brush strokes of gray, green, tan and lavender, juxtaposed to many small areas of bare canvas, recall the familiar effects of Seurat, modified by feelings suggestive of van Gogh and of multicolored mosaics (111). In all these variations upon a single theme, the motif, the essentially identical color-scheme, is never lost from sight. The whole series of experiments testifies to Matisse's resourcefulness, to his versatility, to his ability to combine in distinctive and unified forms values transferred from landscapes and a number of diverse plastic traditions.

Color-Scheme

The wide range of Matisse's color-schemes is understandable when we consider the quality and number of his colors, his feeling for decoration, and his fertility in the invention of designs of which color furnishes the keynote. Primary interest in immediate sensuous quality is revealed in ensembles all the elements of which are sometimes bright and exotic (21, 56), or pervasively delicate (109), or monochromatic (60, 78), or subdued (87); sometimes bright colors are combined with dull (136, 144), or with delicate tones (108). Each ensemble has a characteristic Matisse flavor: vivid contrasts of color, of light, of shape, and of line, in a highly decorative organization. None is a mere exercise in color, it is always also an expression of aspects of traditional forms or of everyday objects and situations of universal interest. For example, effects and values which appeal to us in the external world are rendered by means of individual color-schemes, predominantly light and bright, or dark and relatively somber, or rich and solid. Thus different color-schemes contribute to the ineffable lightness and delicacy of flowers (140), to the weight and solidity of heavy objects (58), or to the textural reality of materials (155).*

The foregoing general principles may be illustrated by a large number of pictures dating from 1917, when Matisse took up his abode in Nice. The palette in these consists, in general, of light and luminous colors near to each other in tone, with a predominance of greatly varied shades of lavender, blue, rose, green and pearly gray. These tones often have a precious delicacy, a quality of Egyptian textiles, of water-color, of pastel, or of mother-of-pearl. A multitude of color-schemes is obtained by variation in the proportions, degrees of accentuation and relationships of these tones, and very frequently by their contrast with areas of more positive color which function as focal points in the color-organization. The focal point may be a jet black (81), a red (90), a blue (86), a green (134); indeed, it so varies in color that it further extends the range of color-effects.

Lavender is the color most extensively used in this Nice color-scheme. Pure lavender, or its nuances in lilac, violet, coral, purple, purplish brown, slate, or deep gray, may pervade the picture (98, 109), or contrast with bright vivid colors (108, 134); it may punctuate by accentuations (90, 98), play a subsidiary rôle in an ensemble dominated by other colors (74, 91, 105), or serve as the foundation of a Matisse version of one or more forms characteristic of other traditions

*Cf., e.g., 50 with 51 and 58; also 95 with 145; and 40 with 140.

(90, 98). Lavender is common also in Hindu and Mughal drawings, Persian miniatures and Japanese prints; Matisse combines the Oriental use of lavender with features derived from other traditions and makes of the lavender the determining and outstanding mark of a new form which, while reminiscent of each of the sources, has its own identity and individuality. Thus a lavender, lilac or violet alters the total effect in a composition built upon Cézanne's distribution and treatment of masses (101), or in one based upon Manet's type of expressive drawing and manner of using black and tan (112).

Thin washes of lavender, in one or more of its numerous tones, function actively in Matisse's modeling of flesh, and thus emphasize the exotic sensuous quality of the ensemble. Sometimes lilac shadows on the flesh, in contrast with a setting of such daring and assertive colors as vermillion, bright yellow and green, constitute one of the most prominent and active features of the color-scheme (175). In another instance a delicate shade of rose-lavender models a relatively two-dimensional figure in a flat decorative design (141). In a different picture the lavender shadows only slightly model the figure and function chiefly as one of the elements in a decorative pattern of patches or areas (119). Again, in a figure drawn with more illustrative detail than is usual in Matisse, the patches of lavender-rose tone which model the flesh diminish the realism of the figure but add to its decorative value in the design (152). In another case a delicate lavender applied thinly in broad contour-lines is the chief element both in the modeling of a figure and in a rhythmic series of subtly varied nuances which forms one of the main themes of the whole design: in the foreground, lavender arabesques are superposed on a lemon-yellow tablecloth; in the background-setting, lavender stripes alternate with bright and vivid contrasting colors (148). When tinged with other tones the lavender may play a secondary part in the design; grayish-lavender shadows in a face, for instance, form a subordinate part of a total gray color-scheme (93). When vivid colors enter into the Nice color-scheme, they frequently reinforce the pervasive lavender tone of the picture as a whole (90, 108, 109, 125). Often the Nice color-scheme is instrumental in the rendering of delicate space-compositions embodying the charm and intime feeling of interior scenes (98, 132).

Experimentation with color-schemes, of great diversity and totally different from that just discussed, extends to Matisse's interpretations of practically every phase of subject-matter. In each case we find as many variations in the treatment and in the individuality of the resulting form as those in the Nice type of pictures. In a triptych, for instance, each of the separate pictures is a different organization of essentially the same colors—green, purple, tan, gray and black. The color-scheme of each differs from that of the others because a different color dominates the ensemble (69–70–71).

EXPRESSIVE FUNCTION OF COLOR

The emphasis which has been placed upon Matisse's patterns must not be understood as a denial to him of expressive color. What was said of his form in general holds good of his color also: the power, delicacy, harmony, reality and drama are genuinely revealing of aspects of the world we all know and care for. Though, as we have seen, he does not convey to us the profoundest values, especially not the more poignant or more exalted, a vast number of the feelings which we encounter in our ordinary moments are in solution in his work, and these lend conviction to his expressive form as completely as do the profounder values in the work of the Venetians, Rembrandt, Renoir and Cézanne. Though usually overlaid by decorative detail which is bizarre and exotic, the solid substance of the world about us is unmistakably present in all that Matisse has done.

Color-power in Matisse is sometimes revealed in a feeling of weight, solidity and strength akin to Cézanne's. It may appear in an ensemble of bright and exotic colors in positive contrasts, enriched by color-chords, and applied in long forceful brush strokes and thick impasto (21); or it may emerge from an organization lacking in bright colors and heavy impasto, but characterized by effective relationships between green, lavender and tan, established mainly by the activity of numerous brush strokes (111). Weight and strength result also from an ensemble of deep bizarre colors used in large expanses (34), or from relatively bright exotic colors which in themselves carry the conviction and reality of textures (145). In contrast to this weight and solidity is the delicate power and charm of ensembles of very light, bright, and greatly varied colors in vivid contrasts (84, 105, 159). In another kind of organization of delicate colors—silvery tones of blue, lavender and coral—a few very positive notes of black add a feeling of strength to the pervasive charm and delicacy of the light tones (81). In each of these different types of color-ensemble the organization has definiteness and individuality and, consequently, power. This depends not so much upon the colors themselves, whether bright, somber, exotic, light, delicate, solid, rich or whatnot, as upon their relationships and the degree to which color becomes an integral part of the form. When integration fails, the colors fall apart, and in the fragments of the form we feel neither power nor charm, neither expressive nor transferred values, and the effect of organized decoration also vanishes with the rupture of plastic unity (171).

Color-movement, that is, color which embodies the feeling of movement, plays no small part in the essential realism and æsthetic appeal of all successful color-organizations. This is explained by the psychological fact that the sensations experienced when we contemplate moving objects in the world provide much of the thrill and interest of everyday life, a fact utilized by all artists. The æsthetic satisfaction is fullest when all the factors in the composition are so integrated that the sense of movement is embodied with complete singleness of effect. The work of art is thus made to live in all its components as well as in its form as a unit.

In all of Matisse's successfully realized designs, the harmonious interrelation of color with the pattern of lines, bands, stripes and arabesques results in a concerted movement which imparts life, vitality, to the whole painting. The movement suggested is of all gradations of rapidity and volume, several of which, occurring side by side in the same picture, frequently furnish an additional type of dramatic contrast (64). The movement may be either quick and sharp, or sweeping and continuous, according as the color-pattern takes the form of a rapidly diversified arrangement of patches and relatively small areas (51, 52, 137), or of broad arabesques (31). Indeed, a group of Matisse's paintings offer an infinite number of diversifications of both the staccato and the swinging, sweeping or undulating types (29, 31, 32, 52, 69–70–71, 84, 94, 96, 123). Technical devices, suitably adapted to achieve this feeling of color-movement, are another flexible means of reviving the memories and feelings occasioned by innumerable kinds and degrees of movement in the world about us. In general, of course, the memories and feelings may occur without recall of the original experience in the external world: the transferred abstract value of movement is engendered directly by color harmoniously merged in the design.

Color as the Unifying Factor in Design

As above noted, Matisse's colors are related not only to other colors but to compositional features and also to drawing and light. Though this is true of all great artists, in Matisse the control exercised by color is more nearly confined to its intrinsic sensuous quality, its mere immediate relations of harmony and contrast, than it does in the decorative forms of any other painter. As most nearly the raw material of painting, since all other plastic elements may be regarded as modifications or aspects of it, color is particularly suited to play this unifying rôle. In Matisse its interrelation with line, light and space is achieved in an infinite variety of ways, of which no complete account is possible except by a detailed analysis of each picture. It is possible, however, to illustrate some of the underlying general principles in his most characteristic designs.

One of the obvious means of effecting unity of design is the rhythmic duplication of color. The ways and means by which this type of color-rhythm is achieved and the different compositional functions of the duplication are extremely varied. According to the particular design, the variation may involve the tone of individual colors, their relations to other colors, their sensuous and surface qualities, the relations of the duplicated units to line, light, space, technique, drawing, modeling, pattern; color-unification, in other words, not only takes many forms, but the choice of a particular form depends also upon the material to be unified. Each of these variations requires further attention to the essentials which make it significant.

Matisse's repetition of individual colors in different parts of a picture follows no mechanical rule: variations in the tone of a particular color, and the plastic purposes served by the repeated tones in relation to diverse contexts, illustrate the artist's ingenuity and versatility in adaptation of means to complex organic ends. Colors identical in hue and tone may appear in various parts of a picture with different relations in each part. A vermillion, for example, is implanted amidst bright colors in one part of a picture and among dark tones in another (144); identical colors may be duplicated in areas differing in expanse or shape (42, 61); or they may be applied by different techniques, as when a smoothly applied lavender-rose tone used to model figures in the foreground is repeated in perceptible brush strokes and thicker impasto in the drawing of a tree in the middle distance (31); a tan occurring in some flat area of a background may be used with marked pattern of brush strokes in a chair in the foreground (80); broad brush strokes of relatively thick paint may duplicate the color of areas of bare ivory-tinted canvas (19, 29). Again, similar colors may be duplicated in units of different representative or plastic functions, as when a bright yellow, used as a decorative stripe in the background, also functions as a plane in a face modeled by color-compartments (56). Sometimes the colors are not identical but very closely akin: different tones of brown, for example, in widely separated sections of a picture, establish a common color-basis in units in each of which they enter into different relations with other colors; these other colors serve a variety of purposes in the total organization, but their common relation to the brown ties them together (64).

Other aspects of rhythmic repetition of color as an adjunct in the unification of design appear when one color is used in great quantity. This color may extend over a wide expanse of setting and provide the common relations which establish the unity of the foreground and background (42, 51, 69); or it may be a large area within the foreground or middle distance which serves as a focus about which the other color-units are organized (84, 123). A single color or tone may permeate all the other colors and determine the character of the total color-scheme, as, for instance, when the picture appears as a symphony in blue (73, 142), in tan (80), in gray (57), or, as we have already seen with reference to the Nice type of pictures, in nuances of lavender (98, 140). Often, too, the pervasive color aids in welding together an organization containing elements otherwise very disparate; thus, for example, a three-dimensional figure modeled with few subtle colors, and a dramatically contrasting flat background of numerous and brighter colors merge harmoniously in a multicolored ensemble dominated by lavender tones (134).

All of the instances thus far cited relate to the part played by a single color, or by shades of one color, in coöperation with other plastic factors in effecting unity of design. We may now consider some of the other and more complex aspects of color as a unifying agent.

Rhythmic duplication of color is not necessarily of a single color: units of several colors may bring about integration by the rhythmic repetition of some of their characteristics, as, for example, when in the same picture the contrasts in different sets of color are subtle (128), or vivid (19, 31, 33, 174), or resounding to the degree that they seem to clash (56). Or one set of color-contrasts, by the position and shape of its constituents, may bring into equilibrium another set of contrasts differing from the first in tone, in sensuous quality, and in compositional function (48).* Often the two contrasting sets of colors are so grouped that they constitute two distinct color-schemes (20, 84, 95, 104, 108, 128). Surface-quality is another aid in promoting unity, as when a dry, pastel feeling per-

---

*Matisse said that his problem in "Portrait of Girl with Cat" (48) was to use a background of opposed colors such as light green and rose, and then set against that a figure in such a way that the component colors of the figure would unify the two contrasting colors of the background.

vades a color-scheme of rose, pink, brown, yellow, light and deep blue, and grayish-lavender white (131) ; or when all colors have in common an exotic solid surface-quality like that of ceramics, wood or metal (104, 175), or a solidity conveying with convincing reality the feeling of stuffs (145). Again, colors radically different in tone may have a sensuous quality in common that establishes harmonious relationships in the ensemble; a composition, for example, may owe its homogeneity to the dark, juicy and rich color of the contrasting units (14), or to their vivid and bright (167), or light and delicate (109), or bizarre and exotic, colors (56).

This rhythmic duplication of color-contrast results in many subtle and appealing effects when the colors are so used and related to the other elements in the picture that the contrasting colors tend to unite the composition because each serves the same plastic purpose. One of the most active unifying agents in Matisse's "Odalisque" in the Luxembourg Museum (119), for example, consists of a decorative motif common to the yellow wall, the blue screen and the red breeches. The same principle operates in another composition, in which a delicate voluminous quality pervades the color-contrasts in the foreground and background, and thus not only ties the picture together but also constitutes a distinctive feature of the organization (150).

Another of Matisse's methods of organizing the composition by color consists in dividing it into two contrasting broad sections of color related to each other by sensuous quality and decorative motifs (148, 154). Quite often the representative units are merged by the interlocking of two distinct types of color-schemes (20, 95, 104, 108), by the rhythmic alternation of the main color-constituents (123), or by the intertwining of the principal color-rhythms (69–70–71). Still another plan of unification is to relate the various colors scattered throughout the composition to one multicolored unit or focus which sums up the total color-scheme (110).

The foregoing illustrates a characteristic of all Matisse's best work; that is, when his design involves problems in the use of the plastic means other than color—e.g., space-composition, compositions in arabesques, linear- or light-patterns—all the elements in the organization are rendered in terms of color. The unification of the color-ensemble as well as the unifying effects of the many aspects of color involve highly complex relations of each factor to the others and to the composite design.

It will be seen from the illustrations given that the question of unification by color is inextricably tied up with the activity of every other factor in the painting, including the particular use of each of the plastic means in drawing, modeling, composition, interpretation of subject-matter. Consequently, the method is always a by-product of the requirements of the design; for example, certain types of organization require particular types of color and color-activity, and these in turn may necessitate a kind of drawing which results in distortion. In addition to the examples given above, color-rhythms are used also as the unifying agent in an array of individual versions of traditional compositional types in which some of the other plastic elements are almost equally active in effecting plastic unification: color in conjunction with space and volumes (33, 106, 135); with broad areas and planes (48); with planes and technique (137); with technique and mosaic-effect (10, 111); with lines and mosaic-pattern (21); with broad linear contour (32); with pattern of bands and stripes (90, 156, 167); with pattern of "islands" (101); with pattern of arabesques (31, 168); with light-and-dark contrast in bands (14); with distorted modeling and linear contour (143); color-contrast in conjunction with light-and-dark contrast (76); color-areas with lines (125). These methods of unification are combined in varying manner and degree, and the list is even yet far from exhaustive.

To sum up, the great unifying force in Matisse's paintings is the color-relations arranged in accordance with universal principles of rhythm and contrast, and acting both directly and through the control which they exercise over the other plastic means. It is obvious, therefore, that in order to understand Matisse's ways and means of effecting unity of design by color, we must study in more detail the other factors in the painting indissolubly linked with it. To that study we may now proceed.

Summary

Matisse's forms depend primarily upon color, both upon its bizarre and distinctive sensuous quality and upon its contrasts and relations; all these combined yield a color-power which is the basis of his individual form. The relations transform colors in themselves crude and displeasing into ensembles which have charm as well as power. The other plastic qualities, whatever their value, are subordinated to color and to Matisse's general decorative purpose, which constantly entails extensive distortions of color itself.

Colors and color-units used by other painters assume in Matisse's work, through new sets of relationships, a quality radically novel. Sometimes unappealing individual colors remain unappealing in the ensemble, but an effect of dramatic contrast is achieved which obviates the need for charm; at other times the totality has an appeal which the individual colors lack, and drama is secondary. This is anticipated in the Orientals but Matisse adds a fusion with light, and a vitality all his own.

Color-contrast, constantly present in Matisse, is of all ranges of strikingness and subtlety, and is accomplished by a wide variety of plastic devices including not only direct contrast in hue, but concomitant contrast in lightness, solidity and other plastic effects. The most obvious form of color-contrast is that between the actual hue of individual colors. Contrast may also be established between sets of colors whether bright or dull, light or dark, and there may even be two interwoven color-schemes. An important instance of the direct functioning of particular colors is in the use of black, both the rich deep black of Manet and a black tempered in a different way with other dark colors. The Oriental influence as it increased led him more and more to use this black as an instrument in setting off bright or delicate colors and in ordering the composition.

The chief importance of the color-contrasts is that they coöperate with the other plastic means to organize the total design. The contrasts, for instance, may be between the color of a contour-line and that of an area; or the color-contrasts may indicate spatial intervals or give the effect of deep distance, of modeled solidity, or of illumination. That is, rhythmically repeated, in varying degree of complexity, the color-contrasts play an important compositional rôle in their varying relationships to line, light, space and modeling.

In the union of color and pattern, upon which decoration chiefly depends, Matisse is unrivaled. Sometimes color is emphasized, sometimes pattern, but always their combination regulates the employment of the other plastic means in accordance with the exigencies of each individual design, and takes precedence by far over considerations of realism; as when a mass is flattened out, simplified, and becomes primarily a color-area in a decorative ensemble, even though it retains recognizable identity. Broad areas of color constantly occur in Matisse; the traditional sources upon which he drew for them are numerous, especially among the Orientals, but the color itself is so changed, as is its function in the design, that his originality is unimpaired. The broad areas are almost never completely uniform; examination reveals such variations as differences in brushwork and shading with light. These broad areas serve many purposes: by their shape they may contribute directly to pattern, or to a sense of movement; by their proximity to areas of broken color they may heighten contrast; or by constituting planes they may aid in spatial organization.

When the contours of the color-areas are accentuated the result is a compartmental color-pattern. This type of pattern is derived from various sources, is always creatively modified, and results in a heightened decorative pattern, little conducive to realism. Usually, but not always, it is combined with vivid color-contrast; occasionally, either with or without perceptible actual lines of black or color, the pattern is predominantly linear and results in a striking arrangement of geometrical or irregular shapes. The color of these lines may itself add an element of contrast with the adjacent area; or the areas may be slightly modified where they intersect and this intermediate area may be varied in breadth, continuity and so forth. All these types of color-compartments Matisse uses in a wide range of variations, even in the same picture, combining them with variations in the other plastic means, to secure transferred as well as direct decorative value.

Matisse's use of color-compartments involves a radical departure from conventional treatments of volume and space. Volumes frequently appear as patches of color, and space and realistic depth are also represented by patterned color. This type of compartmental color-composition projects foreground and background upon a few planes set close together and facilitates their reduction to a common decorative status; but even when an effect of real distance is given, the particular objects in the foreground as well as the extensive areas in the background are constituted by compartments. Whatever the manner of their use, color-compartments are an indispensable ally to Matisse's color-contrasts, linear patterns, rhythms and other unifying means by which the distinctive color-organization is achieved.

Matisse's painting has the fascination of scientific experiment, in which a wide store of knowledge is combined with intelligent adventurousness; his experiments are always primarily in color, a recombination and reconstruction of the separate plastic means as well as of the traditions of painting. Traditional color-schemes are re-created in ways perpetually new, and reworked in novel contexts of lighting, modeling and methods of technical execution. His color-schemes are endless in variety, but each is used consistently, whether monochromatic or embracing many colors, subdued or bright, delicate or exotic; if several are combined, contrast preserves the singleness of effect. In any particular picture, the choice of color-scheme is intelligent: it serves to render the quality of what is portrayed as well as to exercise Matisse's own ingenuity.

This is illustrated by the Nice pictures, in which the palette has recognizable sources, but is indefinitely varied, and is selected with discrimination. It is predominantly light and delicate, with occasional contrasting areas of more solid and positive color to serve as a foil; lavender or one of its shades or nuances is its basis and either the dominant note, pervasively present, or at least clearly perceptible throughout the picture.

This lavender serves a great variety of purposes: conjoined with other colors and various types of drawing, composition and modeling, and frequently contrasted with strongly assertive colors, it yields in every instance a characteristic Matisse transformation.

Matisse's pictures, though their chief significance lies in their color-patterns, succeed notably also in giving expression, by their color-organizations, to the painter's sense of such values as power, delicacy, movement and drama. For example, the conviction of power and weight appears in bright colors, vigorously applied, or simply in the effective harmonization of colors which in themselves are less striking; delicacy and charm result from a combination of light or silvery colors, upon which a few positive color-notes confer also a sense of strength. In every instance the success of the color-design depends upon the constituent relationships: when these are inappropriate or inadequate, the value, both expressive and decorative, vanishes.

Another important expressive value to which Matisse's color contributes is that of movement, which includes all the accumulated interest of our experiences of activity and drama. Color is here especially active in connection with linear effects and patterns, and the movement suggested is of all gradations of rapidity and volume.

Color, to conclude, is the great unifying agent for Matisse: the relationships by which his forms are tied together are primarily color-relationships, and the relations of line, light and space are subsidiary to those of color. The most obvious means by which unity of design is achieved is rhythmic repetition of color. Sometimes the rhythm resides in repetition of a color, in the same or varying shade, in various parts of the picture, with different relationships in each new context. Or the variation may be in extent of the different areas, or in the method of application, or in representative function, or in internal patterning. A wide expanse of a single color may establish a focus of relations for color-units or plastic elements in general; or a pervasive color or set of closely related colors may be the key of a whole picture, often harmonizing plastic units otherwise far from harmonious.

Instead of a single color, the unifying agent may be color-relations or color-contrasts. Direct contrasts, subtle or obvious, reappearing in different parts of the picture, may have in each part widely varying relations with line and space; or they may set off another series of contrasts, as in the above-mentioned case of double color-schemes. They may be conjoined with a common surface-quality or sensuous quality, or with a similar repeated linear pattern or type of spatial organization. The whole picture may be divided into a pair of contrasting color-areas with other elements in common; or two contrasting sets of colors may interlock throughout the picture; or several colors may all be related to a single unit which sums them up. The intimate relationship between color and the other plastic factors makes it apparent that the full significance of color in Matisse's organizations can only be revealed by detailed analysis of his use of those means.

CHAPTER X

MODELING

MODELING is plastically but one of the aspects of drawing, for it is obvious that the voluminous quality of objects must be drawn out as well as their shape, contour and other identifying marks. Each design determines whether volume is to be emphasized or diminished, either throughout the composition or in one or more of its parts. Flatness is the rule in the great majority of Matisse's designs. Solidity is often reduced to the point at which objects and figures function primarily as colored areas in a decorative pattern of which the basic principle is dramatic contrast and rhythmic duplication of color (35, 141, 164). This sacrifice of realism is often carried to such an extreme that a piece of fruit may appear actually less three-dimensional than an adjacent leaf (157); or a flat figure may be plastically equivalent to a fully rounded vase (171); or a whole volume, e.g., a cat, may be flattened into the pattern of a silhouette (48). In other instances the principle of variety calls for changing the three-dimensional quality of various component parts of the same volume in order to effect diverse decorative contrasts and rhythms (134, 143). When Matisse utilizes as a theme a traditional form characterized by solidity of volume, full three-dimensional modeling may be indispensable to his purpose: a close adherence to a Cézanne theme, for instance, may require a rather uniform use of solid volumes (85); in contrast, in a more personal interpretation of the same form, three-dimensional volumes may alternate as a contrasting theme in a flat color-design (173).

As is common in all of Matisse's use of plastic factors, he rings many changes upon each of the constituent elements of modeling, by processes of selection, emphasis and subordination, and thereby attains to variety of method and of compositional purpose. A flat design, for example, is best served by a reduced voluminous quality achieved mainly by line (64).* In a light and delicate ensemble, the modeling of a figure may be achieved by broad lines or narrow areas of delicate lavender tone thinly applied along the contours (148). A boxlike volume, suggestive of Negro sculpture, may be modeled by accentuated lines of contour and large patches of shadow and light, and serve as a focus and point of contrast in a decorative two-dimensional setting (174). An approach to a Cézanne-like solidity results from broad dark lines of contour related to hatchings or planes of color in the substance of the objects (33, 34). Accentuation or diminution of these planes results in modeling that can be made contributory to an extensive range of compositional effects. An individualized version of Renoir's delicacy, for example, is aided either by diminishing the perceptibility of the planes in areas of delicate color (150, 152), or by organizing them in long strips of transparent pigment (109). Elsewhere, the lateral juxtaposition of the planes used for modeling also makes them function as a pattern which is duplicated rhythmically in other parts of the composition (29). Generally, the texture of pigment does not contribute to the modeling and only occasionally do the colors of the planes interpenetrate to yield color-chords. When they do, the surface-quality may be reminiscent of Daumier's when the planes are inconspicuous (11, 34), or of Cézanne's when hatchings, brush strokes and rich juicy color are the chief agents of the modeling (33, 85).

A decorative theme, or a constituent general motif of it, is sometimes repeated in the technique of the modeling, in which solidity is achieved by patterns consistent with the general decorative design, with either large flat areas, small patches, or long alternate strips of contrasting colors as the dominating feature. For instance, strips, bands or patches of color occurring in relatively two-dimensional decorative details of the composition, are rhythmically repeated in the areas of color, or light and shadow, used in the modeling of a three-dimensional object, to which a specific patterned type of modeling is thus given (56, 91, 136, 155, 156).

*For function of line in modeling, see footnote, p. 89.

We have discussed in another chapter Matisse's use of bands
and stripes of color as the dominant characteristic in numerous
designs and therefore the one which determines the treatment of
the individual plastic factors.* The modeling in these paintings,
instead of being effected by a uniform or slightly graduated
color-area, is done with juxtaposed strips or narrow bands
forming a series of parallel broad lines of contrasting colors.
These bands make up the substance of the volume and give it
three-dimensional quality varying in depth from full rounded-
ness to relative flatness (14, 20, 29, 92, 136, 156, 158). A use
of similar bands, for other compositional purposes, is perceptible in the patterned modeling of Byzantine types of mosaics†
and paintings,‡ and in the work of Delacroix,§ Daumier¶ and
Cézanne;** each of these traditional methods is utilized by
Matisse as a point of departure for ventures of his own. At
times the diversity of traditional methods in the same picture
indicates that Matisse has made the painting a means of illustrating the manifold ways in which these bands and stripes of
color can serve as instruments of modeling (20, 29). Usually
the stripe-band modeling is coördinated with definite types of
design; it functions organically, for example, in a space-and-
volume composition characterized by light-and-dark contrasts
(14); as an active decorative element in a color-pattern of
Japanese type (64, 158); as a constituent in a space-composition of heavy and raucous color (20); and as a unit in a poster-
design (156).

An additional decorative feature in the stripe-band type of
modeling is sometimes a serrated line, like the edge of a saw,
which results from the dovetailing of the irregular edges of the
stripes (11, 29, 136). This line may be repeated rhythmically,
with variation in its constituents, in other decorative units of
the picture (29), or it may establish contrast with stripes of
relatively even and continuous line of contact (136). The use
of a serrated linear edge is not new with Matisse; it occurs
in the pattern of early mosaics in the line formed by their ir-

*See chapter on Transferred Values, pp. 36–40.   †E.g., 315, 320, 321.
‡E.g., 324.   §E.g., 384.   ¶E.g., 385, 386.   **E.g., 405.

regular stones of different shapes;* it is also a feature in Cézanne's technique of individual brush strokes.† In the latter as
well as in the mosaics it is chiefly a by-product of technique;
in Matisse it is obviously a deliberately selected motif made to
serve primarily decorative ends. The brush strokes which make
up Matisse's serrated line are unlike Cézanne's, and nearer in
effect to the mosaics, in that they are more often juxtaposed
laterally than piled on top of one another. In Cézanne the device is a means to increased three-dimensional quality achieved
by structural color, while in Matisse it is primarily decorative
and only incidentally expressive. Nevertheless, it does aid in
the expressive function of his modeling, especially when the
zigzag edge of color occupies the most prominent part of the
volume and makes one side of the line function as shadow and
the other side as light. Thus it draws out the essence of voluminous quality, it increases the decorative value of the unit,
and it serves as an ornamental motif repeated rhythmically as
a unifying factor in the design (14, 29, 136).

From the foregoing paragraph it is apparent that Matisse's
use of stripes of contrasting colors is a variant also of that type
of modeling by juxtaposition of light and dark areas common
in painting since the earliest times. Matisse substitutes for the
conventional light-and-dark tone-contrasts of vaguely outlined
areas, definite patterns of bands and stripes contrasting in
color. By still other modifications in technique he obtains the
specious sculpturesque effects of Leonardo (15), or the more
convincingly solid volumes of Cézanne, modeled with color and
light and reinforced by thick impasto and hatchings (21).

Technique is an active agent in Matisse's modeling, in the
form either of brush strokes or of areas or spots of bare canvas. The uncovered canvas functions chiefly as light and highlight, in the ways already discussed in the chapter on Drawing.‡ His brush strokes may be either rather uniformly loaded
with pigment (74), or so varied in quantity of paint and relations of color that the modeling of a rounded volume appears
somewhat disjointed or broken, and thus yields the decorative
effect of a color-patchwork (10).

*E.g., 313, 314, 319.   †E.g., 405, 406, 409, 415.   ‡See pp. 91, 93–94.

It is obvious from all that has been said that the type of design prescribes the kind of modeling; consequently position and color of shadows, incidence and color of light, and the degree of three-dimensional solidity, are habitually varied from naturalism in accord with the design. The distortions are radical and extensive, but the essentials of solidity are nearly always preserved and given a version in harmony with the general compositional purpose of the painting.*

SUMMARY

Modeling is relatively less important for Matisse than for painters whose realistic treatment of space and mass requires a convincing depiction of solidity. Solidity is developed in his work to whatever extent the design requires, but is usually slight. As a rule the plastic function of his masses is to be color-areas, and this function frequently requires that they be flattened to an essentially two-dimensional status; however, even when they are reduced most nearly to flat planes of color, volume is practically always retained in the degree necessary to prevent plastic unreality. Though rhythmic pattern of color is always fundamental, modeling in three dimensions occurs when the purpose calls for it, for example, in the employment of a theme from a tradition in which solidity is the rule; such a theme, set in a two-dimensional context, may also be effective by way of contrast.

Matisse's modeling is accomplished less by the use of graduated light and shadow than by color and line in a wide repertoire of means skilfully adjusted to the requirements of his various types of design. Heavier and darker lines in connection with relatively structural color heighten the solidity; lighter masses are rendered by less perceptible planes of delicate color. In either case the patterned modeling enters rhythmically into relation with decorative patterns elsewhere in the picture. When the fusion of light and color requires a comparative blurring of the contours, the modeling is less linear in conception and

*Modeling of faces is treated in chapter on Portraiture, pp. 180, 181.

enters naturally into designs of which direct color-contrast is the keystone.

Line, however, is constantly used; it is often accentuated and accompanied by color, in the form of stripes and bands or of planes or hatchings. If the design is relatively flat or primarily a color-pattern, the modeling may be mainly by linear contour, or by broad areas lightly shaded along their outline; if a relatively high degree of solidity is desired, contours are rendered in broad dark lines related to more or less accentuated planes of color in the body of the mass. Visible brush strokes of rich color, not fully structural yet attaining a quasi-structural effect by its juiciness, sometimes result in a depth approaching Cézanne's. The lines of contour, the stripes, and the planes or hatchings are varied in every possible way to yield a form of modeling in accord with the general decorative setting, and they exercise a general compositional function in addition to their value for modeling.

A particular instance of decorative modeling is the use of stripes and bands, which may give, when so intended, and at some violence to realism, the effect of solidity in whatever degree the design calls for. Matisse does this often in accordance with traditional methods, but in his own individual manner, and in an infinite variety of ways. Sometimes these adjacent stripes dovetail to yield a serrated edge, which serves also as a motif for rhythm and contrast. The device is anticipated in early mosaics and in Cézanne, but in Matisse it is deliberately adopted for decorative purposes; however, when it is so executed as to create the effect of a light-shadow contrast it gives added conviction to the solidity and so has expressive value as well as decorative. Bare canvas is similarly used as light in modeling, and solidity is heightened also by brush strokes which, when varied in color and amount of pigment, add the decorative value of a color-patchwork.

Both in his tendency to flatness and in his indication of solidity by the schematic means described, Matisse departs far from literalism, but beneath the apparent differences the essentials of traditional modeling are preserved.

CHAPTER XI

LINE

Matisse's varied use of line as an element in drawing and modeling has already been discussed.* This chapter deals with the decorative rôle of line and with some of its manifold compositional functions.

Line, like the other plastic means, is subordinated to the requirements of Matisse's decorative designs; hence he constantly chooses as subject-matter objects in themselves characterized by linear patterns, such as striped or checkered materials (97, 106, 168, 173), window-shutters (64, 90), parquetry floors (49, 61, 67), folded screens (91, 157), balcony rails (64, 73). Linear patterns are freely introduced even when they do not occur in nature or in traditional usage (52, 65, 136).

Linear elements taken from the traditional forms are usually elaborated into patterns; the brush strokes, hatchings and contour-lines of the impressionists or post-impressionists, for example, are accentuated by Matisse to make decorative linear patterns rather than to convey the essential quality of atmosphere or of solidity (21, 28, 29, 40, 42, 110). Similarly, the flowing arabesque-like contour of the Japanese is expanded to convert areas or even volumes of color into linear arabesques (31, 32), and the bold linear contour of color-areas of Byzantine mosaics and Egypto-Roman panels is extended in decorative range by breaking the contour into several linear fragments and by increasing the vividness of contrast between the color of the lines and that of the contiguous areas (21, 42, 48). A thin, all-enclosing, unbroken contour-line, reminiscent of Egyptian frescoes,† is occasionally used by Matisse with the fluid, graceful, classic quality of early Greek sculpture‡ and of the linear decorations on early Greek vases.§ This line becomes in Matisse an element in a complex pattern which includes also

---

*See chapter on Drawing, pp. 89–91, and chapter on Modeling, pp. 127, 128, 129.   †E.g., 302.   ‡E.g., 300.   §E.g., 301.

area-lines of contrasting color and various other linear effects occasioned by contact of color-areas, by narrow strips of color or bare canvas, and by broad linear areas of color (31).

Linear contour of objects and figures, usually accentuated by Matisse, is always incorporated in a system of linear patterns, and thereby functions as a decorative element in the design at the expense of realism. Thus in a still-life, two lines of dark blue upon a large area of lighter blue serve rather as a superposed linear pattern than as instruments in the drawing of a table or its definition in space (50). In other pictures linear contours in some parts of the composition make of the color-areas they enclose, units of pronounced three-dimensional quality, but their greatest activity is as part of the linear pattern in a total decorative design characterized by rosette-formations (134, 143), by bands and stripes (20, 167), or by a pervasive arabesque-movement (31, 32).

The arabesque, in more or less complete form, is a feature of many of Matisse's linear patterns, and its range extends from the simple arabesque of lines to a similar formation in the most complex plastic units. Ornaments or objects are often converted into linear arabesques of color, sometimes superposed upon a broad area of different color (64), and often contrasted with adjacent areas of unpatterned color (64, 168). Frequently figures and objects are drawn with accentuated curvilinear quality to fit in with the linear arabesque-formations in incidental objects, so that the design becomes a thematic development of the arabesque-motif (32, 84). Very often curvilinear rhythms of areas and volumes of color are so related to each other that the composite effect suggests a complex arabesque-movement of color (31, 168). Sometimes, an arabesque-formation makes of a figure the focus of the total decorative organization (32, 84, 167).

The compositional activities of line in Matisse cover such a wide field that we shall attempt to illustrate only the outstanding types. Since his pictures are fundamentally decorative compositions of color-compartments, pronounced linear effects support the major purpose. The lines defining the color-compartments work in close coöperation with the rhythms and contrasts of the other plastic factors and contribute their share to unity of design. In other words, his composition depends as much upon the sequence of linear rhythms and contrasts from one color-area to another as upon the ordering of the color-areas themselves. Linear pattern becomes in reality compositional pattern, as when a network of lines extends from one unit to another, the lines in each meeting, paralleling, contrasting, counterbalancing, or continuing the lines in the others (31, 64); or when broad accentuated contour-lines of luminous black increase the sensuous quality of the enclosed areas of light colors, emphasize the patchwork of interpenetrating planes, and constitute a solid framework for a composition of contrasting color-planes (52). Again, lines of contour, together with a linear pattern of bands or strips of color, unify a series of color-areas by holding them within a definitely organized linear framework (86, 90). Elsewhere an intricate linear pattern of contours, bands, stripes and arabesques is related by its movement to the sweep and swing of the color-areas (31, 32); in a relatively monochrome gray color-scheme, a set of deep black lines bring together in some sections, and abruptly separate in others, the various constructive parts of the dramatic spatial contrasts which characterize the composition (57).

Other examples of this practical identity of linear and compositional pattern are furnished by designs quite different from any of those just mentioned. In compositions formed by a condensation of foreground and background in a small number of planes, the pervasive linear rhythms help to establish a decorative factor common to all sections of the picture (148, 154). In another type a theme of light pearly tones is rhythmically punctuated by a subsidiary theme of dark linear accents so focalized in various sections of the picture that they assist considerably in giving form and unity to the widely-distributed and contrasting constituents of a space-composition (98). Again, in ensembles of relatively dark colors (51, 67) or of tones tending to monochrome effect (60), continuous broad dark lines encircle both objects and their constituent parts, as in stained-glass windows, and create positive contrasts of light and dark as well as of color. Occasionally too, the effect of a positive linear flow is obtained less by actual lines than by the coördinated sequence of areas, planes and volumes of color in space (69–70–71).

The organic interrelation of line with color, illustrated by the foregoing examples, brings up the question when a line ceases to be a line, or when a color-area acquires characteristics intrinsic to line. The answer is found in the psychology of perception: if our attention is engaged in tracing linear pattern, strips of color are felt as lines; if we are analyzing the composition from the standpoint of color-areas, the same narrow strip or broad line of color is perceived as a natural part of the pattern of color-areas. In Matisse a narrow band of color often functions as a wide line of color and may be considered an area-line when in direct relationship with the actual linear contour of objects, the direction and movement of which it duplicates rhythmically (29, 31, 32). Vice versa, lines defining contours are often so broad as to function equally as narrow areas of color (7, 20, 26). Matisse, as we have seen, frequently uses area-lines for both decorative and compositional purposes, as well as for drawing and modeling. Even when used sparingly, the area-lines effect rhythmic color-contrasts in a design of colored planes (31), they lend variety to decorative organizations of stripes and bands (20), or they duplicate and emphasize the arabesque character of volumes (32). Occasionally, area-lines constitute the leitmotif of the total pictorial form: they are varied and deployed, and build up a symphonic organization of color in linear formation (29). The similarity and the difference between Matisse's use of area-lines and that in Byzantine mosaics and Egyptian textiles are pointed out in another section of the book.* Infinitely numerous as Matisse's linear effects are, in all but an inconsiderable number of his works they are fully synthesized in his form as a whole.

SUMMARY

To realize the full decorative possibilities of line, Matisse not only frequently selects subject-matter for the sake of its

*See chapter on Creative Use of Traditions, p. 70.

actual richness in linear pattern, he also adds linear effects when they have no counterpart in nature. Traditional practices such as brush strokes are similarly given an added, and for him fundamental, status as line; the arabesques of the Japanese become areas or even volumes essentially linear in character; his lines are very often broadened and colored, and related to the color of the areas bounded to achieve heightened ornamental value. The continuous, fluid, fine line of classic sculpture is also used in complex patterns, which are diversified and enriched by area-lines and various other plastic elements which yield a rich decorative ensemble. Literal reproduction is as always sacrificed in favor of decorative design, or to create the characteristic vehicles of transferred value.

Arabesques, ranging from simple linear arabesques to the most complex organizations, constantly recur in Matisse's work. A whole mass may be distorted into an arabesque color-area or color-volume, with a curvilinear quality imposed upon it, to bring it into relation to similar motifs elsewhere, and a figure so drawn may serve as the focus of the whole composition. This arabesque-motif is used in various ways, especially as a means of contrast, either in color-quality with the groundwork of the areas so decorated, or in opposition to parts of the picture destitute of pattern.

Since decoration in Matisse fundamentally takes the form of compartmental color-pattern, the importance of line is obvious. The sequence and rhythm of line coöperate with the relations and contrasts of color as a means of compositional organization: not only does the network of line cover the picture with its own, often intricate and elaborately balanced and rhythmic, composition—a sort of skeleton to which the color-areas are related—but the color of the lines, when they are broad and accentuated, directly heightens the effect of the color itself. The linear framework may also in some areas bring together and in others sharply separate the enclosed areas; or, when the areas form planes in space, the line may both aid in establishing spatial distinction and furnish a common decorative factor to the nearer and more remote spatial regions. This is accomplished by the continuity and sequence of line, and by its color-value. The color of the line also, by force of contrast with adjacent areas, may add an effect of illumination or darkening.

The effect of Matisse's broad lines, black or colored, may be regarded either as a matter of line or color. Geometrically speaking, they are not lines at all but narrow, elongated areas of color. Nevertheless, as defining contour and maintaining a sequence of linear flow, they function as line. The paralleling of linear contour by broader lines of contrasting color gives rise to area-lines, and these, in addition to their extremely effective decorative rôle, play a part in the modeling and spatial organization. This fact again illustrates the intimate fusion of the various plastic means in Matisse's designs.

CHAPTER XII

LIGHT

LIGHT in Matisse, though it is most closely related to the impressionists',* is made distinctive and personal by adaptation of traits from other traditions. Thus, as may be required by the specific character of the design, the impressionists' spots of light are broadened into large areas, as in the post-impressionists (31); the surface of the color is modulated with light by thin washes, as in Renoir (151) or in early Chinese painting (77, 94); a mottled effect of light reminiscent of the Japanese prints is obtained by the paint's being slightly scraped from the surface (89); large areas of bare canvas function as light, as in Japanese prints (90); light and shadow are used for modeling in a modified version of Leonardo da Vinci's familiar form (14, 15); sharp contrast of small units of color and light, a practice of van Eyck's, is modified by the sensuous quality of color and the broad simplified drawing (141, 174); light adds a sheen to color and textiles, as in Vermeer (90, 108, 136); juxtaposition of accentuated light and heavy dark color yields a pronounced Spanish effect (44, 76); irregular patches of accentuated light in relative isolation from adjacent color-patches give to a patterned composition a surface-character not unlike Cézanne's (26, 101); areas of light still more isolated and often circumscribed by contour of line or shadow produce the "islands" of early Chinese painting (26, 36); focalized light yields dramatic effects reminiscent of Théodore Rousseau (7, 72).

In each of these adaptations, the light, because it forms an inextricable part of Matisse's color, achieves more specifically decorative effects than in the original. That is, Matisse's pri-

*See chapter on Creative Use of Traditions, p. 46.

138

marily decorative designs impose upon light a corresponding decorative function, which is exercised to the utmost. Light enhances the sensuous appeal in drawing, composition, line and space by its fusion with bright, daring and exotic colors (21, 40, 50). It forms patterns of spots and areas greatly diversified in size (10, 31, 80); it appears in patches in contact with areas of darker colors to constitute light-patterns which are an organic part of the color-composition (14, 19). These patterns emphasize sometimes the contrast between light and dark (14), sometimes that between an area of light itself and one of color (19).

Traditional methods of using light are often selected as a theme upon which Matisse builds an organization of his own; thus we find color-compositions which are also designs of light-and-dark contrasts, subtle as in Manet and the Chinese (77), heavy as in the Spaniards (44, 76), translucent as in stained glass (51), or luminous as in Manet (100, 113).

Light is often the most active element in imparting both the luminosity and the sensuous quality which characterize the color (33, 53, 100, 113, 170), the space (Nice type of pictures), or the texture of materials (107, 108, 150, 152). Related to space in a number of ways, light becomes a major factor in the decorative organization of space-composition: it may be focused at the back of the picture (31, 50, 51), or in the foreground (89), or it may form an enveloping radiance which lends luminosity to distance and to all objects and spatial intervals in the composition (Nice type of pictures). As already pointed out, light is a very active constituent of Matisse's greatly diversified drawing,* and it serves also to give many of the distinctive qualities to the patterns of color and the dramatic color-contrasts which determine numerous different types of composition.

Light is also very active in contributing to the identity and form of the decorative motifs encountered so frequently in Matisse's work. The sunburst-rosette motif is mainly a fusion of light and color in equal parts (56, 70); and what we have termed "islands," or irregularly shaped patches which seem to

*See chapter on Drawing, p. 91.

float, are essentially areas of light surrounded by shadow. These islands, often seemingly isolated or detached from the structure of the ground, tree, sky, etc., heighten the decorative value of these objects, and also form a part of the general pattern of irregular shapes which determine the type of organization. This island-motif is in reality a flexible compositional device which, by variation in its elements—light, shape, color, contour, solidity—yields effects reminiscent of Renoir (133*), Cézanne (26,† 101, 137), the Chinese and Japanese (26, 36, 114, 133), and of such diverse material objects as mosaics (101), Carrara marble (36), or soft downy cotton (133).

Matisse's ingenuity and technical skill enable him to make of light one of his chief means of converting into a form distinctively his own the raw material drawn from other painters and traditions. Gauguin's color-scheme, for instance, when used by Matisse, is made more luminous and more varied by a more resourceful use of light (41, 53). A similar transformation is effected in his derivations from Japanese prints: the bright exotic colors of the originals are enlivened by light, which is modulated, accentuated at various points, and organized in internal patterns (156).

Matisse, like all other artists, sometimes fails to realize his purpose, and then we find pictures falling far short of that unity of effect which makes paintings convincing as works of art. His failure is nearly always due, as we have already seen, to such overemphasis upon the decorative aspect of subject-matter that it becomes an isolated element, without organic ties to the form as a whole. Such faulty compositions reveal too great a stress placed on one or more of the plastic means, which in consequence stand alone, that is, lack the support of the relationships which, in every work of art, establish the form. In Matisse's misadventures, it is light that is most often responsible for tawdry effects: overaccentuated light makes a picture seem flashy and superficial (165); a surface-sheen replaces adequate expression of structure of objects (107); or an accentuated pattern of light, decorative in itself, may destroy unity of volume (103).

*Cf., e.g., 429.   †Cf., e.g., 407.

SUMMARY

Matisse's light is derived mainly from the impressionists, but always with such characteristic modifications, based upon other traditions, that the effects are quite non-impressionistic and novel. The impressionists' spots of light are usually made much larger, and light is often rendered by thin washes of paint or by areas of bare canvas, and occasionally also by slight scraping of the painted surface. Varying traditional methods of using light are resorted to upon occasion but each adaptation—whether from van Eyck, Leonardo, Vermeer, Théodore Rousseau, Cézanne, Renoir, the Japanese, Chinese, or the Spaniards—by its intimate fusion with Matisse's color, produces an effect more strikingly decorative than that to be found in the original. Sometimes these traditional methods are employed as themes for original development, as when a pattern of light-and-dark contrasts is integrated with a general composition of color-areas.

The most important general function of light in Matisse is that of heightening color, to which it gives vividness and power, as well as such occasional specific effects as that of delicacy in the Nice pictures. It takes the form of colored light, and forms patterns of spots and areas which are organically related to the composition of color-areas; sometimes these patterns appear definitely as light-and-shadow, sometimes their effect is that of contrast between light and color. This light is particularly important as an agent in the luminous color-effects in the Nice pictures, but is indispensable also to the patterns of contrasting color in other types of composition. It plays a very important part in the representation of space, either by establishing a focus at a particular point or by its presence as a pervasive luminosity, and it is no less valuable in the rendering of textures.

Light is usually an element in Matisse's decorative motifs. Its most striking contribution in this aspect is its formation of "islands," which not only heighten the decorative effect of objects but enter into the general compartmental composition of the picture. By their aid Matisse is able to produce a personal version of many traditional effects and to simulate the quality of many textures. In general, light is with him a sovereign means of assimilating to his own form the work of other painters and diverse traditions. A foreign color-scheme by it is made more luminous, or given internal patterns and varying emphases.

When his pictures fail in plastic integration the fault is usually to be found in the overaccentuation of light, which may take the form of exaggerated pattern, or of such an isolation from structural color as to cause the objects modeled by it to fall into superficiality.

CHAPTER XIII

SPACE

THE variety of spatial relations in the real world is literally inexhaustible, and equally so are our emotional reactions to them. The sense of illimitable distance in the open sea, or in the sky with a range of mountains rising into it, gives us a sense of expansion or freedom; a crowded room, a narrow valley may make us feel cramped and hampered in our movements; a combination of restricted space with ample elbowroom about each object may seem pleasantly sheltered and intimate; and all these effects may be conveyed as well by depiction of a scene as by the scene itself. The employment of spatial effects is determined partly by the interest of the particular artist, partly, no doubt, by the characteristics of the natural environment in which a tradition grew up (as shown by the difference between Dutch and Umbrian painting), and partly also by the specific purpose underlying a particular design. In general, the presence of spatial relations in three dimensions is the *sine qua non* of fully expressive form. Color, line and light all lend themselves to exploitation in flat ornamental design, but the power of a painting to make us feel ourselves in the presence of reality itself is seriously compromised by projection of objects upon a single plane, and evisceration of them to a degree of flatness that leaves no room for solidity or ordering in three dimensions. Spatial organization alone is not sufficient to assure reality, but its complete absence is the sure mark of a purpose that aims at decoration and nothing more.

Matisse's psychological complexion finds expression in a treatment of space in which its decorative possibilities are picked out and developed in accordance with the particular design. In the space-and-volume type of composition, spatial intervals are fittingly emphasized as units born of the relation of color, light and line (20, 33, 51, 85, 150). When the illustrative aspect of a picture is accentuated, space is correspondingly

143

realistic (133). To accord with one type of poster-design, space is rendered by bands of dark color contrasted with stripes of bright color in the decorative motifs of the background (167). In an exotic color-pattern, space functions chiefly as areas of bizarre color (175); and when bare canvas is an active element in drawing shape, solidity, lightness, and so on, space too may be rendered by areas of bare canvas (19, 36, 89, 90, 115).

Matisse's spatial effects may be classified in three broad general categories: (a) realistic, as in the few of his pictures which are conceived, more or less, as illustrations (133); (b) non-realistic, with the salient characteristic a reduction in the number of planes to blend all the elements of the subject-matter in a decorative organization, which may even approach compression into a single plane (25, 164); (c) non-realistic, with positive distortion of space to attain novelty in decoration, as when still-life objects and the intervals between them, though retaining recognizable identity, appear to merge in the pattern of the background (89).

Very frequently in Matisse's highly individualized color-patterns and in his experiments with color-schemes and color-contrasts, one or more of the traditional treatments of space are utilized, in manifold and novel interpretations, as part of his working material. For example, Chardin's subtle and charming spatial intervals appear in novel contexts of pattern and color (80, 90, 155); the precise and clean-cut space-relations of le douanier Rousseau become part of a more vivid color-pattern (87); organization in compact planes, characteristic of the primitives and the cubists, appears in more exotic relationships of color (52); the Chinese handling of space in loosely defined areas of color acquires a new meaning by the way in which Matisse relates it to objects drawn in the impressionistic manner (123, 133); aerial perspective and the illusion of infinite distance, slightly reminiscent of Claude, emerge from a setting of brighter color in areas more definite in shape and more simplified (73).

Matisse's fascination by the dynamic relationships of space and volumes in the work of Cézanne is reflected in forms achieved by a technique sometimes close to Cézanne's, sometimes quite different. The bizarre effects of levitated objects, common in Cézanne, are obtained by Matisse, but for a different purpose: in Cézanne, the levitation increases the feeling of movement of volumes in space; in Matisse, it heightens the dramatic contrast of volumes and spaces (57), or helps to organize a sequence of decorative rhythms (152).* He achieves Velásquez's and Manet's subtle effects of free full space by means similar in principle but different in execution and plastic function; that is, a large color-area with slight tonal variations, covering most of the background and extending like a continuous sheet of color to the lower part of the foreground, becomes an active participant in the total color-pattern (51, 57, 66, 88).† This feature is common also in various forms of Oriental art.‡

Elements from the many different treatments of space in Oriental art are also placed by Matisse in contexts essentially new. Thus the Persian rendering of an equivalent of perspective by vertical juxtaposition of planes is sometimes closely followed by Matisse to obtain individual effects in pattern, movement and contrast of color (34, 64). For similar purposes, he avails himself of the decorative activity of the lines of perspective in Japanese prints (156), and of their use of a screen or door to serve the dual purpose of emphasizing and relating two contrasting themes of space-composition in a single picture (81, 90, 119).§ These Japanese traits are woven more firmly in the total form than they are in the originals, and spatial intervals and objects are arranged more compactly.

Whatever the traditional or individual treatment of space adopted by Matisse, all the plastic means make a perceptible contribution, though color, in one or more of its aspects, is always dominant. Primarily decorative and always in characteristic contrasts, whether it be bright, dark, delicate or exotic, Matisse's color gives a novel effect to traditional space-forms and an unmistakable individuality to the transformation. For instance, a picture in which the quality of roominess is heightened by conventional linear perspective and by a clear swimming

*Cf., e.g., 414.   †Cf., e.g., 356, 387, 388.   ‡E.g., 335a, 351.
§Cf. illustrations, pp. 282, 283.

atmosphere worthy of Carpaccio, owes its distinctive charm not
only to the space but also to a set of color-relations between
areas of pale pink, bright blue, ivory and coral-lavender around
a focus of vivid vermillion (90). Again, it is color-contrast
which, in the bands of a patterned background, makes an element of deep space also an integral part of a decorative setting, as when a dark oblong band is juxtaposed with bands of
brighter color, and their color-relation, by giving in essence
the effect of perspective, projects the darker band into infinitely remote distance (150, 157, 158, 167). Sometimes too, a wide
vertical band of dark color extends the whole height of one
side of the picture and, by its contrast in color and tone with the
other sections of the composition, stands out as the plane foremost in space, in relation to which all other color-areas recede.
This broad band may represent part of a window or shutter
(16, 22) or a figure at the extreme side of the foreground
(117), but irrespective of shape or representative significance,
the chief characteristic is one of a plane emphasizing space by
color-contrast.

Distance may be so adapted to the particular decorative color-
design that it also is rendered in terms essentially decorative
as, for instance, when a large plane of color rises precipitously
from the foreground toward the upper part of the background
and serves as a setting for the color-compartment composition
(34, 84, 175), or when the perspective of the plane of a table-
top in the foreground runs parallel to or continuous with the
vertical plane of the background, thus making of the foreground and background a pair of decorative elements, united as
a single area upon which are set the objects of the middle
ground (147, 148, 154).

Other factors may play an equally active part with color in
rendering space; for example, in pictures with emphasized
color-pattern, the space around a figure or object may be drawn
by the sharp contrast of the pattern and color of the object
with the pattern and color of its cast shadow; in other words,
the shape and the tone of the colored areas combine with the
color itself to give the space its particular character (66, 134,
173). Lines also fulfill a similar purpose in color-organizations

of the stripe-and-band type; that is, the lines are as active in
the depiction of perspective as in the pattern (156).

Light also functions directly in Matisse's decorative treatment of space. Light is focused, for example, on a foreground
object and gradually diminished in the adjacent objects; this
throws the latter into receding space, and the light-pattern, resulting from the relationship between the focus and the areas
of reduced light, works its way through space from foreground
to background (89). Conversely, a focal point of light in the
background may determine the convergence of aerial perspective and intensify the feeling of infinite space (31).

Specific technique is often an indispensable aid in rendering
space for a particular compositional purpose. Brush strokes,
for example, may function as broad lines or as patches of color
which, by their rhythmic relations to each other, carry the
movement of objects into receding space (111, 114). Bare canvas, in spots, lines or areas, on or around contour of objects,
functions as light, and this bare canvas, in relation to the light-
values of adjacent colors, fixes the position of the volumes or
planes in space (50, 88).

Spatial organization may be effected by variations in atmosphere from the clear and luminous to the blurred and hazy. The
result in each case is due to a fusion of all the elements by
which space is rendered, and the differences are due to the way
in which this fusion is effected. Clear and luminous aerial perspective, more common than haziness in Matisse's work, is
drawn out by the relationships between the sensuous quality of
bright and delicate color, a suffusion of clear light, and clean-
cut linear elements. This is exemplified in that large group of
Nice pictures in which the roominess of an interior as well as
the expanse of sky, sea and landscape seen in vistas are so treated that the whole picture has the clearness of crystal (90, 98).
The reverse effect, haziness of space, is a resultant of loose
contour related to ill-defined areas of bare canvas, a soft and
fluid color-scheme, and areas mottled with diffuse patches of
light (99).

Composition in space may be defined as an organization
in which the reciprocal relationships between objects and spa-

tial intervals are directly productive of æsthetic feeling. The simplest form is mass-composition occasioned by the harmonious relationships between flat objects and relatively two-dimensional spatial intervals. Plastically this is a product of line, light and color in flat masses and surface-space, all so composed that the relationships establish a definite form, a fusion of all the components in a new entity. Such flat design, while satisfying for what it is, remains comparatively meager in fulness of conviction and reality. When deep space enters into the picture, color, line, composition and design acquire new possibilities of individual and interrelated treatment, which increase greatly the painter's power to evolve new and more complex plastic forms with a multitude of values impossible in flat painting. Mere spatial depth, however, and three-dimensional quality are not, *per se,* the factors which determine the relative worth of flat or three-dimensional painting, since either becomes a mark of ostentation or virtuosity if attained speciously by tricks instead of by the harmonious coördination of all the plastic elements of the design.

Matisse is a master of composition in both two-dimensional and three-dimensional painting. His distribution of objects is always picturesque and usually novel, whether he coördinates them and their spatial intervals in a rosette-formation (108) or in a steplike or accordionlike in-and-out movement of planes (64, 81); whether he organizes them in a compact sandwich of planes (131) or in volumes wedged into small areas of space (136); whether, finally, he alternates intervals and objects equally throughout the entire picture (172), or establishes a contrast between the compact space-composition of an interior and the expansive volume-and-space arrangement of an out-of-door scene (81, 98).

In general, his space-composition takes the form of relationships between areas or patches of color arranged in compartments of varying degree of accentuation or diminution in accord with designs ranging from the sharply compartmental (56) to the relatively diffuse (94).

Composition, both two-dimensional and three-dimensional, is successful in proportion as its elements are conceived not spatially only, but in terms of color, line and light also. To bring about the integration, Matisse uses his entire repertoire of color and technique. The space-composition of a picture may owe its novelty and picturesqueness to the coördination, through the medium of numerous small brush strokes, of a particular color-scheme with an accentuated light-pattern (111). Again, exotic colors in daring contrasts related to equally dramatic contrasts between rosette- and stripe-motifs, may give the space-composition its striking individuality (33). At other times, color-movement, sweeping arabesques, and sharp patterns of light, may characterize the total design as well as the space-composition (31).

The sacrifice of realism for the sake of decorative value, so prevalent in Matisse's work, often leads to bizarre effects in space-composition. Decorative motifs on a drapery or table-cloth may be, as we have seen, so drawn and modeled that they appear as volumes or planes of color detached from the fabric and actually surrounded by space. These distorted motifs become active units in the space-composition formed by the relations between solid objects, and thus contribute to the dynamic power characteristic of the Venetians and Cézanne (33, 150, 152). The particular plastic purpose served by these distortions is avoidance of the flatness which would result from a realistic treatment, when the design calls for three-dimensional space in that area of the picture. Another bizarre volume-and-space effect appears in numerous pictures of the poster-type. Normal solidity of objects is reduced, as are the spatial intervals between them, but often the distance between foreground and background is more realistically rendered. The contrast between the two styles of spatial treatment adds much to the novelty and picturesqueness of the design, as when the surface of a receding table-top in the foreground constitutes a decorative feature about equal to the background in the extent and prominence of its color-pattern (147, 148, 154). This is but one of the many ways in which Matisse obtains varied effects of three-dimensional space in his poster-designs.

Whatever the method or the particular effect, the compositional plan of the color-design is carried out consistently in the treatment of space. Even when Matisse's theme is the interpretation of the traditional volume-and-space organization characteristic of the Venetians, Courbet or Cézanne, neither the volumes nor the spatial intervals ever lose the imposing content of color-values and color-patterns (14, 20, 33).

SUMMARY

Matisse's treatment of space is very versatile and is always appropriate to the type of his design. His means of realizing it are unconventional, consisting on occasion of such devices as stripes and bands, or spots of bare canvas, but the means are effective and the spatial intervals, even when least apparent, are an integral part of the form.

Space-relations in Matisse's work are sometimes, though rarely, realistic; usually they are either compressed, with a very considerable reduction in number of planes, or radically distorted, as when all the objects seem to be projected upon a single flat surface. The fundamental design of color-areas determines the mode of spatial organization, but it admits of considerable latitude, and within this Matisse employs many of the traditional renderings of space. Precise definition of a large number of intervals, or even the illusion of infinite distance, appear on one hand; on the other, organization in compact planes or in the Chinese type of loosely defined areas of color, always in a context of simplified drawing, bright color or individual technique. His treatment of space owes much to Cézanne's and Manet's, but with characteristic difference in purpose. The Persian elevation of distance is much used, but with new effects in pattern and contrast of color, as are also the Japanese lines of perspective and employment of a door or screen in distinguishing and relating spatial units, but Matisse's units are usually brought into closer juxtaposition.

Though line and light also are active in the realization of space, it is always color that operates primarily to integrate the spatial relations in the form of the picture. When deep space is employed, it is not the space merely, but the color-relations, including contrast, which confer upon the space-form an essential part of its rôle in the design: indeed it is often by virtue of color-relation that an object exercises the function it does in effecting spatial organization, as when juxtaposed bands of color are felt also as planes in a space-relationship. However, line may also be important in rendering the effect of space, as when the defining line of bands or of the shape of a shadow or colored area is what determines perspective, though the space-effect is secondary to the pattern-effect. The same is true of light: diminishing from a foreground focus, the degree of its diminution may point to a parallel recession in space; or focussed in the background, it may carry backward indefinitely the eye, or at least the imagination. Bare canvas may function as light, and so determine space, and the relation of brush strokes may intensify the spatial function of color. Atmosphere, whether clear or misty, is determined by an appropriate fusion of all the plastic means; when it is clear, the color is usually bright and delicate, the light is clear, and the line relatively clear-cut; when misty, line is diffuse or broken, the color soft and fluid, and the light distributed in diffuse patterns.

Composition, at its very simplest, is a relation of flat masses in two-dimensional space, and is satisfactory when the masses and intervals, including relationships of color, line and light, fuse in a definite form. The limitations of flat design, however, are so great that composition does not become really satisfactory until depth is added, though the mere addition of depth means nothing unless it is effectively handled. Matisse's arrangement of objects, both on a flat surface and in deep space, is masterly, and his types of composition are numerous and original, though they are always chosen with an eye to decorative effects, such as those of the rosette-pattern or of a step-like formation. As might be expected, the spacial relations are always reinforced, and their fusion made more intimate, by color and technique. Unity of color-scheme, harmony or contrast of particular colors, light-patterns and decorative motifs of every sort, any one or several of these, pervading the spatial elements, may serve to knit the composition firmly together and to give it identity. However realized, the spatial relationships are invariably part and parcel of a network of color-relations.

Matisse's decorative distortions lead to a number of extremely unusual spatial effects. Bizarreness is achieved by the separation of decorative motifs from the fabric to which they belong, and their establishment as detached volumes with independent spatial status; by this means flatness is avoided when it would mar the compositional unity of a particular type of design. Or the background as a whole may appear to be on one plane or on a small number of closely-set planes, and the foreground on another, but the space between the two may be realistically rendered. These distortions, however, are not arbitrary; like every other feature in Matisse's handling of space, they are the necessary corollaries of his general decorative color-design.

CHAPTER XIV

COMPOSITION

In the chapter on Plastic Form and Design, composition was considered briefly in the conventional acceptation of the term, that is, as the placing of masses in either two or three dimensions. It became immediately apparent, however, that the real meaning of the word could not be confined to this technical usage, since for the purposes of design an area of color may exercise the compositional function of a mass, and the sequence of masses may serve to outline the picture as a whole. In the present chapter we shall observe this process of expansion of meaning going on, as each of the plastic means becomes effective in ordering all the details of a painting, in effecting its total com-position. The general factors of design, especially the principles of rhythm and contrast, are operative also in composition, and the more general requirements of unity and personal distinction in design of course apply equally to composition.

Matisse's compositions exhibit an accentuated decorative pattern which, though never the sum and substance of the design, is always its framework. Over and above the pattern there is invariably a sufficient degree of representative and expressive form to raise the painting above the exclusively decorative level; however, the emphasis, as we have repeatedly seen, remains upon decoration, and pictures in which there are not spatial compression and diminution of solidity are the exception, not the rule, in Matisse's work. Pattern in itself may be one of the important features of a composition of high order, as witness the fact that in paintings by El Greco and Cézanne, patterns of line and color are composed in a unit with a single æsthetic effect. But in the work of these artists, as in Matisse's, the pattern is the skeleton for the flesh and blood of a fuller form without which it would lose much in individuality, and everything in deeply expressive value. The patterns of Matisse, like those of

El Greco and Cézanne, are almost invariably also compositions in three-dimensional space even when the space is distorted for the sake of decorative enrichment. Rarely, except when Matisse's obvious intention is to exploit surface-pattern, are his compositions completely flat. He constantly utilizes the æsthetic effects of composition in three dimensions—i.e., thrust and counterthrust of solid volumes and accentuated spatial intervals—to increase the variety and appeal of his decorative forms.

According to the requirements of design, an individual area may operate directly in the composition, or it may be combined with other individual areas in a group which makes a single compositional unit. In the latter case there is a subsidiary composition within the group, just as each of the several movements of a symphony or stanzas of a poem is in itself a unified composition. The condition of success in such grouping is always the artist's ability to make all the elements hang together in a unified form which embodies his feeling for symmetry, order, balance and rhythm, as well as the flavor of his individuality. A striking example of this sort of organization on a large scale is a Matisse triptych, a set of three separate pictures, each of which is a compact group of figures organized in a composition with its own identity, and at the same time an integral part of the total composition formed of the three pictures (69–70–71). The three compositions are tied into one by the rhythmic sequence of masses and spatial intervals in a graceful rise-and-fall and in-and-out movement, which involves great variety of color, drawing, modeling, perspective and use of planes, in each of the compositional units.*

Matisse's primary interest in decoration extends its sway to composition without impairing his ability to render traditional types of composition and to retain their essential æsthetic effects as, for instance, when he achieves a decorative version of the Cézanne style of mass-composition by a series of new relationships and dramatic color-contrasts between the volumes and spatial intervals (33, 173). His composition ranks in importance with that of the best masters in picturesque distribution of masses, in variety and novelty of relationships of vol-

*See analysis, p. 399.

umes and spaces, and in the union of these in well-knit organizations. Such is the case, for instance, when the sequence of masses from the foreground backward coincides with an accentuated sweep of decorative units moving in space from one corner of the canvas to the corner diagonally opposite (33, 49, 94, 136). This diagonal ordering of the principal masses has been a favorite plan of organization with Tintoretto and many later painters. In Matisse this traditional type of composition is retained but is made an incident in new types of design characterized by sets of contrasting rhythms. Sometimes the counterbalancing rhythms are vertical, horizontal and oblique (136); at other times the diagonal mass is the oblique-longitudinal focus of a concentric arrangement of variedly colored enframing area-lines receding in space (94). The rosette type of organization, i.e., a grouping of masses such that the constituents converge toward a center and describe around it a radiating wheel-like rhythm, is still another traditional compositional framework which Matisse utilizes and modifies by added features prescribed by primarily decorative designs (40, 108).*

In general, Matisse plays havoc with academic rules relating to composition. An instance of this is a bizarre decorative organization effected by placing a large object or figure at the extreme left foreground of the picture and other smaller volumes to the right and in the distance. The large unit thus becomes a mass or plane in space, and also, because of its shape and treatment, one of the components of a unified pattern of stripes and bands (91, 117). But Matisse's infractions of academic rules always result in organizations which satisfy the instinctive desire of human beings for symmetry and balance; moreover, they do it in an unexpected manner with decorative and dramatic enrichment of rhythms which give distinction and individuality to the composition. These adventures in composition are made more interesting because of the by-products of his exploitation of the decorative possibilities of subject-matter. Masses as such are often less important to his design than planes (31), dramatic color-contrasts (136, 174), or

*Cf., e.g., 353.

transferred values (53, 167) ; in other words, the masses are vehicles for specific compositional effects.

An adequate study of Matisse's composition falls in three main subdivisions: organization of color, relationship between foreground and background, and rhythmic organization of decorative components. The first of these topics, **organization of color**, has been treated in detail in the chapter on Color* and need be mentioned here only to recall that color-relationships and color-patterns are the very foundation of his compositions, all of which are organized color-rhythms.

Certain aspects of the **compositional relationships between foreground and background** have been treated incidentally in other parts of the book. It was noted that usually Matisse's plan of organization is to establish, in all parts of the picture, a common denominator of decorative quality by daring and radical distortions of the objects themselves and of their natural relations to the background. Solid objects in the foreground are often rendered lightly and decorative objects in the background are given additional increased prominence to accord with a decorative design which aims at harmonious fusion of background and foreground. The sacrifice of realism frequently reaches such an extent that solid objects in the foreground and ornamental motifs of draperies in the background have an identical function as decorative-expressive units in the homogeneous design (147, 148, 154, 164, 166). Variety of compositional effects is attained by many such changes in the degree of realism in the solid objects, so that their compositional value accords with that of the decorative motifs.

Compositional equalization of foreground and background may be effected by introducing in both sections such factors as broad geometrical color-areas (56, 63, 165), wavy area-lines (29, 94), pattern of technique (25), decorative motifs (131, 141), or three-dimensional volumes (33, 150, 152). Often in this last-mentioned type of composition, ornaments of draperies or screens in the setting appear detached from the fabric and thus become a series of quasi-solid units with

*See pp. 101–102, 104–106, 108–109, 116–121.

free space around them; these rhythms of volume and space
in the setting are continued in the other parts of the picture by
the relationship between volumes and spatial intervals in the
more realistically rendered objects of the subject-matter. In
other words, the composition is a novel version of the traditional space-and-volume type. A hint of this distortion of decorative ornaments to transform them into volumes set in space
is found in the work of Tintoretto* and of Cézanne,† but Matisse carries the distortion much further by means of dramatic
color-contrasts and accentuated linear patterns which more
completely break up the flat texture into a pattern of volumes
and spatial intervals.

In those of Matisse's designs in which the background is
subordinated to the foreground, the unity of both sections is
achieved by a wide range of compositional devices appropriate
to the particular design. Sometimes color-areas pervade foreground and background and determine the type of composition
(48, 133). At other times accentuated volumes and color-
contrasts of the foreground are echoed in the background (21).
The common compositional factor may be a set of semi-rigid
elongated areas of color that lend to the total design a graceful
rigidity reminiscent of primitive Negro sculpture (176); or it
may be a rhythm of curvilinear elongated areas making up a
three-dimensional space-composition, the patterned organization of which recalls the enframing device common in primitive art (94‡). The color of the background may serve as a
foil to that of the foreground either by vivid dramatic contrast (42), or by subtle relationships of sensuous quality (69–
70–71). Still another unifying factor is a sheetlike setting,
continuous in color and tone from the top of the background
to the immediate foreground, with its center constituting the
focus about which the subject-matter proper is placed (51, 66,
88). This all-inclusive and continuous area of background and
foreground is a variant of the device used by Velásquez and
Manet in their subtle rendering of deep space.§ In Matisse's
version, deep space is rarely stressed, and the continuous area

*E.g., 354.   †E.g., 412.
‡Cf., e.g., 357.   §E.g., 356, 387, 388.

of color may function, according to the design, as a large plane
upon which are superposed parallel planes of contrasting color,
tone, shape and size, which build up the volumes and patterns
of the subject-matter (66) ; or the space may take the form of
a series of dramatic contrasts involving all the plastic factors
(51, 88). An illustration of the latter is a flowerpiece in
which the continuous setting is a sequence of slight volumes of
colored atmosphere which envelop, as in a pocket, the sharply
contrasting, crisply defined vase of flowers (88). In this instance the unifying agents are the shapes and volumes of color,
their patterns, the sensuous quality of the color, and the element of contrast common to both foreground and background,
but ranging from accentuation to extreme diminution.

A background more prominent than the foreground is not
uncommon in Matisse. For example, an entire foreground, including part of a room with figures and furniture, may form a
sort of enframing setting for a background-landscape seen
through a window: vista and setting are unified by alternate
interrelated rhythms of color-areas, bands, stripes and arabesques, all incorporated in a steplike organization of planes
with space distorted as in the Persian miniatures (64). In
pictures of the poster type the accentuated background is
brought into harmonious relationship with the foreground by
diminution of the space between the two sections and by
rhythmic duplication, in each, of the patterns and color which
occur in the other (141, 148, 167).

The third subdivision in our study of Matisse's composition, **rhythmic organization of decorative components,** inevitably overlaps the other two, since every one of his compositions resolves itself into a rhythmic ensemble of its
plastic constituents, and each of these is essentially a decorative element. In general, it is the rhythmic repetition of color-
areas, linear patterns, patches of light or even brush strokes,
which gives identity, and therefore compositional unity, to his
dramatic color-patterns and space-compositions. The ways and
means of effecting compositional unity by rhythmic repetition
are literally innumerable; a few examples will be cited here,
merely to illustrate the principle.

Repetition in the landscape-setting of the curvilinear pattern of the foreground-figure, with variation in color and plastic function, may link the two units of the subject-matter in a harmonious plastic form dominated by tones of blue (32). A constant practice of Matisse's is the repetition, in different parts of the picture, of a single color or set of colors, slightly or perceptibly varied, by which a common factor is established in objects belonging to background and foreground (56, 120, 144, 166, 167). Again, plastic unification may be effected by repetition, with suitable modifications, in subsidiary parts of the organization, of the general type of drawing of the principal compositional factor; in a portrait, for instance, color-compartments of loaded pigment, together with areas of bare canvas, give character to the drawing of the face and are repeated in larger and less defined areas in the blouse, hat and background (21). Frequently a decorative motif on flat objects reappears in the three-dimensional modeling of a volume, as when the stripes of a background-plane recur in a figure (167), or when the familiar rosette-motif pervades the design even to the pattern made by the volumes in space (108, 152). Not only the possible but the actual uses by Matisse of this device of rhythmic repetition are far too numerous for cataloguing: they merge into one another by such imperceptible gradations that it is constantly possible to regard a particular duplication as no less, for example, one of light than of line or color.

In the above discussion Matisse's composition has been studied from the viewpoint of color-organization, relationship between foreground and background, and rhythmic organization of decorative components. These three modes of compositional unification are not mutually exclusive: all of them may on occasion be found in a single picture. They represent not pigeon-holes in one of which every composition must be placed, but distinguishable aspects; and the number of variations in each, and in their combination, testify again to Matisse's resourcefulness and command of traditional forms.

Summary

Composition, in the narrow sense of ordering of masses, tends inevitably to broaden its meaning to include a use of all the plastic means to achieve a unified design. The initial problems of composition are those of placing of objects with reference to one another, and of relation of foreground to background, but the means by which such unification is accomplished quickly reveal aspects which go beyond mere spatial relationship.

The foundation of Matisse's composition is a decorative pattern, within which there may be sub-patterns, areas which form a relatively independent composition, though in a successful picture this is always integrated in the design as a whole. Both in the design as a whole and in the sub-designs, Matisse's decorative interest usually affects composition by flattening the masses and compressing the space, though both solidity and deep space are at his command when he desires to use them. He adopts a number of traditional types of composition, such as a mass-and-space organization, a diagonal recessive ordering of volumes, or the rosette-motif in deep space, but always with an individual development of their decorative possibilities. His treatment of all types of composition is extremely non-academic: sometimes the largest mass is put at the extreme edge of the canvas, but without disturbance of balance, since for him masses are as a rule primarily planes of color, or stripes and bands, or groups of ornamental motifs, and so may be balanced by similar plastic elements elsewhere.

In addition to the already-discussed organization by color, Matisse's composition proceeds on several other principles. Foreground and background are usually brought into relation by treating each as a set of decorative motifs: objects and figures in the foreground are frequently devoid of any real weight, or ornamental motifs in the background are given separate existence, and appear as if suspended in space. This device was not original with Matisse, but no other painter ever used it so systematically or so constantly. When the background is subordinated to the foreground, the two may be unified by pervasive color-areas, by corresponding voluminousness of objects and degree of color-contrast, by color-relations either of harmony or of contrast, or by a continuous sheetlike setting, to which the main objects of the subject-matter are attached by a variety of plastic relationships. Not infrequently, the usual order is reversed, and the point of chief interest is the background, to which the foreground serves as a setting. In this second aspect of compositional organization, the principal unifying agents are distorted space and rhythms of color and pattern.

A third principle of compositional unification is rhythmic organization of decorative components, a repetition of color-areas, patterns of line or light or brush strokes throughout the picture. The repetition, always with modification in either quality or context, may be of curvilinear pattern, of color or color-relations, of a general type of drawing, of some particular manifestation of the familiar bands, stripes or rosette-motifs, and so on indefinitely.

The three principles of unity in Matisse's composition— color-organization, relation of foreground to background, rhythmic organization of patterns—are not mutually incompatible; in practice they overlap; but any one of them may dominate the organization of a particular picture.

CHAPTER XV

THEMATIC VARIATION

PRACTITIONERS of all the arts constantly introduce into their own work elements taken from their predecessors. Such elements may be general methods of using color, line, light and space, in which case we say merely that a painter stands in or employs a tradition; however, they may also be more or less specific forms or fragments of forms, and then we say that an artist has taken over a definite theme. In literature, for example, innumerable plots, situations, and characters have been, in essentials, used by many men—Shakespeare's borrowing of his plots is a famous illustration—and in music the practice is no less common. Provided the borrowed plot or melody is modified and developed, given a new set of relations and made an integral part of a new form, the originality and integrity of the artist remain unaffected. Brahms, in his "Variations on a Theme of Haydn," does precisely what the title indicates; his theme is lifted bodily from Haydn, but as the composition progresses the melodic intervals, the harmony, the orchestration, the whole spirit and quality, are so changed that the music is as organically Brahms's own as if he had himself invented the melody which served as his starting-point. In the finale of the same composer's C-minor Symphony, the second theme is strongly reminiscent of the broad, swinging melody in the last movement of Beethoven's Choral Symphony. When the resemblance was pointed out to him, he replied "Any fool can see that," with the implication, clearly true as a matter of fact, that the difference in use and development of the borrowed theme made any initial resemblance unimportant.

Matisse likewise levies tribute upon the great traditions of painting for plastic themes which he reworks into forms essentially new and bearing his own unmistakable stamp. Often, too, what amounts to the same theme is employed in a number of separate pictures, with differences so numerous and important that each picture has its characteristic identity and cannot for a moment be confused by a discerning observer with any of the others. This principle of thematic variation is so abundantly employed by Matisse in sets of pictures, and its application throws so much light on the variety of his designs and his resourcefulness in their execution, that the subject calls for discussion at some length.

In general, all well-organized compositions are resolvable into themes which, varied individually or collectively, enter into forms expressive of many shades of difference in the reactions of the artist to the world about him. A theme is a subject, or topic, or proposition, presented in the medium through which the artist expresses himself. A theme in a picture may take the form of a specific item or type of subject-matter, a color-scheme, a type of space-composition or decorative presentation, a quality of feeling, or indeed any plastic unit or traditional form of organization. Variations upon any of these give rise to a great diversity of highly individualized plastic forms, as we have already seen in the discussion of Matisse's versions of landscape, types of drawing and color-organization.

Subject-matter to an artist may be merely a point of departure, a source of themes to be so varied by his creative use of the plastic means that the familiar representative values are almost entirely subordinated to the new set of meanings embodied in the form. This relative independence of subject-matter and its plastic expression may be illustrated by a consideration of Matisse's varied treatment of one of his favorite topics, the odalisque.

To the untrained observer, Matisse's many presentations of a nude reclining or sitting amidst decorative surroundings, may look so nearly alike as to suggest obsession or poverty of resources. The monotony is only superficial, however, for of the score of these pictures, no one is repetitive of another: each plastic organization has its individual identity established by variation upon themes which draws out not only the qualities of the subject-matter but the decorative possibilities of its plastic ingredients. In many of these pictures the compositional framework may be a pattern of geometrical areas of contrasting color, but variations in the character and relationships of the constituents produce in each painting a perfectly individual plastic form, often radically different from that in any other.

The foregoing point may be illustrated by a comparative study of three renderings of the odalisque in which treatment of space is the theme upon which interest centers. Space is accentuated in one (152), diminished in the other (174), and minimized in the third (164). As a result of these variations, each coördinated with the compositional activity of the other plastic factors, the designs acquire widely divergent transferred values. The first composition resembles in general form a flowered cretonne, but its individuality is established by a rosette-pattern of accentuated space-and-volume units. The total effect of the second picture is that of a gaily-colored flag: its numerous stripes, bands and arabesques of vividly contrasted colors are organized as a flat setting against which is placed the boxlike figure of the reclining woman. A cretonne-effect, in the third odalisque composition, differs radically from that in the first picture, because the space is reduced to such a point that the figure becomes merely one of the decorative units in the flat ornamental ensemble.

Another group of pictures containing the same subject-matter—a set of still-life objects, including a bowl of goldfish, in a blue-walled studio opening into a pink-and-green garden—are also radically different plastically (50, 51). One of these compositions is lightly executed, its objects sketchily drawn and slightly modeled, and the bright and delicate color-scheme is dominated by extensive areas of a light, almost transparent blue (50). The theme of this picture, lightness and brightness, is born of the interaction between bright, delicate, light colors, diminished space, accentuated light, and simplified drawing. This major theme is reinforced by variations upon another theme, bare canvas, which is used extensively to define contour, heighten illumination, vary tone, and as an active element in modeling. A second composition of this "goldfish" series is formed by variations on three major themes which by their interaction yield a radically different type of design, and a corresponding difference in effect (51). One theme consists of the contrast of comparatively few small areas of bright, light colors, with larger areas of deep and weighty tone. Another theme is an exercise in space-composition, that is, in the dynamic relationships between accentuated spatial intervals and volumes and planes varied in degree of solidity. The third theme is the geometric shape of the color-areas forming the compartmental framework within which the first two themes are developed in a great variety of ways. As our attention shifts from aspect to aspect, this picture emerges as a sharply-defined pattern of color-compartments, or as a very individual version of several traditional forms of space-composition, or as a lively interplay of daring and dramatic color-contrasts. But it is the interaction of the three themes which gives character to the total picture as a solid and weighty organization, diametrically the opposite of the light and delicate picture just discussed.*

Another illustration of thematic variation in pictures dealing with similar subject-matter is offered by two paintings which represent the same figure in Spanish costume seated at a table covered with a decorated tablecloth, and set against a patterned background (147, 148). The difference between the two in plastic form is due to changes in the color-scheme and in the organization of the decorative elements. Both pictures are cretonnelike in general appearance, but one is a harmony in blue (147), the other a multicolored ensemble of vividly contrasting areas, stripes and arabesques (148). Moreover, while in each composition the figure merges with the rhythmic pattern of the background, it plays a different plastic rôle in the organization. In the blue picture, a theme of volume-and-space relationships requires that the figure be relatively fully rounded to correspond with the floral ornaments of the drapery, which appear as slightly three-dimensional volumes partly detached from the fabric. In the other picture, the figure is flattened and becomes a rhythmic constituent of the compositional theme, a two-dimensional color-pattern of stripes and arabesques.†

*For further analytical data on 51 see Appendix, p. 382.
†Compare also, as illustrative of the same point, 95 with 97.

Other illustrations—even more striking—of the independence of subject-matter and plastic form, illustrations which indeed show the radical difference which may exist between the two, are offered by pictures with subject-matter almost completely identical in detail, even to position and compositional distribution of objects. Two paintings, for example, represent the same corner of a room in which the same figure and objects are arranged in like positions (106, 115). In one of these (115), the components of subject-matter are organized as a decorative ensemble of juxtaposed color-areas; the whole has a lightness, delicacy and floating quality reminiscent of both Renoir and Pascin; it is loosely drawn and lightly executed with the aid of much bare canvas, light washes of color and swirling brush strokes. Instead of this delicacy and lightness the form of the other picture has solidity and weight, it is primarily an integration of figure, objects and room in a compact, tightly-knit space-composition, and its more positive drawing is executed by deeper color, accentuated linear contour and color-pattern, thicker paint, and fewer areas of bare canvas.

Thematic variation of the type in question may again be illustrated by two compositions quite similar in the pose, costume, type and distorted modeling of figure, and in the colorful setting decorated with rosette-motifs (134, 143). Specific color-scheme and relationships of color and light produce in one picture (143) a vivid, almost flashy, ensemble of positive color-contrasts, while in the other a pervasive tone of lavender tempers most of the colors, diminishes the degree of color-contrast, and lends subtlety to the intricate plastic interrelations of color, line, light and technique.*

Types of pictorial organization are extensively used by Matisse as themes in a great variety of designs. One of his favorite organizations is an all-embracing pattern of dramatically contrasted color-areas; the variations on this theme involve the relationships of all its plastic constituents, with a special emphasis upon differences in the sensuous quality of color. Variety in aspect and treatment of this theme is illustrated by a number of pictures, each having broad, well-defined compart-

*For analytical details see Appendix, p. 419.

ments of bright and exotic color juxtaposed in daring and dramatic contrasts (34, 56, 141). One of these pictures (56) is primarily a pattern of audacious colors that clash, but their relationships are such that the very feeling of clash is an indispensable part of the harmony. Another picture of this category (141) is pervaded with nuances of lavender which give the tonal key to the pattern and, by removing the feeling of clash, diminish the intensity of the contrasts, though without impairing either the exotic, bright quality of the color or the emphasis upon color-compartments. In a third version (34) a flag-like background of a few extensive compartments of relatively deep and weighty color makes a sharp contrast with a figure more actively patterned and lighter in tone.

Another sort of variation in color-compartmental design becomes in itself a theme of pictorial organization, within which Matisse develops a series of individual forms. Its general plan presents a condensation of the color-pattern into two large contiguous color-areas, placed one above the other, each patterned with ornamental motifs; in these areas a whole set of distorted volumes blend to form a decorative ensemble. The decorative motifs in the two areas are similar in general type but differ in color and shape, and these differences emphasize the contrast of color between the two areas and also help to integrate the distorted features of the subject-matter proper—figure or still-life objects—in a total form which looks like a suspended tapestry, comparatively heavy in the upper part and light in the lower. With this ensemble of general characteristics as a theme, and by a play upon line, light, color and space, Matisse elaborates different plastic organizations. In one of them, a still-life, the decorative motifs of the background-drapery are drawn solidly with color and accentuated linear contour so that it is they, more than the actual objects on the table, that function as volumes in space (154). In another picture, based upon the same compositional theme, a figure in decorative raiment becomes part of a flat, brightly striped background, and has about the same degree of prominence as the decorative setting (148).

Space-composition with accentuation of both spatial interval and volume is another fruitful field for Matisse's thematic variation. One version of it is characterized by a type of modeling which is a synthesis of elements taken from Cézanne, Renoir and the seventeenth-century Dutch genre-painters (150). The identifying mark in another is an accentuated pattern of broad color-compartments in which, while color-contrasts are ample, a large expanse of a single color, blue, dominates the picture as a whole (51). In still other renderings of the theme, the volume-and-space composition is essentially in the manner of Cézanne and is drawn and modeled in the Manet-Cézanne style, but the exotic tones make of it a distinctively Matisse organization (33, 157).

Planes of color, moving rhythmically in space, are the outstanding feature in many of Matisse's versions of space-composition. Planes grouped compactly are obviously very different in effect from planes widely separated. The latter arrangement is illustrated by a composition of large, widely distributed curvilinear planes of color that by their interrelation in deep space produce the feeling of a large color-movement, which includes in its sweep all the component figures and objects (31). The other extreme is exemplified in that poster-type of design in which the planes are closely packed (131, 141), and in that category of color-organization represented, for example, by decoratively treated portraits in which the unification of figure and background is again accomplished by means of a compact series of flat planes of color (48).

Both of the foregoing types of thematic development of the plane as a compositional factor are occasionally used alternately in the same picture (52, 56), and also, at times, in conjunction with the space-and-volume theme in one or more of its possible versions (51, 80). Indeed Matisse's work as a whole offers an unending series of variations on the spatial interplay of volumes and planes, along with other themes into which enter all the plastic elements. Here, as always in plastic organization, it is the interaction of the constituent factors that establishes the individualizing relationships of the design.

Pattern in space-composition is another theme prolific in variations. Often the space-composition is organized in a sort of triangular or pyramidal unit of space formed by converging planes, within which figures or objects are set at various intervals (76, 109, 155, 156). The background-setting is thus a pattern of three planes, representing, for example, the walls and the floor of a room or the top of a table, with the meeting-point of these planes the focus of the perspective, which may be near the center of the composition or to the right or left. Volumes or planes within this pyramidal space, as well as its three constituent planes, are treated differently in each picture to accord with its general plan of organization. In one instance (156), each of the three constituent planes is subdivided by variously colored bands, stripes or lines, which serve two compositional ends : they set off by contrast, and also rhythmically respond to, the bright, exotic, vivid patterns of bands and stripes in the figures and objects in the foreground. Here compositional unity is largely due to bands and stripes in a pattern of colors. In another composition (155), the pyramidal form of the spatial setting is repeated in an upright pyramidal arrangement of volumes in the foreground. The three component planes of the pyramidal space, by contrast between their colors and by their sharp linear junctions, accentuate the perspective and the roominess of space between and around these objects in the foreground. The resulting total design is one characterized by dynamic relationships between volumes, planes and space, in all of which modeling and drawing are accomplished by patches of contrasting color.

Further variations in the component elements of the pyramidal space-setting give rise to designs of totally unlike effect. In one picture the few broad areas of thick color make of the pyramidal unit of space a positive and dramatic pattern of light-and-dark contrasts with a pronounced feeling of heaviness (76). The compositional triangular formation, in another picture, is part of an ensemble characterized by delicacy and lightness of color and by subtlety of contrast within a generally lavender-gray color-scheme (109).

Matisse's familiar rosette-motif is another pattern which is often extended to include all the elements of spatial organization, and which varies in treatment and function according to the particular design. A rosette of solid volumes in well-defined spatial intervals may be an accentuated form of the theme which pervades the subsidiary parts of the organization in minor degrees of distinctness (152). In contrast to this solidity of volume and this alternation of emphasis and diminution of the rosette-pattern, another composition has the shape of the pattern well defined in most of its parts, and the rosette-formation of the total picture is formed by a compact group of radiating color-planes (131). In this same picture, a bizarre variation upon the theme of space-composition establishes one of the main characteristics of the design; that is, the major planes from foreground to background are vertical, parallel to each other, and set close together, so that the effect is a compact sandwich-like alternation of flat objects in space. A contrasting variation of this sandwich-like arrangement is achieved in another picture by making the parallel units relatively three-dimensional and widely separated (135).

The intrinsic ornamental nature of the arabesque makes it particularly eligible as a theme for variation in Matisse's designs. Sometimes it is so all-pervasive that the total picture is a highly complex arabesque, formed by subsidiary arabesques both in the foreground and background as a whole and in their component units (31, 32). Sometimes a comparatively flat figure forms a large arabesque, and this motif is repeated on a small scale in the contrasting background of bands and stripes (167). In the first of these instances, the arabesque is predominantly one of moving volumes in space; in the second it is chiefly of two-dimensional patterns.

Matisse also employs as plastic themes several types of compositional surface-pattern, i.e., of the pattern described on the canvas by the general framework of the design. Such a patterned plan of organization is the diagonal arrangement of objects from an upper corner of the canvas to the opposite lower corner, which divides the surface of the picture into three main sections. The diagonal sweep, in one of his adaptations of the theme, is basically the traditional conception of space and volume but with emphasis upon the decorative elements (152). In another picture, the diagonal pattern is a scene for the exploitation of the values of ancient Hindu and Negro sculpture, re-interpreted by Matisse in a bright and exotic color-scheme of clashing contrasts set in a pattern of bands and stripes (136). A third version of the theme offers a central undulating diagonal area, paralleled on either side by wavy bands of subtly contrasting color, which gradually recede as they extend toward the borders of the picture (94).

In this general type of compositional pattern, the central diagonal area is often the framework for the pictorial distribution of the principal objects of the subject-matter, and is treated differently in each plastic organization in accordance with the character of the design. In two still-lifes, for instance, Matisse develops this theme with widely varying degrees of elaboration in the decorative and expressive detail (33, 49). Both pictures offer contrasts between the relative flatness of one series of objects and the pronounced three-dimensional quality of adjacent ones; but the stress upon three-dimensional quality in one picture (33) and upon flatness of decorative pattern in the other (49) determines the character of design in each. The still-life objects in the first composition (33) are volumes modeled by hatchings and related to each other in comparatively deep space; this theme of volumes in space is repeated rhythmically, in the tablecloth and screen, by the floral ornaments so drawn and modeled that they seem like detached volumes. In the second still-life (49), conceived in terms more nearly those of decoration, the objects in the sweeping diagonal pattern are relatively flattened to harmonize with the large arabesque-motifs of the tablecloth. These variations in thematic development of the oblique pattern achieve in the first still-life a highly individualized interpretation of a Cézanne form; in the second, a new version of a Japanese decorative compositional arabesque.*

We have already discussed Matisse's methods of making a similar color-scheme serve multifarious ends by varying the proportions and relationships of the individual colors.† Further consideration of this topic, from another angle, and with especial reference to the color-scheme of the Nice type of pictures,

*Cf. illustrations, pp. 258, 259.   †See chapter on Color, pp. 109–111.

will illustrate more fully the importance of thematic variation in giving identity to design. The outstanding feature of the Nice color-scheme, as we have already noted, is a pervasive sensuous quality of delicacy and freshness reminiscent of early Egyptian textiles, water-color, pastel or mother-of-pearl. Matisse shuffles, as it were, the component colors, and obtains an infinitely large number of subtle and significant variations in design, without sacrifice of the essential formal qualities of the theme.

One type of variation upon this theme consists in so extending, repeating and emphasizing one of the colors—a blue, for instance (73), or a tan (80)—that it gives the key to the color-design of the picture. Overtones of lavender pervading various colors (98), or a large area of red (84) or green (123) serving as a setting for smaller color-units, may similarly dominate in the color-scheme. It is not, however, simply a matter of accentuation of color that gives the design its individuality and force, for in each case variations in drawing and other plastic factors coöperate with the color to bring about the composite effect. The pervasive lavender in one of the instances just referred to (98) would not work as it does except for the support of simplified drawing and accentuated linear contour. Likewise, the red picture (84) obtains its chief characteristics through the bizarre position of objects and of decorative arabesque-motifs. The blue picture (73) is individualized by the rhythms and contrasts in its pattern of stripes and by subtle and varied effects of space; the pictorial character of the tan picture (80) depends upon reinforcement of the tan by reddish and ivory tones closely related to it in feeling, and upon the contrast between the comparatively rounded figure and the flat patterned background of floor and wall. In all four compositions the sensuous quality characteristic of the Nice color-scheme serves as a theme, with effects varied by correlative modification in the other plastic means, which gives the color new meanings by its context of linear patterns (73), space-and-volume units (80), bizarre color-patterns (84), or contrasting treatment of space-composition (98).

Matisse's many poster- and cretonne-effects are likewise

produced mainly by variations on a decorative compositional theme. Novel aspects are achieved as the emphasis is laid upon the voluminous quality of objects and their spatial intervals (152), upon multicolored stripes and bands (56, 174), arabesques (31, 167), monotonal merging of colors (140), or upon vivid contrasts of color-compartments (53).

As we have already seen, Matisse is fond of selecting a traditional form as a theme to be reworked into compositions of his own, much as musicians employ their predecessors' themes. A familiar theme of Cézanne—the sharply patterned arrangement of still-life objects modeled by planes and hatchings of color—is utilized by Matisse as the foundation for several new types of design. In two such compositions, for instance, he increases the decorative value by diminishing the solidity and by flattening the deep space of the prototype (33, 173). The result differs in each picture: one is a series of semi-voluminous objects drawn in patches of bright contrasting exotic color dominated by tones of blue and by numerous complex and highly decorative patterns (33); the other is a simple, somewhat rigid and angular pattern of relatively broad and uniform color-areas with no one dominating tone (173).

Also, at times, Matisse plays upon a Renoir theme and attains to a variety of designs which, while pervaded with a general Renoir quality, have none of his drawing, color-scheme, or compositional arrangement. One of these variations achieves the lightness, the delicacy, the grace and charm of Renoir through the medium of a rhythmic pattern of oblongs and stripes in delicate light tones of water-color quality, so subtly contrasted that they blend into the harmonious pearly lavender-gray ensemble (109). In a second version the Renoir qualities are set in a matrix of patterns composed of two contrasting sets of color enlivened by Oriental curvilinear motifs and large units of bright color reminiscent of Persian miniatures (95).

Matisse's heavy draft upon characteristics of Oriental art has been already treated in considerable detail.* It will suffice here to indicate briefly how ingeniously he has varied one of these Oriental themes, the treatment of space, to obtain novel

*See chapter on Creative Use of Traditions, pp. 54–72.

and very striking effects. As we have seen, the Oriental handling of space, especially in Persian miniatures, often consists of juxtaposing, one above the other, in an upright plane, those portions of space which in reality recede into the far distance. Matisse adopts this general compositional principle and introduces features of his own that increase the bizarreness of the effect and extend the decorative activity of the spatial units. One of his interpretations makes of an ornamented red rug covering the floor an obliquely vertical decorative setting for a figure and objects of furniture done in contrasting colors (84). Space in another composition is rendered by an ascending series of planes contrasting in color and pattern, and organized in a steplike formation from the bottom to the top of the canvas; these planes are also compositionally active in the total color-pattern of vertical and horizontal bands and stripes (64).

A space-form found in the Chinese, Japanese, Velásquez and Manet—an uninterrupted plane of space extending from foreground to background—is so manipulated by Matisse that it may serve as a color-setting to a compositional group of colorful volumes related to each other in deep space (51); or as one of the principal agents in a design of space-contrasts (57); or as an extremely light, delicately colored circumambient atmosphere in which swims a brightly colored, crisply drawn bouquet of flowers in a vase (88), or as a plane of solid color in a patterned composition of planes (66).

The foregoing study of Matisse's variations upon themes could be extended by innumerable illustrations of like creative adaptations of other themes taken, for instance, from Manet's drawing (66, 121), color-scheme (66, 100), and subject-matter (100, 114); from Japanese prints (69–70–71); Persian tiles (104, 175); Byzantine mosaics (21, 24, 48); and a large number of other traditional forms. Most of these themes have been or will be referred to parenthetically elsewhere, and no complete account of them is possible except by analysis of every plastic feature in each design. A selection of particular themes for detailed treatment has been made here in order to indicate the extraordinarily wide compass of Matisse's thematic developments as determinatives of his designs. His prolific metamorphosis of plastic themes involves not only the constituents of each theme but, to a still larger extent, the complex intertwining of a number of them. Matisse's profusion of resources in effecting thematic variations proves his rich comprehension of the pictorial possibilities of subject-matter, his assimilation of the æsthetic significance of traditional forms, his amazing control of the plastic means, and a prestidigitator's ingenuity and skill in adapting themes, fundamentally alike, to individual and greatly diversified new plastic expressions.

SUMMARY

Like all artists, Matisse draws from the traditions of art not only general methods of organization, but specific themes, already organized in a definite form, and so reorganizes them that they become integral parts of new forms definitely his own. Such themes in his hands are extremely prolific, and any one, suitably modified and placed in a variety of contexts, may give birth to an almost indefinite number of particular pictures. Sometimes these themes as a whole can be definitely placed in the traditions, sometimes they are, as ensembles of plastic factors, original with Matisse; but in any event they are varied and interwoven with other themes in so many ways that their employment does not become mechanical or monotonous.

In a series of odalisques, for example, which superficially are much the same, there is extensive variation upon the theme of space. According to the degree to which the space is accentuated or diminished, and the remainder of the plastic context varied, the pictures acquire radically different transferred values. Another group of pictures, all treating the same subject-matter (the "goldfish" series), also differ plastically from each other; of two of them, for example, one is dominated by a theme of lightness and delicacy with much use of bare canvas; and the other by an interplay between a theme of color-contrast, a theme of space, and one of marked color-compartments. Again, in two pictures of a figure at a table, because of changes in color-scheme and arrangement of decorative detail, the first is relatively homogeneous in color and organized in deep space, the second is multicolored, with elaborate linear patterns but practically no depth. In another pair of pictures with subject-matter even more completely identical, one is a closely organized space-composition, with relatively heavy, solid color, and positive drawing, line and pattern; the other is a set of delicate color-areas, loosely drawn and lightly executed. Other instances of plastic variation with similar subject-matter are indefinitely numerous.

Variations in which the theme is a type of plastic organization are extremely numerous. The familiar patterned organization by contrasted color-areas has many sub-forms, each of which is capable of wide variation. The variation may consist in modification of the sharpness of the contrasts, and of the sensuous quality of the component colors. In a type of organization in which there are two general color-areas, containing decorative ensembles of flattened volumes and ornamental motifs, by variation in the line, light, color and space, the volumes may be made of equal importance with the ornamental motifs, or the emphasis on solidity and space-organization may be even shifted to the decorative motifs of the setting.

Space-composition is another familiar theme in Matisse's work. Conjoined with a fairly heavy and realistic modeling it is varied in a series of pictures, one of which is differentiated from the others by an accentuation of color-compartments dominated by blue; in another the volume-and-space organization is more especially in the manner of Cézanne, and there are characteristic Matisse exotic colors. Spatial organization in planes alternates, with intermediate forms, between compact flat planes and curvilinear planes sweeping in three-dimensional space; occasionally both variations occur in the same picture, or are combined with the heavy modeling just mentioned.

Patterns in space-composition may be similarly varied. A pyramidal arrangement of space, with the apex forming the focus of perspective, may be treated in very varying styles: in one instance each of the three constituent planes of the pyramid is a pattern of bands and stripes which contrasts with, and also rhythmically repeats, similar patterns elsewhere; in another instance, a pyramid of space in the setting is counterbalanced by one of volumes in the foreground, with the result that space-composition is accentuated, and additional color-contrasts are obtained. Similarly the rosette-motif, as a form of spatial organization of volumes, may be less completely reproduced in the subsidiary parts of the composition, or voluminousness may be practically eliminated without detriment to the essentials of the rosette-form. A sandwich-like arrangement of objects may be given either by a series of compactly placed vertical planes, or by volumes and intervals of deep space. The arabesque-motif, as a means of spatial organization, may pervade the picture by appearing in its component parts, or it may be utilized in some units and thus form a contrast with a background of bands and stripes ornamented with arabesque-motifs.

Compositional surface-patterns may also be varied. A diagonal succession of objects across the canvas may appear as a decorative version of the traditional arrangement of volumes in space or, in the form of contrasting bright colors set in stripes and bands, it may reinterpret motifs from primitive sculpture. This central area generally forms the axis about which the subject-matter is distributed, but the detail is never twice the same: there is always variation in degree of flatness or voluminousness, in color-contrast, in elaboration of ornamental detail, and so on.

Another form of variation is in color-scheme, which is illustrated in the Nice pictures. Always retaining its essential delicacy, this particular color-scheme may be dominated by any one of a number of colors, which is either pervasive or present as a large dominant area. Various decorative motifs, spatial effects, types of modeling and linear arrangements, are all in keeping with this light and graceful form, and variations in all these parallel the variations in color.

A frequent result of Matisse's play upon decorative themes is a type of composition which has the general effect of a poster or cretonne. Diversity is attained by emphasis upon, respectively, the voluminous quality of objects and their spatial intervals, stripes and bands, or one or more of the aspects of color.

Matisse is also in the habit of selecting themes from the traditions of painting and putting his own stamp upon them. Cézanne's heavy modeling by planes and hatchings of color and his arrangement in deep space are varied by flattening the space and lightening the weight; and this general variation is further modified by brightening and altering the character of the color and adding numerous complex decorative patterns, or by making the composition one of broad uniform color-areas. In similar fashion the delicacy of Renoir is on occasion adapted and varied.

Oriental space-forms are extensively used and manipulated. Representation of distance by elevation to the top of the canvas is varied by the introduction of obliquely placed masses in contrasting colors against decorative settings similarly placed, or by making successive planes at once a series of steps and of bands of color. A single sheetlike plane connecting foreground and background is made the means to a great variety of plastic relationships: the fundamental theme is the same, but it serves on one occasion as a color-setting, on another as a means of spatial organization, on a third as atmosphere, on a fourth as an element in a design of color-planes. Further instances could be multiplied indefinitely.

Although in his variation upon themes Matisse does only what all artists do in some measure, the very unusual extent to which he carries the practice, and the extraordinary wealth of forms he achieves by it, testify again to his superlative power of organization, resourcefulness, and ability to make apparently slight changes instrumental to far-reaching plastic effects. They demonstrate conclusively how great a wealth of plastic organization can be derived from illustrative material comparatively slight in body and narrow in range.

CHAPTER XVI

PORTRAITURE

PORTRAITURE, in the sense of realization of the character or personality of the sitter, is so rare with Matisse as to be almost negligible. Many of his ostensible portraits are in reality primarily adventures in color-contrasts or in patterns in which the figure serves either as a focus of the color-organization (21, 42), or as a unifying factor in bringing disparate colors or patterns into an ensemble (34, 48, 56, 74). Matisse's oft-quoted remark, "It is *not* a woman—it is a *picture*," makes futile any criticism of wide departure from resemblance to the sitter or of absence of the personality of the subject.

Considered as pictorial organizations, his portraits have plastic characteristics which make them distinguished entities even in his extraordinarily rich repertoire of forms. The faces are practically always drawn in accordance with a design which makes gross distortions inevitable. Facial features, for instance, may be indicated by dark or brightly colored lines and strokes, or by dabs and patches of color, in order to make them an integral part of complex line- and color-rhythms which pervade the picture (21, 22, 42, 48, 56, 62, 65, 69–70–71, 74). By playing upon traditional types of portraiture through appropriate variation within each organization of the facial features, and adaptation of the new unit to a specific type of design, Matisse paints heads reminiscent of the Egypto-Romans (21, 42, 48, 62), the Byzantines (56), the Orientals (93, 168), Manet (74, central figure in 71), Cézanne (28, 103), Modigliani (176). Often the head owes much of its individuality to the plastic activity of elements taken from several traditions. Gauguin's color-scheme, for instance, is introduced as the groundwork of an organization in which facial features are rendered in the Egypto-Roman style (168): the line of the eyebrows is continued down the center and length of the nose, and is flanked by a strip of shade on one side of the nose

179

and by a band of light on the other. Moreover the loose and flowing lines in garments and background give to the color-pattern a diffuse effect somewhat reminiscent of the Chinese.

Faces in Matisse's portraits often consist of a series of color-compartments used partly as planes in the modeling, as in Cézanne, but more fundamentally as color-units in a color-pattern type of design ; in other words, Matisse transforms the three-dimensional structural function of Cézanne's superposed planes into the decorative activity of relatively flat and juxtaposed areas which make up a pattern of contrasting color-compartments (21, 42, 48, 56). Changes in the constituents of this general type of ensemble, such as variations in quality of color, in degree of accentuation of contour of areas, in technique, or in intensity of contrast, provide for great diversity of plastic effects. For instance, in the modeling of a face, a set of relatively flat areas of bizarre colors clash, paradoxically speaking, in unison, to make an exotic ensemble of dramatic contrasts, and this theme of the face is repeated throughout the picture, with variation in size, shape and color of the areas (56). Another design also based on Cézanne's use of planes is characterized by a series of volumes, richly decorative and dramatic, that pervade the figure and background and unify the greatly diversified colors, line- and light-patterns, and technical devices (21). A third variation of the compartmental color-pattern design consists in the union of small planes of color ill-defined in contour in the face, with large planes of color of more definite shape in the setting (48). In these versions of the Cézanne color-planes the decorative values and technical effects of early Byzantine and Egypto-Roman portraits, accentuated in varying degree, are woven into color-organizations typical of Matisse. Accentuation or diminution of one or more of the characteristics of the above-mentioned traditions (Cézanne, Byzantine and Egypto-Roman) results in an array of varied designs determined by the new relationships. For instance, exaggerated linear drawing of a face harmonizes with accentuated linear patterns in a Byzantine type of compartmental composition (48, 69–70–71) ; attenuated linear facial patterns blend with less emphatic lines of contour (24, 153);

black lines in the features fit into a somber Goya-Manet theme of portraiture (68), and lines of different colors into a design of color-contrasts (21). In most of these cases, by a simplified technique of broad brush strokes and dabs of color, Matisse introduces a note from Manet which materially transforms the Byzantine effect.

Matisse's manipulations of the Egypto-Roman type of portrait result in a great variety of patterns in which the facial features, especially the eyes, become outstanding characteristics both by their intrinsic quality and by their activity as rhythmic compositional units. Features so drawn contribute conspicuously to the pronounced Oriental flavor which pervades many of Matisse's paintings (42, 64, 69–70–71). At times he adopts a Cézanne practice which so exaggerates the Egypto-Roman shadows that the eye seems to be embedded in a deep pocket of color, a pocket varied, as the plastic purpose varies, in intensity of color, depth and completeness (32, 82*). In other types of design, the Egypto-Roman form, fused with Manet's simplifications and Cézanne's color-hatchings, yields the effect of mosaics (21, 48).

Sometimes the modeling of a face is simplified to a smooth homogeneous effect like that of a mask, in order to make it a consistent part of Matisse's color-compartment composition; the face is rendered in very few areas of color which tend to merge in a single area only slightly patterned by the linear definition of the eyes, nose and mouth (93). When the continuity of the masklike effect is perceptibly broken by patches of color and by linear pattern circumscribing the features, the mask comes to have much of the specific quality of Negro sculpture (48, figure to left in 69, central figure in 70).

One of the most interesting points in Matisse's experiments in portraiture is the way in which he handles the problem of relating the figure to the background so that the two become partners in the total decorative design. His backgrounds, as is natural in view of his general decorative purpose, are more active than in conventional portraiture: a single area of intense color tied up compositionally as a theme with a contrasting

*Cf., e.g., 411.

theme constituted by the multicolored figure (42), is much more picturesque and decorative than the broad background-area of neutral color common in portraiture of the usual style. Again, a background of two or more areas of contrasting color may serve as an organic part of a design of contrast and balance in broad compartmental areas of exotic color (34, 48). In another picture, vividly colored geometric patterns of broad areas and bands are factors common to both background and foreground (56). Areas of exotic color in arabesque-formation, and commensurate distortions in drawing of figure and setting, make of another foreground and background a harmonious single effect (168). A background of irregularly shaped patches of color in planes emphasizes the maplike division of an entire composition, in harmony with the face modeled by Cézannesque planes (23). Again, a set of bright exotic areas of planes and volumes repeat in the background the bizarre highly decorative treatment of the figure (21) ; or, by the same principle of rhythmic duplication, multicolored decorative motifs in the background strike the keynote in a composition in which the figure is a cognate unit (148). Shapes themselves may constitute the unifying factor by being repeated in all parts of the picture, as when long vertical bands of color in the background are related in tone, shape and pattern to the column-like neck, egg-shaped face, long thin arms, and oval hat of the figure (176).

The foregoing discussion shows that portraiture for Matisse is not the medium for psychological characterization of the sitter, but, like his painting of still-life, landscape and interior-scenes, is merely another field for exploitation of those aspects of subject-matter which lend themselves to primarily decorative designs.

SUMMARY

Matisse's portraits are not psychological characterizations, they are compositions centered about a figure, compositions of which the purpose is as always primarily decorative. Faces, consequently, are usually violently distorted: the features are drawn, whether as detailed patterns or mere patches of color, to harmonize with the total design, not to suggest personality or emotion. In accordance with this design, they may be executed in the style of any one of many traditions, from the Egypto-Roman to Modigliani; and often a single face combines the qualities of several traditions.

In a face the design is often a series of color-compartments reminiscent of Cézanne's, but the planes, instead of being a means of achieving solidity, are decorative units, variation in the qualities of which provides for a great diversity of effects, rhythmically duplicated elsewhere in the picture. The duplication may be in color-contrast, pattern in light and line, technical execution; or there may be contrast between small planes of color in the face and large planes in the setting; or line, either accentuated or attenuated, may be present in both. These variations are accompanied by a great number of motifs taken from other traditions, notably the Byzantine and the Egypto-Roman, and from Manet.

The Egypto-Roman portraits are drawn upon by Matisse for a style of design in which the facial features, especially the eyes, give the portrait an Oriental character; sometimes the eyes are embedded in color-pockets in harmony with other colored shadows elsewhere in the composition; sometimes the effect of the whole is that of a mosaic. In contrast to the complexity of this style, faces are sometimes modeled in a form almost like that of a mask, in color-areas with features lightly indicated by line; when the line around the features is more apparent and patches or hatchings of color appear, the effect approaches that of Negro sculpture.

In accordance with his generally decorative purpose, Matisse gives to the setting or background of his figures greater importance and a more active plastic rôle than is usual in conventional portraiture, chiefly by embellishing it with more color, more vivid color, and often a wealth of linear patterns, and by making of figure and background coördinate units in a general composition of contrasting colors, patterns of definitely shaped compartments and bands, or arabesques. Decorative motifs in the background may call for a similar treatment of the face; vice versa, the type of modeling may determine the character of the decorative setting; or again a background of long bands may fit in with extension of any part of the figure in one direction, and compression in another.

A sitter, in brief, is for Matisse a field for plastic, not psychological, exploration.

CHAPTER XVII

BLACK–AND–WHITE WORK

COMPARISON between Matisse's work in black and white and his paintings reveals anew the extreme importance of color in his form. As an artist in black and white he is less important than as a painter: the loss of color very seriously impairs the plastic conviction of his black-and-white forms, though the line and its relationships have sufficient plastic force to form effective decorative ensembles. Much of his black-and-white work constitutes studies for paintings, and the measure of his greatness as a colorist becomes apparent when we compare the sketch with the finished product.* Subordination or neglect of expressive aspects, in both his painting and black-and-white work, often leads to repetition of substantially identical poses and facial expressions. In his paintings the subject-matter proper and its setting, while successfully related, retain distinctive diversity in detail; in the black-and-white work their treatment is more nearly identical throughout. This involves distortion, sometimes relatively slight (205), sometimes gross to the point of caricature (210). Considered as a whole, this work reveals a relative poverty of resource which is far from characteristic of Matisse's paintings.

The **drawings**† fall into three general types.‡ The characteristic note of one of them is modeling both of figures and objects by juxtaposed areas of light and shadow (206, 208) which are accentuated in varying degree to yield corresponding variations in three-dimensional quality. Objects of all sorts are given the shape of fairly definite geometrical forms, and their composition produces a sort of irregular checkerboard- or

*Cf., e.g., 166 with 207.
†For the sake of convenience, the term drawing is used here in its conventional sense, and refers to black-and-white work done by pencil, pen and ink, crayon, charcoal, etc., as distinguished from the mechanical processes involved in etchings and lithographs.
‡Cf. illustrations, pp. 351, 354, 358.

patchwork-effect. This effect, indeed, is so constantly repeated that, in spite of the variations employed, it comes to stand out as a cliché, a piece of banality which is probably nearer than anything else in Matisse to academicism.

In another type of drawing there is a shift of emphasis from light and shadow to linear pattern (215). Distortion is here more pervasive and more consistently extreme, the drawing as a whole emerges as primarily a linear pattern, and shadows are reduced to such a point that they do not seriously compete for attention with the line. Absence of the mechanical, repetitive use of light and shadow, makes the drawings of this second type vastly superior to those of the first as manifestations of imaginative design.

In a third type, shading completely disappears and the lines become long and continuous, often in the manner of Ingres (216, 219). The plastic quality of this line is so considerable that the absence of light and shadow does not compromise the modeling, which remains adequate to the decorative purpose of the design. The general effect in drawings of this third type is akin to that found in Japanese prints, especially those of Hokusai and Utamaro. The long lines form a series of arabesques defining irregular shapes; often the areas in immediate juxtaposition show contrast in that one is, one is not, embellished with internal decoration (216).

In all his drawings, and most notably in a series depicting a figure reclining on a divan (216, 217), Matisse's usual ingenuity in decorative design is exercised in variation of the position of the parts of the body, of the immediate setting— e.g., chair, sofa, garb—and of the general background. This variation makes for a great diversity of effects both in pattern and in relation of decorated areas defined by linear contours. Particularly varied are the direction, length and degree of movement of the line.

Matisse's **lithographs** and **etchings** contain a combination of the characteristic effects of the three types of drawing above noted. Sometimes the conjoint action of light and shadow is predominant, with the proportion of each widely varied (203, 205, 210), though the frequent repetition of the light-and-shadow areas has the same academic effect upon the lithographs and etchings as that already noted in the drawings. Sometimes the linear aspect is entirely unsupported by shading (204, 209, 211, 213, 218, 220, 221); here, as in the drawings, his play upon arabesques makes for variety in design. The decorative rhythms of line, repeated throughout the picture, may yield the effect of a tapestry-pattern (210, 213), and frequently tapestry or decorated fabrics are actually depicted, also in lines without shading (202, 211). Some of his black-and-white work are much like Ingres's in general effect (212); others show the same degree of resemblance to the Japanese (201, 214, 218); quite often there is also a very strong suggestion of the Hindu-Persian miniatures (217). The combination of line like Ingres's with the Japanese or Hindu-Persian general decorative theme differentiates completely the final result from either of its sources.

SUMMARY

Compared with his painting, Matisse's work in black and white is inferior in plastic quality and technical resourcefulness. His distinguishing gifts are those of a colorist, and the absence of color makes his black-and-white work much less interesting and forceful. His decorative concern is here as accentuated, but in this medium his resources are so limited that his work at times seems repetitious and monotonous, and the distortions sometimes merely grotesque.

In one type of his drawings, modeling is accomplished by juxtaposed areas of light and shadow. Familiar objects appear as geometrical shapes so arranged that their combination yields the general effect of a checkerboard, but with a lack of variety that makes the work as a whole wearisome. In the second type, linear pattern strongly overbalances light and shadow; a consistently greater degree of distortion results in a more free and varied series of forms, so that the compositions as a whole are much better than those of the first type. In a third type, light and shadow are entirely eliminated, and the long continuous line, often like Ingres's, has in itself sufficient force to achieve modeling. The drawings of this type resemble Japanese prints in their sweeping arabesques: the areas included in the arabesques vary as regards presence or absence of internal decoration, with the result that their effect sometimes approximates that of a tapestry.

His lithographs and etchings combine, in varying degree, the qualities of the three types of drawing, and are on about the same plastic level.

CHAPTER XVIII

DEVELOPMENT

Two types of development in plastic creation may be distinguished. The first is a growth in depth and breadth of vision, in which the promise of a painter's early work is continuously and in larger and larger measure fulfilled. The second is a growth in technical range and resourcefulness, in which there is little or no profound development in the way in which an artist sees the world, although he finds new means of varying and embroidering it. The first type of growth is illustrated by Renoir and Cézanne; the second, by Matisse. In order to throw the characteristics of Matisse's development into more clear relief, it will be advantageous to begin with a brief sketch of the way in which Renoir and Cézanne enlarged their personal insight at the same time that they added to their repertoire of technical resources.

Renoir in his earliest, pre-impressionistic period, leaned somewhat upon the Dutch and Spanish traditions but more especially upon his immediate predecessors, Courbet and Manet.* With the rise of impressionism, he adopted to a very large extent the typical impressionistic manner of showing the effect of direct sunlight by visible brush strokes and divided color; but from the start his individuality was revealed in his finer feeling for relationships, his richer yet more delicate color better organized and more deeply integrated in the structure of his masses.† As time went on he varied the impressionistic technique and used it instrumentally to incorporate in his form most of the values of the great traditions. He achieved new compositional and expressive effects, the movement of volumes in deep space with rich circumambient glow as in the Venetians,‡ the epic expanse of landscape characteristic of Claude,§ the human values of Titian,¶ the monumental quality of

*E.g., 430.   †E.g., 428, 436, 437.   ‡E.g., 416, 419, 431.
§E.g., 427.   ¶E.g., 433, 435.

Giorgione,* the grace of Watteau and Fragonard,† the poised movement of Velásquez,‡ the voluptuousness of Rubens,§ the graceful pose of Greek statues,¶ all with a delicacy quite his own. Starting, in other words, with the impressionism current in his time, he extended and varied it to make it the means of recasting and enriching almost the whole tradition of painting, and achieved a form which is both completely individual and one of the permanent and outstanding achievements of plastic art.

Cézanne's development shows the same cumulative character, though it proceeds along dissimilar lines and to a different end. Delacroix and Courbet furnished him with points of departure;** then followed a version of impressionism which he took from Pissarro, but which he modified by color broader in area and more solidly structural, also derived from antecedent traditions.†† The combination in his hands was powerful from the start, and its power showed a steady increase as his personal form emerged more clearly. His color acquired a greater degree of depth, internal glow and structural solidity. More and more he brought out the essential reality of his subject-matter, whether landscape, human figure, or still-life; and his means became increasingly individual—accentuated planes of color and distortions reminiscent of El Greco but used for utterly different purposes and with an effect radically novel in the history of painting.‡‡ These planes and distortions not only draw out the essentials of the subject-matter, but make up decorative patterns which relieve the severity of his expressive forms. There was a continuous growth in his command of all the plastic means and a translation of all of them into terms of color, through which they were more fully unified in his own type of design. Michelangelo, Tintoretto, El Greco, Manet and the impressionists were transmuted into something new and distinctive, which, like Renoir's form, added a new plastic embodiment of human values to the traditions of painting.

No such evolution appears in Matisse. There is undoubtedly

*E.g., 420, 434.   †E.g., 418, 424, 426.   ‡E.g., 432, 438.
§E.g., 417.   ¶E.g., 419.   **E.g., 401, 403.
††E.g., 404.   ‡‡E.g., 402.

growth; unlike Picasso, he does not veer about in obedience to the latest wind that blows; but what is added as time goes on is not new breadth of vision, not a view of life organized at deeper and deeper levels as the purport of past traditions is absorbed, but an always increasing range of means for expressing a vision at substantially the same level. His growth is in erudition, and so in resourcefulness; his intellect has more material to use in logical constructions and so he becomes more fertile in inventiveness; but after attaining maturity, the command of his medium and the way of seeing which is his own, his artistic stature does not appreciably increase. The history of his growth is therefore primarily an account of accumulation, of quantitative enrichment, not of organic assimilation of profundities.

This statement does not apply, of course, to the period in which he was attaining his own specific manner, style, or form. His earliest pictures, apart from the copies of old masters which he made in the Louvre, show clearly the influence of the painters dominant at the time. Chardin's influence was in the air, and it appears in Matisse's paintings of the early 1890's, but with none of the qualities which make Chardin important (1, 4). Others of his early pictures also show exercises in the technique of the impressionists and post-impressionists: thick impasto in modeling by light and colored shadow, drawing by broad brush strokes, with the brush strokes sometimes elongated as in van Gogh and combined with hatchings reminiscent of Cézanne (5, 6, 12). All this is the work of a young man feeling his way; it is unoriginal and lacking in plastic force or conviction. The experimentation which is a permanent part of his artistic career has begun, but its results are as yet negligible. However, even his early copies show great technical skill in the use of light, line and space, and feeling for color-relations of all sorts (2, 9, 13). The general tonality of color in much of his earliest work is dark, but his command of varied effects is skilful (1, 4, 5, 6, 11). This proves that his choice, later, of extremely bright colors and of an apparently outré manner of painting was deliberate, not the result of any inability to paint in a more conventional manner.

The attainment of his artistic majority coincides approximately with the year 1898. By that time his definitely decorative interest, his consequent susceptibility to Oriental influences and extensive recourse to distortion, his ability to organize a picture both in general and by means of color, his choice of unusual, striking and exotic color, are all clearly apparent (7, 8, 10). In general his impasto is growing thinner and is less extensively applied, and though both Manet's brush strokes and Cézanne's hatchings of color are still much in evidence, as indeed they are in all his later work, they are modified and used with discrimination, as the design calls for them. The ability to borrow from various sources what is needed for a particular design, recombining what is borrowed into a new synthesis, is already in evidence. In short, Matisse's form as a distinctive entity has made its appearance. Its essential originality is shown by the fact that he was everywhere hailed as wilfully fantastic, although, as we have earlier seen, it is genuinely an outgrowth of the traditions, directed to a definite end, and wrought out of materials deliberately chosen for that end.

The years following 1898 were devoted to the perfection of Matisse's individual form and technique, and by 1906 he had painted pictures (21, 27, 31) as powerful and as valuable æsthetically as any belonging to a later period. By this time his great gifts were fully developed: his marvelous command of color, in its sensuous aspects, its relations, its ability to give the essential quality of light, line and space, and to compose the canvas as a whole; his mastery of patterns of light and line; his decorative use of space. His version of Cézanne's modeling and Manet's drawing had taken on its definite identity, he had already employed decorative features derived from the Orient; and such distinctive effects as those of the poster, stripes, bands and mosaics were lending to his designs their transferred values. His limitations were also apparent: his inability to make any real advance in the more profoundly expressive use of the plastic means, however completely he might master, diversify or recombine uses made by others; his necessary reliance upon an invention relatively cerebral instead of upon a profound plastic imagination.

In the period from 1898 to 1906 a type of effect occurs which appears less often, and in modified form, in Matisse's later work; it is that of the mosaic. Sometimes this effect is achieved by pointillist technique and exotic color (10, 25); on other occasions it is due to scattered spots of color between which areas of blank canvas intervene, so that the Oriental quality is that of Russian embroidery (17); finally it may be due to a combination of hatchings like Cézanne's, brush strokes and impasto like van Gogh's, Byzantine linear patterns, and Matisse's own set of vivid color-contrasts (21).

Subsequent to this period, his erudition increased and with it the range of his resources; his ingenuity had at its command more devices to shuffle and recombine, but there is little or no advance in penetration or power of synthesizing at a deeper level the significance of his derivations from traditional forms. When the old motifs recur, as they do constantly, it is usually their context, not their essential quality, that is new. In a Renoir painting of 1910 the total form is broader, deeper, more fully expressive, than in a picture of 1890, or of 1870, and every detail, the use of all the plastic means, shows the effect of a progressive development of scope. The same cannot be said of Matisse; his investiture of old motifs with fresh ornamental detail, however skilful, cannot alter their essential sameness of plastic significance.

This aspect of Matisse's development may be illustrated by tracing the recurrence of definite types of painting throughout the whole period of his activity. As we have seen, the influences most persistently active in him are those of Manet, Cézanne, and the Orientals, but in addition to the constant and pervasive effects upon his work so exercised, there are also a number of pictures in which the influence of Manet or Cézanne is strong enough to determine the general cast or quality of the picture, though never to submerge its identity as a specific Matisse form. The features of Cézanne's work thus operative are usually the distribution of subject-matter on the canvas, modeling by hatchings, and the compositional function of the planes, and they appear at intervals all through Matisse's work. In 1898, for example, we find them in a context of exotic color used in broad areas, dramatic light, and linear contour (7); in 1905 typical Cézanne arrangement and technical treatment of still-life are modified by a new set of dramatic and bizarre color-relations, and by an organization of the plastic constituents in a pattern of bands and stripes: the effect is that of an Oriental rug (20); in 1906 a Cézanne type of landscape is used as a point of departure to achieve a new organization of small, bright, contrasting color-units dominated by Chinese-like arabesques (26); in 1907 a still-life very Cézannesque in composition and three-dimensional expressiveness has also a highly decorative Oriental quality attained by exotic color merged in a harmony of blue tones (33); in 1918 a still-life, perhaps closer to Cézanne in composition and technical treatment than any earlier picture, differs radically in the sensuous quality of the bright colors, in the vivid contrasts between such tones as rose, light blue, deep green, coral and gray, and in the presence of fewer but longer brush strokes (85). In "Repose" (145), a painting of 1923, which represents perhaps the high-water mark in Matisse as regards fulness of individual expression, the solidly structural color recalls Cézanne's, but the technique, with total absence of hatchings, is radically different. Even in the latest Matisses, those since 1924, one or more of the Cézanne characteristics reappear unmistakably in some part or the whole of a painting. Often the derivation from Cézanne is as close in these later pictures as in those painted twenty years before (150, 157, 161, 173).

Manet's influence upon Matisse, though even stronger than Cézanne's, is in most of the pictures of his early maturity revealed mainly in his drawing by simplification or elimination of representative detail; but in 1916 we find a still-life which is frankly a play upon a Manet type of composition and color-scheme, given a Matisse quality by a novel use of superposed planes (66). In 1917 appears a Manet form embedded in elements from the Chinese (74, 77); and in 1919 an interior-scene, the appearance of which in general resembles Manet's, has also emphatic Japanese elements (92); in 1920 a Manet theme is simplified for the sake of color-pattern (102), and in 1921 a still-life of Manet's general type is modified by dramatic color-contrast and an interplay of patterns of bands and circles (121). In still other Matisses, Manet's effects of black-and-white contrast are simplified and made more decorative by broad areas of contrasting color (114); in 1925 Manet's drawing and type of face are combined with markedly Oriental colors (160). Instances might be multiplied, but the case is already clear enough: Matisse consistently reverts to the devices used long before, always intelligently recombining them, but rarely making a significant plastic advance over the expressive version previously rendered. Perhaps the most notable exception to this rule is "Repose" (145) which, while reminiscent of Cézanne and Manet, is a more fully plastic expression than his previous pictures painted under the same influences: color is of greater structural quality and approaches very close to the power and solidity of Cézanne's and Renoir's.

An important difference between Matisse's work of 1898–1908 and that which began about 1917, when he started to paint in Nice, is a shift from weight and vigor to grace and delicacy. Most of the Nice pictures treat figures in interiors, with sea visible through an open window (73, 86, 90, 98, 108, 109, 118, 125, 132); but when subject-matter of a different type is handled it is usually with the same color-scheme and style, airy, luminous and delicate, which are appropriate to a scene on the Riviera (81, 84, 88, 95, 105, 106, 107, 108a, 140). The plastic elements derived from Manet and Cézanne are still employed, but with many modifications and stronger Oriental influence. The charm of these pictures often allies them with Renoir's, and they include works as important as any Matisse has ever done. A characteristic instance of Matisse's reversion to previous forms is found in pictures painted in 1921, 1922 and 1923 (111, 127, 137, 138, 146), after his Oriental experimentation had gone to extreme limits. In them he suddenly returns to his earlier impressionistic manner, with color-scheme, technique, expressive drawing like Manet's and Renoir's, and actual choice of subject-matter nearer the originals even than in the early pictures painted when he was more directly under the impressionists' influence. These pictures, however, are made definite creations through Matisse's elaboration of several of the impressionistic features into characteristic decorative organizations.

In the course of his Nice period Matisse began increasingly to interest himself in a new effect, that of the poster. Although this effect is apparent also in some of his earlier pictures (31, 50, 56), after 1917 it appears in constantly increasing measure and after 1921 becomes one of his chief prepossessions (130, 136, 141, 144, 148, 156, 165, 167, 171, 174, 175). Its bright flat color-areas, simplification of detail, and rendering of objects in foreground and background as units of equal compositional value, are an obvious reflection of his interest in Oriental designs. The Oriental influences, including linear patterns from the Byzantines and Egypto-Romans, exotic and vivid colors from the Japanese, islands of light and arabesques from the Chinese, and Persian delicate color-patterns and distorted space, have become stronger as Matisse has grown older, and their effects have been increasingly shown upon the poster-pictures done after 1921. In an odalisque composition painted in 1928, a poster-effect, with general Oriental character, is invested with a solidity like that of ceramics by the introduction of color almost as weighty as Cézanne's, though the weight is primarily decorative and not expressive (172).

In the later work the decorative effect of cretonne comes to be increasingly in evidence. At times it is united with the poster-effect (50), at other times it furnishes one of the dominant themes of the painting (118, 140, 154, 166). The decorative patterns on draperies or wall-papers in the cretonne-like compositions are often so accentuated that they stand away from their background, as though separated from it in space. This of course is an extreme departure from realism; the first appearance of it is comparatively early (33, 42), but its more frequent occurrence in his later work attests the increase in his decorative interest (89, 147, 150, 152, 154, 166). The combination, in varying degree, of the poster-effect and the cretonne-effect adds greatly to the striking novelty and force of Matisse's later decorative designs (148, 154).

Matisse at all periods painted pictures in which the usual sources of his effects are relatively disregarded, and other men and movements are drawn upon for specific traits or effects. In 1899, for example, he employed an effect of color reminiscent of Daumier (11) and in 1901 he painted several compositions with marked influence of Courbet (14, 15). His addition of patterned stripes and bands of color, and of color-areas in dramatic light-and-dark contrast, assimilates these compositions to Matisse's own form. In 1912, 1913 and 1914 cubism affected him slightly, but the new form remained distinctively Matisse's: sometimes color and patterns of dramatic contrasts gave a personal note to his interpenetrating large planes (51, 52), or the cubistic color-scheme of gray was worked into a dramatic space-composition emphasized by linear patterns and contrasts of light and dark (57).

Matisse, in brief, though he attained the fulness of his growth at a comparatively early stage of his career, and has attained no heights greater than those scaled by 1905–1908, has since then advanced by extending the range of his effects. His energies have not flagged nor has his form deteriorated or decayed. He has rather added new types of plastic design to the array of his accomplishments, reaching in them the level set by his earlier efforts and enriching plastic art by a series of decorative masterpieces which suffer by comparison only with the supreme achievements of expressive painting. His development has never been arrested; only, after a certain point, it has consisted in an exploration of new decorative realms, not in attainment to a more exalted status. In 1923 he painted a perhaps greater number of important and individual pictures than in any earlier year,* not excepting the years from 1905 to 1910, the period of those masterpieces of his early career which are now in the Museum of Modern Western Art at Moscow, and in the Barnes Foundation. His best pictures are far apart in years, but they occur in his early and middle periods as well as in the later (21, 31, 33, 37, 43, 51, 54, 55, 64, 69–70–71, 73, 84, 89, 90, 104, 106, 108, 118, 119, 121, 131, 132, 134, 136, 140, 141, 145, 152, 156, 157, 167, 168, 172, 175).

*See Data on Works of Art Mentioned, pp. 443–444.

SUMMARY

Some artists reach the limit of their growth in insight and artistic stature relatively early, and therefore do not develop in essentials, though they may add new means to their repertoire. Others continue to grow all their lives, and consistently give evidence of fresh perceptions and more profound understanding. Renoir and Cézanne are instances of the latter type, Matisse of the former. Renoir, having acquired at an early age the vision which had crystallized out of the traditions in the work of Manet and Courbet, soon learned to see with the impressionists, though then as always there was a distinguishing personal quality in his vision. It is only at this period, however, that his individual development really started: upon impressionism and its technique he engrafted the contributions made by nearly all the great figures in the history of plastic art, so that there is scarcely a value, human or plastic, to be found in the traditions of which some indication is not found in his work. Cézanne shows a similar development, though the process and the result are quite different: he started from another point, was less obviously affected by impressionism, made use of fewer traditions, yet by a steadily cumulative growth advanced to a personal vision and style entirely his own, to a profound mastery of human and plastic values.

Matisse shows advance in artistic growth up to a certain point, at which he had also attained a distinctive vision and style, authentic and personal; but the advance ceased much earlier and reached a level appreciably below that of the greatest masters. Thereafter there is further development but no real increase in stature: what he has to say is said in more varied and skilful ways, but with no more profundity of expression than before. The account of his development therefore falls into two parts, an account of his attainment of maturity, and then an account of the enlargement of his repertoire of means.

His earlier work is chiefly an exercise in assimilation of the influences current in his youth, especially those of the impressionists, of the post-impressionists, and, to a limited extent, of Chardin. In spite of great technical skill and feeling for color, these earliest paintings show scarcely any originality in the adaptation of his models, and are of little intrinsic importance. The attainment of his artistic majority, in 1898, came with his definite adoption, with decorative modifications, of certain features of the work of Manet and Cézanne, and his ability to realize a unified decorative form in terms primarily those of color. During the next few years he made himself master within his own field, acquired a command over all the plastic means, began his increased drafts upon the Orientals, and developed his distinctive decorative devices. At the same time his limitations were revealed, his lack of interest in or command of any very deep human or plastic values, his inability to do more than recombine effectively and with genuine novelty what others had shown him.

During this period he developed one effect, that of the mosaics, which rarely appears afterward in such pronounced form. After it he mastered other devices which constantly reappear in subsequent paintings, though usually without essential increase in depth of vision. He enriched his repertoire, but made no further progress in expressive fundamentals. Throughout his later career he constantly reverts to earlier styles, and paints pictures close in form to those of previous years. Certain typical plastic traits, for example Cézanne's modeling and use of compositional planes, and Manet's drawing, are common in his work at all periods, from 1905 to the present, though they are always given a characteristic Matisse setting.

There are, however, fairly definite periods, each with its own characteristics. His early mature work is vigorous and weighty; beginning with 1917, the Nice pictures show a predominant lightness, grace and delicacy, a greatly increased Oriental influence, and sometimes a suggestion of Renoir's style. Yet after this period was well under way, he painted a few pictures quite as impressionistic in general effect as some of his earlier work, but with more elaboration into a primarily decorative form. It was during the Nice period that the poster-design was more consistently developed, reflecting in its flat color-patterns, linear decorations, vivid exotic color, arabesques, islands of light, and distorted space, Matisse's increasing interest in Oriental art.

At the same time the cretonne-effect, with its even more radical departures from naturalism, became apparent, and was frequently combined with the poster-effect.

Throughout his work Matisse shows incidental and transient influences of men, e.g., Daumier, Courbet and the cubists, lying outside his chief sources of influence. In short, unlike the greatest artists who show a continuous development in all the phases of their art, in personal vision as well as technical resourcefulness, Matisse acquired his distinctive way of seeing things and his mastery of the appropriate means comparatively early, and he failed to press on constantly to levels essentially beyond those already reached. Yet the widening of his range constitutes in itself a phase of development, and in his wide exploration of the possibilities of plastic decoration, he produced, on his own level and within the limits set by his restricted purpose, masterpieces; they are less than the greatest because decoration even in its highest estate is something less than complete plastic expression.

CHAPTER XIX

MATISSE'S RANK AS AN ARTIST

In the foregoing chapters we have paid tribute to Matisse's marvelous versatility, to his intellect, his intelligence, his indefatigable and adventurous curiosity about all the aspects of his world. We have seen the richness of his resources, his ability to look at things through the eyes of other painters, seeing them with his own eyes too, and so not falling into academicism or eclecticism. We have seen also his command over his medium, his ability to put down on canvas what his lively imagination has seen, without faltering or stumbling, so that we rarely feel that he failed in doing what he set out to do. The time has now come to assess the value of his accomplishment as a whole, to compare it with the accomplishment of other painters, of the great masters of painting, and so to estimate his position in the hierarchy of plastic artists.

A brief résumé of several points in our earlier chapters will facilitate this estimate. First, as to the different types of formal organization to be found in a picture. In what we have termed "expressive form," the organization of the plastic means is intended primarily to effect a revelation, to exhibit what the painter found essential, significant or moving in the object before him. The revelation is both of plastic values and of human values; of plastic values, in that we are made to see the full colorfulness of things, their solidity, their spatial organization, their outline as this indicates motion, rest, poise, equilibrium; of human values, in that these plastic qualities are so selected and emphasized as to bring out the aspects of real things and enrich their significance for human feeling. All the very greatest painters convey to us, not as a substitute for, but over and above, intense plastic reality, an expression of some such quality as awe, majesty, exaltation, peace, compassion, the pride and triumph of life.

In contrast, forms may be fundamentally decorative, dependent upon pattern conjoined with the sensuous quality and organization of color. The purpose is more primarily ornamental than interpretative; it does not carry our minds through the picture to the reality beyond, it keeps them fixed upon the picture as something in itself charming or exquisite, or as a reminder of values transferred from another realm of experience. The primarily decorative status of the picture tends to become assimilated to that of an *objet d'art,* a rug or tapestry. When the element of essential realism is wholly excluded and the picture becomes entirely decoration, form becomes pattern pure and simple, as it does in most cubistic pictures. Profound human values vanish, imagination is degraded into ingenuity, and we say of the painter, not that he is an artist, but a mere craftsman.

Matisse, as we have seen, is primarily an intelligence, an intellect, he lacks the impulsiveness that results in untrammeled spontaneous expression. In all his vitality, his eager interest, his adventurousness, he never loses the calculation, the sobriety of a judge or banker, and with him creation is largely a matter of skilful and ingenious manipulation. Consequently, his effects seem weighed and measured. He has far too much insight, too great an interest in his world, to be a mere decorator, but it is impossible not to feel that he is interested less in objects for what they really are than in the ways in which they can be woven into decorative designs. His imagination, never sinking into mere adroit ingenuity, yet remains at the plane of invention: it rarely rises to the level of profound inspiration. The extent to which this temperamental deficiency removes him from the first rank in art will be indicated in the following series of comparisons.

In Giotto we find an undoubted decorative organization to which all the plastic means contribute; we find in addition a vast dignity, repose, and religious peace, achieved not by merely illustrative means, but by spaciousness, a transfiguring color-glow, and a quietly expressive line. With a much greater number of actual colors, and a drawing incomparably more varied and intricate, Matisse gets nothing at all of Giotto's deep mysticism, and little or nothing of the human dignity of Giotto's figures. A group of figures in Giotto plays the rôle of a group not only plastically but as a human or dramatic assemblage, a religious procession, or a group of mourners; Matisse's groups are seldom much more than a set of pictorial units.

Between Matisse and El Greco much the same difference holds, though it is accentuated by the fact that El Greco's patterns are much more elaborate than Giotto's, and so challenge a more direct comparison with Matisse's. We have in El Greco the very essence of movement, expressed by iridescent color, flickering light, writhing line, a lurid ghastly drama dominated by a sense of religious exaltation, almost intoxication. The serpentine line, the phosphorescent color flecked with light, the dramatic light itself and the pattern of light, the distorted figures, all are put into an elaborate, perfectly unified form which adds to highly decorative value an expressive quality, a sense of deep religious mysticism, of human tension, suffering, and transfiguration, of which in Matisse there is never a hint. Both men's work is highly patterned but when in Matisse there is some sense of ecstatic drama, the drama, humanly considered, is relatively slight because it is incidental to forms that are primarily decorative (31). The rich residue of decorative forms is unaffected, but a whole realm of values remains unevoked.

A similar deficiency, though of a different kind, appears in the contrast between Matisse and the great Venetians. Plastically considered, the difference depends perhaps chiefly upon the difference in color. Though not nearly so prolific in striking contrasts, their color has a richness and a structural quality which Matisse approaches even distantly only at rare intervals, and most often scarcely attempts. Giorgione has a sensuous charm, an immediate richness of color, a softness of texture without feebleness, which assure ample decorative quality; at the same time his lyric charm is an added human value to which nothing corresponds in Matisse's generally coldly calculatory treatment of his material. The poetry of the Nice pictures is of a light and delicate type and does not involve the full, deep values of life. Titian, though in him drama replaces the poetry of Giorgione, has a depth and splendor of color which Matisse has not. Titian's work at the best has a solemnity, dignity, moving drama, a quiet but profound religious emotion, to which again we find in Matisse no analogue. That Titian is capable of patterned designs on a large scale, employing all the plastic elements in richest profusion, is shown by his "Assumption," but in this too he never finds it necessary to sacrifice or dilute human value in the interest of decoration. In the same fashion the movement and drama present in both Tintoretto and Matisse are in the latter, primarily and mainly, a play of color, light, line and mass; in Tintoretto it is drama and movement of man and nature also.

The painter who stands most completely at the opposite pole from Matisse is Rembrandt. The pattern in Rembrandt is extremely simple, and is chiefly organized by a highly accentuated chiaroscuro; color, line and space are rather functions of this chiaroscuro than independently executed elements of the form, though the effect of color, of space, of contour, is given convincingly. Rembrandt's use of means is subtle in the highest degree, yet by signs in themselves almost imperceptible he gives the essence of space and mass, of textural quality, and along with them a sense of human personality in its mysterious depths. His too is a poetry near at hand and yet mystical. This poetry and this sense of humanity is never evoked by Matisse's work: the persons in his portraits, no less than in his compositions, are primarily assemblages of plastic traits. He lacks not only Rembrandt's religious sense of human personality, but also interest in characterization of the sort that appears in Dürer, Goya, or Daumier. He might have said with Théophile Gautier, "I am one for whom the visible world exists," with the implication that what is not visible gives rise to nothing deeply significant.

As the painter whose total decorative achievement, because of its union with expressive values, is probably the greatest in the history of plastic art, Renoir is on the whole the most profitable subject of comparison with Matisse. Since Renoir's fusion of line, light and color is so intimate, and the flow of all the plastic means throughout his canvases is so continuous, his pictures appear only slightly patterned; but his color, creamy and velvety, and of the utmost richness and variety, has the same directness of sensuous value and the same organizing function as Matisse's. Utterly different as the colors are in other respects, they are in each man the fundamental plastic element, and in each they supply the basis, the keynote, for the organization of light, line and space. Yet Renoir's color, like the Venetians', is deeply structural, and the added conviction which this gives strengthens his color-organization as a whole and with it the entire framework of the picture. In addition, like the other painters contrasted with Matisse in this chapter, he expresses a gamut of human feelings that Matisse almost completely lacks. He has Rembrandt's feeling for human personality, a poetry like Giorgione's, though less elysian, more intimate; he has also a feeling of the charm of landscape, the warmth of sunlight, the mystery of distance, all the varied glamor of nature. To Matisse nature and personality are mainly counters in the decorative game he plays. This is not to describe his pictures as specious or plastically unreal; they have substance solid enough to keep them far above the level of pattern, and the essential quality of the subject-matter is brought out sufficiently to make it definitely a part of the real world. But his pictures are comparatively poor in human significance, in stirring emotional reality, and in spite of their sensuous richness, the wealth of their plastic relations, of rhythms, daring contrasts, subtle interplay of patterns of all the plastic elements, they remain the work of an extraordinarily intelligent and learned inventor sensitive to every nuance of pictorial relationship. Renoir, in the richness of his color-chords, the luminousness of his flesh, the pearliness of his atmosphere, the jewel-like quality in many areas of his surface, has the fullest possible decorative charm; he has also what Matisse usually lacks, a realization of nature, both in its majesty, as in Claude, and in its small-scale episodic character, as in Constable, and the intimacy of Chardin.*

*Exception must be made in deference to Matisse's Nice pictures which, in their spirit of place and not inconsiderable human values, exhibit a marked sense of the *intime*.

In actual technique Matisse's form is closer to Cézanne's than to Renoir's. The two men have in common a composition of color-compartments, with color-relations operating powerfully as the unifying agent, and this involves extensive distortion of all the plastic means. In both there is notable simplification and accentuation of planes which, interpenetrating and balancing each other, form the solid framework of the picture. Cézanne too was an experimenter and his designs show the same evidence of reflection. At this point they diverge. Cézanne's color-areas are not only units in the pattern, they actually build up objects and make them real, and these more convincing objects are dynamically related in a more real space.* Cézanne's color, deep and rich enough to assure ample sensuous charm, has as its prime function that of bringing out the essential quality of objects, that which makes them what they are, with their meaning enriched by the artist's profundity of insight. Since no embellishment is allowed which might detract from this end, he has a stark strength, a rugged, austere force, unlike anything in Matisse. Matisse has power, but it is more the power of the superlatively able and competent designer, craftsman and organizer, master of his material but attempting no ambitious flights; it is not the epic sense of abstract power.

What human value, as distinct from plastic, Matisse's work has, is as a general rule the value of the picturesque. He can depict, with a considerable degree of essential realism and an eye to natural lifelike quality, the pictorially striking but relatively homely or quaint aspects of things. A bourgeois interior, a still-life, a figure strikingly clad and posed, are far from being a mere means to decoration: their pictorial qualities are emphasized and an added appeal is lent them. Matisse's omnivorous interest in what is about him fastens itself most naturally upon subject-matter of this description, dwells upon it, and brings out, from every point of view, what is essentially characteristic of it no less than its decorative possibilities. If we consider the union of expression and decoration, these are his most satisfactory pictures, since in them there is nothing to suggest those aspects of existence to which his genius is un-

*Cf., e.g., 33 with 414.

equal. To say this, however, is in itself to place him in a position in the hierarchy very appreciably below the highest. He is an artist, a genuine artist, and, in his own sphere, even a very great artist, but his sphere is not among the greatest.

The plastic limitations which result from the preponderance of Matisse's interest in decoration confirm this conclusion. If, by way of exception, he does paint a portrait which attempts psychological characterization, his distinctive style disappears and he becomes mainly an adapter; not Matisse himself, but someone else, is directing his brush (83). The same thing is true of his attempts at genuine realism: if a peach in one of his still-lifes seems real, the form of the peach is Cézanne's (85); a beach scene, with expressive figures, follows so closely the drawing of Manet that it is not entirely Matisse's own (100, 102). Expressive forms, in other words, when they appear are not radically modified: their context is new, and they fit harmoniously into the decorative scene, but except in a very few paintings (145) the elements which give them expressive significance are not completely recast.

Much more serious is the fact that Matisse's assimilation of the plastic contributions of the greatest artists, while complete enough for his purpose, has not the profound and organic significance of the originals. If anything comes to him from the Chinese by way of Manet, it bears the marks of its history: Manet's fingerprints remain on it (36). His work is never eclectic, for his admirable judgment and sensitiveness always guide him to the new contextual setting in which a borrowed element may fittingly be placed. The more profound originality which comes when the deepest significance of the various traditions are worked into the fibre of a painter's mind, so that without his explicit consciousness, without any deliberate planning, they color all that he sees, manifest themselves in all that he does, has so far usually eluded Matisse. Decorative interest, it would thus seem, does not arouse a sufficient depth of feeling to create artistic personality in its profoundest form.

Hence, no doubt, the fact that while Matisse has developed a perfectly definite and unmistakable form which constitutes a part of the permanent capital of plastic art, he has created no form of such magnitude as those of the greatest masters of painting, the great Florentines and Venetians, El Greco, Rembrandt, Velásquez, Renoir and Cézanne. From all the indefinitely numerous organizations of which he is the author, there emerges no individual imaginative insight into that profound and comprehensive reality characteristic of the greatest artists.

His most constant defect is the incessant recourse to drawing like Manet's and to hatchings of color like Cézanne's. Even though these are usually assimilated into his own form they lose the force which they had in their original setting, and are used with such frequency that they sometimes seem mechanical. His modeling by light and shadow is also, at times, too close to the academic manner and without sufficient significant modification to create a style of his own. A similar approach to academicism appears in the placing or grouping of the components of subject-matter in some of his still-lifes and landscapes, which too closely approaches that of Cézanne (85, 101). Matisse is also prone to repeat himself too much; a tilelike area, for example, will be used again and again in a series of pictures, with variation in context sufficient to yield novelty in the total form of each, but not with sufficient change in detail to avoid the impression of mechanization (79, 81, 104).

The effect of some of Matisse's devices also tends toward speciousness because they attain an end by some easy and obvious method when the end ought to have been the outcome of a more imaginative plastic insight. A sharp plane of color representing, for example, an open door may extend through the center of the canvas from top to bottom, and by thus dividing it in half set up a contrast by facile means (81). A device more or less legitimate is the introduction, in part of a picture, of some material object which suggests by direct association the quality of the total effect. But when a Matisse picture as a whole has, for example, the transferred value of Oriental drapery, an actual rug, realistically painted, may too obviously give the clue (166), or a Spanish shawl may be used as a signpost in a design of general Spanish character (46). Sometimes a black or other dark color is introduced at some critical point in the color-composition for the sake of emphasis or bizarreness: this dark color, if uninteresting in itself, is a facile way of securing an effect which, if obtained by elements with their own intrinsic appeal, would be justified (27).

The following effects, also specious, depend upon the use of devices specifically technical. Often part of the canvas is deliberately left bare, in the manner of Cézanne (7, 40, 49). With Cézanne, this is accidental or incidental, a detail in the working out of his form, something not counted upon but found to be appropriate when execution had reached a certain point; in Matisse the effect is obviously calculated, and so often repeated as to appear mechanical. Similarly the canvas may not be left bare, but after paint has been applied it may be rubbed or scraped so as to allow the canvas to show through the pigment and give the effect of the surface-quality of drapery (89), or to function as a patch of light (166), or a pattern of white lines (86). Textural quality, linear quality, or light-effects are thus gotten easily but speciously, instead of by plastic relationships. A similar defect appears in the literal admixture of white in the color in which textiles are painted: the sheen so secured is no more integral to the form than are cosmetics on a face (53,107). Again, exaggerated ridges of paint may give movement to a figure, but movement so rendered is not plastic, it is adventitious, a literal suggestion like the mystery of La Gioconda's smile (165). Finally, there is now and then a tendency in Matisse, present in his earliest work and never completely outgrown, to produce "flashy" pictures, pictures in which an overemphasis of obvious bright contrasting colors serves to attract attention (24), or such studio devices as draperies, furniture, and windows opening on the sea, are mechanically arranged to make a factitious picturesqueness (75).

Although the characteristics just noted constitute a failure to live up to the requirements of the highest plastic standards, they are rather shortcomings than positive blemishes, and they occur only intermittently, in his less successful pictures. What may appear as a more serious drawback, is the comparative aridity of his surfaces which, particularly in his later work, are usually devoid of the richness imparted by color-chords. This, however, is not *per se* a defect, since the nature of his color-organization depends largely upon a relatively bleak surface; when color-chords do occur, they are usually derivative, sometimes from Daumier (11) or Renoir (151), but most often from Cézanne (33, 34, 85). Though they may contribute to the individuality of some of his color-effects, they are chiefly a decorative incident, not an integral part of a fully expressive form as they are in Cézanne. Matisse's work at all times lacks Cézanne's and Renoir's surface-richness and variety, and in his latest work color-chords have practically disappeared. His surfaces are often dry and hard: the paint itself is uninteresting, like the paint on a fence, and has none of the immediate surface-charm and decorative quality of Renoir's, Cézanne's or Soutine's. This surface-bleakness is usually accompanied by a lack of differentiation in the texture of different objects, so that the textural qualities of an area of flesh, a door, a wall, a drapery, a sky, a piece of fruit, are substantially the same. This, however, is consistent with the primarily decorative character of his designs. On rare occasions the only actual *feeling* in the surface is that of the literal paint, the pigment: expressive quality is then entirely absent, and decorative quality also is seriously compromised (165).

Made of a lesser man than Matisse, the foregoing criticisms would be captious, but he, as far and away the foremost painter of the day, challenges the closest possible scrutiny of his real status as an artist. Compared with the magnitude of his achievement, the gravity of his deficiencies is exceedingly slight. In the last few pages we have not been drawing up an indictment, we have been seeking to determine the position of a painter great enough to sustain comparison with all but the greatest masters. The sum and substance of his offending comes to this: that by centering his interest upon decoration he misses the supreme values of painting. This is a relative matter, and does not affect his individual integrity. To quarrel with a man's natural bent is as foolish, to use Santayana's expression, as to quarrel with the color of a child's eyes. Subject to the limitations of temperament and choice, as just noted, Matisse is a very great artist, a man of keen sensitiveness, vigorous intelligence, and enormous erudition; he is intensely alive and adventurous; and from his fecund imagination have come a wealth of plastic achievements unequalled by those of any other painter of his generation.

CHAPTER XX

MATISSE COMPARED WITH HIS
CONTEMPORARIES

In the preceding chapter we have seen Matisse's standing in relation to the great artists of the past; in the present chapter a placing of him among his contemporaries will be attempted. We have already described him as the most important living painter, but without discussing the specific resemblances and differences between him and the men who challenge comparison with him. These are Soutine, Picasso and Derain: Soutine, because of their common interest in color; Picasso, because of his ability to organize a painting; Derain, because of the extent of his use of the traditions, and his very great technical skill.

Soutine's form, like Matisse's, is founded primarily upon color. Soutine, also, succeeds in making the effect of his color highly decorative, but in him the primary interest is upon expression. We have already seen that Matisse's distortions, when compared to Cézanne's, indicate clearly his concern with the less profound aspects of the world, and the same may be said of them in relation to Soutine's. Remote as Soutine's paintings are from naturalistic imitation, his forms seem to convey the actual quality of their subject-matter, the drama and power of nature, as these impress themselves upon a temperament keenly alive to the forceful, even the strident, aspects of things. This is reflected in extraordinarily heavy impasto, color of extreme richness, juiciness and immediate sensuous appeal, and in expressiveness in every unit of the painting. At his best, Soutine rivals in color-power the great Venetians and Cézanne; more specifically, he achieves the drama, the *élan,* of Tintoretto; and on those occasions, unfortunately infrequent, when the organization of line, light and space is adequate, the result will bear comparison with the work of any of the great masters.* In these rare instances he is the superior of Matisse: both have color-power, but Matisse's is comparatively abstract, dependent upon the relations between areas which in themselves lack the richness, juiciness and expressive intensity of Soutine's.

The difference between the two men is indicative of a psychological difference which goes far toward explaining the merits and the shortcomings of both. Matisse, as we have seen, is the reasoner, the intellectual; he has sensitiveness, of course, and a consuming interest in the world about him, but never seems to be carried away by his emotions. With Soutine emotion is primary, he has passion and rapture, the tendency to be carried away by his feelings, to let himself go utterly. Matisse is the always interested, but also always detached, spectator of a drama in which he is not himself a completely engrossed participant; we feel about Soutine that at every moment he is in the thick of events, participating in all that is going on. Hence the power of his forms when all his emotions work together, when every aspect of his subject is really drawn out and related to every other; hence also his failure to do justice to the aspects—more especially the spatial—which do not seem to have for him the appeal which the colorful always have. Matisse, with his even, deliberate control of himself, can almost always control also the means he takes to his end. Hence his balance, his orderly utilization of the capital which he has accumulated from many and diverse traditions.

Soutine, also well versed in the traditions, shows little ability to use the contributions of men not temperamentally in accord with him. In diverse ways, he profited by what he had learned from Tintoretto, Daumier, Renoir, Cézanne, van Gogh and Negro sculpture, but little or not at all from men so different from himself as Chardin, Ingres, or Courbet. Matisse's marks of assimilation and organization, however, because we feel them to be much more calculating, leave us comparatively much colder: the fire and glow in Soutine awaken, when he is at his best, a corresponding heat in ourselves.

*E.g., 462, 463, 464, 465.

Unlike Soutine, Picasso is not a great colorist, and in this respect he is not to be compared with Matisse. He does challenge comparison, however, by his very personal use of the traditions and, in his more successful work, by his capacity for organization. He is at his best when his interest in illustration finds adequate play; his sense for design, his plastic ability, are adequate to the task of giving convincing integration to his illustrative themes. His failure in integration is chiefly a failure in the organization of his personality as a whole. Sharing Matisse's experimental and adventurous mind, he does not share the lifelong devotion to a single purpose, the assiduous attention to all the means available for realizing a single chosen end. Hence we feel in him the lack of single-mindedness and resoluteness, the recurrence at all periods of promises which later work shows have remained unfulfilled. Nothing which he has done has given ground for revision in essentials of the estimate of him published seven years ago: "Psychologically considered, Picasso's art represents a great natural sensitiveness and fertility rather than a reflective, resolute and well-directed search for an individual æsthetic conception. . . . It is true that he shows advance, but the successive styles seem less cumulative, less like stages on the way to a goal which has been foreshadowed all along, than they do in Cézanne or Matisse. In this sense, Picasso is unreflective, as is shown by the fact that his later work does not always show an improvement in the fulness and strength of his plastic form. In his Renaissance period, for instance, solidity does not seem a real augmentation of his resources, but rather a reversion, since it suggests that a new interest had appeared which was in the nature of a distraction rather than of fulfilment of his earlier and more natural interests. In the same way, his cubist paintings are in most respects less satisfactory than those of his Blue Period. Such veerings marked with partial retrogression suggest an impulsive temperament, going off at a tangent from the line of maximum advance. . . ."*

The breaks in the continuity of Picasso's development did not begin until his career was well under way. Prior to the ap-

*The Art in Painting, pp. 392–393.

pearance of his interest in cubism, his work indicated a clear advance in command of medium, assimilation of traditional forms, and the formation of a style in which his great natural gifts found an appropriate expression. Beginning with a bent for illustration,* he gradually added to qualities taken chiefly from Toulouse-Lautrec and Degas a sensitive perception both of the specific sensuous qualities of color in harmony with his design, and of color-relations which, within a rather narrow compass, seem right in themselves and adequately expressive. This was the time of his Blue Period and Rose Period, during which he eventually achieved forms embodying many of the plastic qualities of Raphael, El Greco and Cézanne, in which real and moving human values were given a new plastic setting with conviction and charm.† His efforts to achieve a Cézannesque solidity in masses, however, were never more than partly successful, and his sense of frustration obviously drove him to the panacea of cubism,‡ with disastrous effects upon all his subsequent painting.

Cubism was based upon a metaphysical pseudo-psychology not merely false but fantastic. All masses, the argument runs, are composed of intersecting planes; to give the effect of mass, therefore, the painter should actually isolate a number of the planes discernible in an object, place them adjacent to one another on the canvas, with emphasis upon their angles of intersection, and by some mysterious geometrical alchemy the natural expressive values of a solid body will be discovered in them. Unfortunately for the theory, no truth in psychology is more certain than that we perceive things as continuities, not as sets of isolated aspects: as William James says, our perception of a river is not a perception of spoonfuls or bucketfuls of water. Picasso's natural ability enabled him to organize the disembodied fragments scattered on the canvas in a pattern which did at times attain to some movement of planes and volumes in space, but which more frequently remained on the level of decoration pure and simple, and of course did not retain a vestige of any significant human values. In this respect cubism is related to plastic art in the same way that spelling out the

*E.g., 459.   †E.g., 449, 450, 451, 452, 453, 455.   ‡E.g., 456.

words in a poem would be related to a reading of the poem itself.

In his next attempt to obtain solidity, Picasso went to the other extreme, and by heavy modeling with light and shadow painted a series of compositions in which the figures resemble nothing so much as Roman statues.* He achieved solidity, but it was realistic rather than real: he diverged abruptly from the line of his natural development in the use of color. His cubistic pictures, whatever their general plastic eccentricity, were painted in the quiet tones, generally gray but with subtly effective suggestions of other colors, which were natural to him. About 1921 he began to use bright and varied colors in patterns which developed from his adventures in cubism; but since he had no flair for colors of this sort, his pictures of this group are interesting chiefly as evidence of the complete disruption of his artistic personality. The comprehensive exhibition of his work, held in Paris in 1932, was replete with this hybrid combination of patterns more or less cubistic with bright and exotic colors which were clearly imitative of Matisse's.† The result is a travesty of both his own form and Matisse's. Yet throughout the course of these vagaries, he was painting pictures in his own natural vein, in which without ostentation or sensation-mongering there was a rich union of expressive and decorative values.‡

The lack of consistency betrayed by Picasso's career taken as a whole is discoverable in his individual pictures, and this is true even of his best work. In his large group "Strolling Players" (458), for instance, there is a unity, but in the parts, not in the whole: each unit is well organized, but the units are not composed in a single pictorial form. This is never true of Matisse's characteristic paintings. However divergent and sharply contrasted the sources from which the elements of his work are drawn, he is able practically always to fuse those elements into a single, coherent plastic form.

Unlike Soutine and Picasso, Derain is not a great artist, and comparison between him and Matisse reveals not the difference between types or degrees of artistic achievement, but the differ-

*E.g., 460, 461.   †E.g., 457.   ‡E.g., 454.

ence between the shadow and the substance of art. He has in common with Matisse an eye for the picturesque, a mastery of his medium, and an extremely extensive acquaintance with painting of all the great periods of art. These resources, however, are applied to ends totally different in the two men. Unlike Matisse, Derain cannot in any accurate sense be said to have learned from the host of painters whose methods are clearly revealed in his work. He appropriates their methods, but he has not seen for himself what his mentors saw, and his borrowings from them accordingly become not means or methods for personal vision and creation but a set of tricks of technique by which the surface-effects of authentic artists are imitated. Even his smooth rich texture, which has undeniable æsthetic appeal, is not his own, it is lifted from Chardin, Daumier and Cézanne. So great is his cleverness in mimicking the effects of others that a connoisseur was recently heard to say, when a new picture was brought to him for judgment: "I'll have to look at it carefully before offering any opinion about its authorship: it may be a Derain." Unlike Matisse, who utilizes the traditional forms as a foundation upon which to build for himself, Derain has nothing of his own with which to build. His superb craftsmanship, his archæological lore, and his contact with contemporary movements have done nothing to make him an artist, though they have made him one of the most adroit eclectics of all time.

CHAPTER XXI

MATISSE AND STRAWINSKY

THE quality of Matisse's form is closely paralleled in the field of music by that of Strawinsky. The immediate effect of each, upon the unaccustomed observer, is one of surprise, even of shock, and this is true both of their actual sensuous quality and of the extremely varied and daring relations in which the elements of the form are set. Both are extremely colorful, but Matisse's color and Strawinsky's sounds seem raucous and at variance with what in other artists we have learned to expect. In both forms, also, the effect of familiarity and methodical analysis is to reveal beneath the strangeness the traditional sources which supply the groundwork. More specific resemblances appear in their common employment of themes taken from the primitive and the exotic, and in their decorative emphasis. Indeed, so numerous are the points of analogy that detailed comparison strikingly illuminates the artistic quality of each man's work.

The immediate effect of Strawinsky's music is one of stridency, a result partly of his orchestral color, partly of his frequently insistent rhythms, partly of his violent transitions and contrasts. The resemblance here to Matisse is too obvious to need pointing out. We are constantly surprised by the audacity of both men, surprised to the point of being disturbed; but though these effects may cause a sense of frustration, we are reassured and reconciled to them when we have learned to see the grasp of traditions out of which the startling novelties proceed.

Strawinsky shares Matisse's talent for organization, and though the former's assimilation is less thorough and he is consequently less far removed from eclecticism, he too is able to incorporate in a single composition actual themes, the spirit of other themes and composers, and transferred values drawn from widely diverse sources. He has at command all the traditional resources, though he follows them with very different degrees of fidelity. Bach and Mozart are present pervasively and in solution, though, of course, none of Strawinsky's characteristic compositions is in the literal form of a fugue or sonata; the influences are felt in his use of counterpoint and in his thematic development. Occasionally also there are definite reminiscences of Bach's highly figured themes or of Mozart's singing crispness and charm, usually retained only for a second, set in contrast to some heavy rhythm or series of dissonant chords in weird orchestral color derived partly from a totally dissimilar source, partly from no source but his own creative ingenuity. The presence of Beethoven is to be felt in his command of rich expressive forms and in occasional bursts of orchestral color, as well as in obbligatos of French horns, and in the transferred value of a song sung at a country festival. These borrowings are always overlaid and transformed with new rhythms and motifs, and further varied by the sounds of actual instruments which did not exist in Beethoven's day or were not used by him.

A more immediate debt is owed to the pioneer work of Wagner and Strauss, who enriched the orchestral palette, broke up the relatively fixed keys in use since Bach's time, and introduced very much more varied and voluminous harmonies. Also to César Franck, in whom there are many reminiscences of Oriental notes, as well as a rich orchestral warmth to which Strawinsky's tone-color often closely approximates. In the finale of "L'Oiseau de Feu" he follows so closely the climax of Franck's Symphony in D Minor that he invites the charge of plagiarism, even though he introduces modifications of his own and makes the passage a fitting climax to a personal organization.

These contributions from the great men and traditions in music are alternated or fused with folk melodies of all sorts, Russian, Chinese, African and Irish; sometimes the two types can be heard simultaneously, as when a passage comparatively close to the traditional style is played against a background of strongly rhythmic monotone. This resort to folk music has been common, but is not so frequent in the great composers; when it occurs, the manner of its use indicates that the composer felt the composition to be unimportant.* Strawinsky made extensive and systematic use of primitive elements; indeed they are ubiquitous in his music. Their presence constantly alters the effect of even the most traditionally conceived and executed passages, either by their juxtaposition, or by subtle changes in the way the technical passages are varied in tempo, rhythm, harmony or orchestration. A parallel case in Matisse is his use, in a design based primarily upon a traditional form of the Venetians or of Cézanne, of traits derived from primitive Negro or Hindu sculpture, or from the Byzantines. In such of Matisse's designs, as those of Strawinsky, the introduction of personality is obtained by the dramatic entry of stridency and dissonance. Matisse rarely follows the originals so closely as Strawinsky.

The composer to whose work Strawinsky owes most is Debussy: indeed the relation between them is closely parallel to that between Matisse and Cézanne or Manet. Just as Matisse took whole compositional forms from Cézanne and Manet, modifying them in characteristic ways but leaving the general derivation so apparent that it can be mistaken by no one with an eye for plastic quality, so the Debussy line, orchestral color, pictorial quality, and the pervasive attitude of expectancy of the auditor, are constantly reappearing in Strawinsky, again with characteristic changes, but unmistakable none the less. Debussy's gentle dissonances never sharpen into violent discords as Strawinsky's constantly do, nor does he introduce the tom-tom effect of primitive music; the suavity and elegance always present in the former are in Strawinsky many times replaced by the shock of barbarous rhythms, blares of crude sound; but at bottom the musical essence of an extraordinary number of Strawinsky's devices are anticipated in Debussy. Examples are long sweeping lines with a sound very suggestive of that of a shepherd's pipe, and the extremely numerous and varied uses of expectancy due, in some instances, to complete suspension of sound, to rests; in others, to prolongation of a phrase be-

*E.g., 466.

yond the point at which we expect it to pause, and then its abrupt termination by a burst of sound not strongly related to it either in melody or harmony. Such a passage occurs at the end of "L'Après-Midi d'un Faune," and may be paralleled in "L'Oiseau de Feu" and in numerous other passages in Strawinsky's work. The analogy here to Cézanne and Matisse is clear: however great the sense of power in Cézanne, there is never the shock, the assault on our sensibilities by sheer sensuous quality of color or bizarre pattern that is so constant in Matisse.

A very striking point of resemblance between Strawinsky and Matisse is their common emphasis upon decoration. Both men attempt fully expressive forms very rarely, and then episodically; when they do, they are usually most like their predecessors, just as when each uses color of sensuous appeal he is least himself, closest to his sources.* Strawinsky is always highly patterned, not in the manner of Haydn or Mozart, with their use of definite pauses or breaks recurring at fixed intervals, but in a manner quite his own. Indeed he converts even strident sound into a pattern of insistent rhythms, much as Matisse does with raucous color. Strawinsky's pattern in some of its phases is determined by one or another of the primitive traditions: "Les Noces," for example, has throughout a rhythmic pattern very strongly reminiscent of the tom-tom of a primitive Negro chant. The primacy of intricate decoration, comparable to the complex rhythmic forms in Negro music, is well illustrated in "Le Sacre du Printemps," in which the music to the dance is so complicated that no human body could make movements or gestures corresponding to all the nuances of the score. To say this is to say that there are decorative features in the music to which no commensurate expressive aspects correspond.

Strawinsky's music, like Matisse's painting, rarely or never attempts a rendering of the major human values: there is nothing in it that corresponds to the Credo in Bach's B-minor Mass or to Beethoven's Eroica Symphony; if he attempts a phrase or a brief passage in the style of Beethoven it is, like one of the

*Cf., e.g., 85 with 468.

isolated tilelike areas in Matisse, an episode skilfully reproduced in essentials and without mere imitation of surface-effects, and admirably woven into the fabric of the form, but actually a note of contrast in a totality dominated by a different
conception and style of execution. In his adaptation of primitive themes, what stands out may be bizarre or barbaric, but
there is no sustained temper of the terrible or tragic. He is, in
a word, like Matisse, concerned with the picturesque.

He is like Matisse also in his extensive use of transferred
values. We constantly hear echoes of such things as the melody
of a hurdy-gurdy, the conglomerate sounds of a military pa-
rade or a country fair, and even roars, sometimes rumbling,
sometimes thunderous, which catch the quality of a passing
train or a storm; and they do so without the literal imitation
which makes program-music so objectionable.* A very frequent
motif is a broad strongly rhythmic type of theme, something
which we should expect to hear from a hurdy-gurdy, and which
carries the spirit of an out-of-door festival; the rhythm of this
pervades "Petrouchka" from beginning to end, and is combined
with long sweeping melodies much in the manner of Debussy.
Its decorative function is almost exactly paralleled by that of
Matisse's rosette-theme, which, when it serves as the general
principle of organization, is constantly repeated in the detail,
and is there also united with entirely different, and strongly
contrasting themes. We find in Strawinsky Matisse's habitual
switching from one tradition to another for motifs relevant to
new and individual forms. Both artists show infinite versatility
in dealing with a single theme, in deploying it, resolving it into
its elements and recombining them, or in surrounding it with
relations that lend it essential novelty and freshness. Again,
Strawinsky's succession of disparate passages—for example, a
lullaby followed by a highly patterned and lively primitive
motif—is analogous to Matisse's organization of two distinct
and sharply contrasting sets of color, one of them light, delicate
and tranquil, the other vivid, intense and lively.†

Like Matisse, Strawinsky is a very-much-alive individual in
a complex, varied, and many-sided civilization. Both have at

*For the opposite, cf. 467.   †Cf., e.g., 84 with 469.

hand resources, not of a depth, but certainly of a diversity never paralleled before. Both are adventurous, able to seize upon the essence of traditions, and in consequence to wander far from conventional forms without losing the solid substance of the past and present. Their wanderings naturally make them seem strange, even wilfully obscure, but their very strangeness is a challenge to an inquiring mind. Bewilderment gives way to satisfaction and a rich store of new æsthetic experiences, as the fundamental purposes are grasped and the key found to the original and powerful sets of relationships.

ILLUSTRATIONS

No. 6.

No. 7.

No. 10.

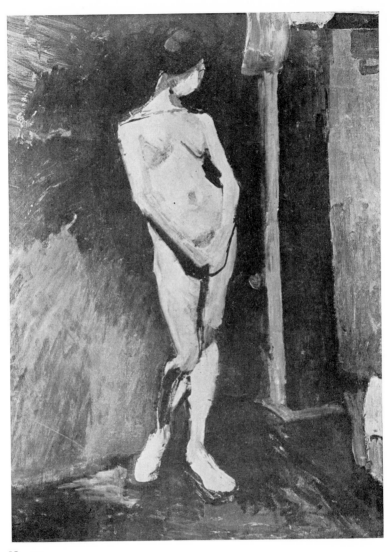

No. 11.

No. 14.

No. 378.

This Japanese print and the Matisse opposite have the same coalescence of patterned figure and patterned background into a single arabesque design.

No. 19.

No. 305.

No. 313.

The Egypto-Roman portrait above and the mosaic below show the source of the accentuated pattern of facial features in the Matisse opposite.

No. 21.

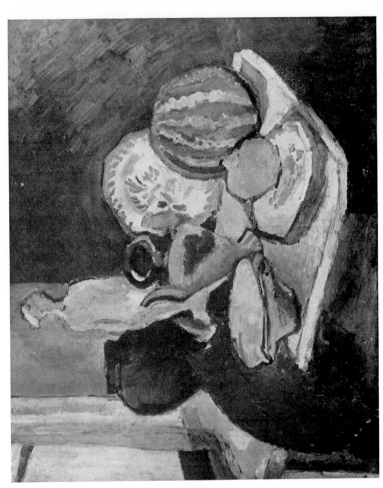

No. 20.

No. 27.

238

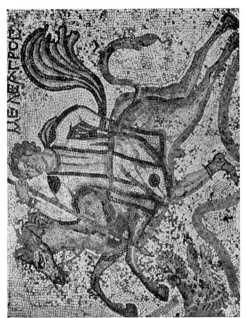

No. 320.

No. 307.

The Egyptian textile on the left and the Roman mosaic on the right employ internal patterns of bands and stripes as an instrument in modeling, in ways which anticipate Matisse's. (Compare with painting on opposite page.)

240

No. 25.

This sketch for the picture opposite, indicates which aspects of the latter are plastically fundamental, and which are incidental to detailed execution.

No. 31.

Analysis, page 369.

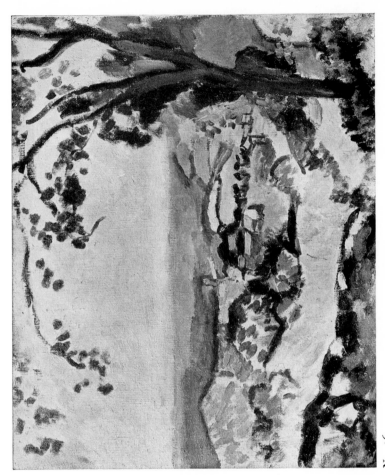

No. 26.

No. 33.

Analysis, page 373.

No. 30.

No. 34.

No. 365.

This Japanese print is similar to the Matisse opposite in its
all-over fluid, angular, arabesque pattern, in its recurring "islands" and in the compositional
distribution of its units.

No. 36.

Drawing very much in the manner of Manet here introduces, in place
of the miniature-effects in the Japanese print opposite, looser contours in a bolder pattern.

248

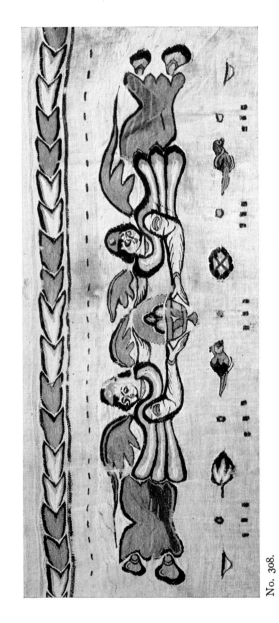

No. 308.

This Egyptian textile is an anticipation of the type of distortions by which Matisse transforms a figure into an arabesque-pattern, as illustrated on the page opposite.

No. 32.

No. 37.

No. 40.

No. 42.

Analysis, page 379.

No. 43.

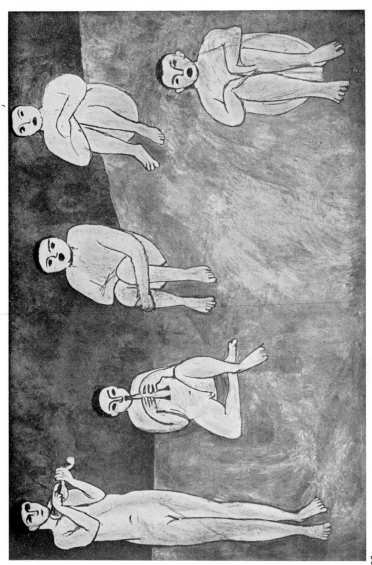

No. 47.

No. 326.   No. 304.

No. 323.   No. 325.

Early Italian, Egypto-Roman and Byzantine prototypes of the linear drawing of facial features and of the rigid, non-naturalistic decorative pattern
in the Matisse opposite.

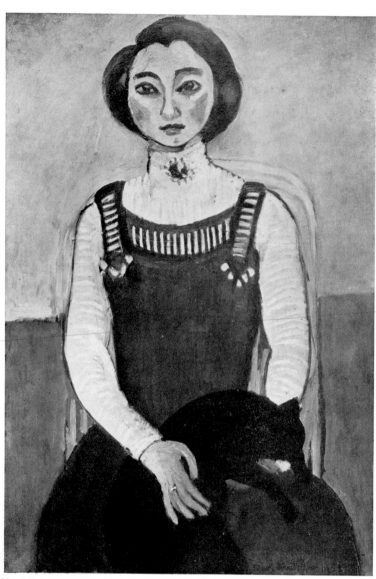

No. 48.

258

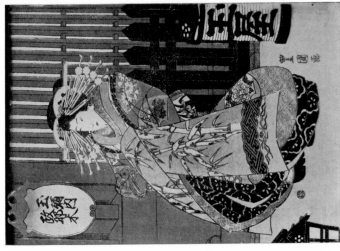

No. 368.

No. 345.

The diagonal sweep of the figure, against a striped background, in the Japanese print on the right, is compositionally identical with the foreground masses and setting in the Matisse below. The Turkish tile, on the left, anticipates the patterned drapery in the same painting.

No. 49.

No. 50.

Simplified drawing, diminished space, and generally light execution give
to this picture the light, delicate quality of a cretonne.

No. 51.

Essentially the same subject-matter is treated here with more emphatic line, more solid modeling, and accentuated perspective; the result is a composition in deep space which gives, incidentally to a feeling of power, the effect of light shining through heavy stained glass.

Analysis, page 382.

No. 54.

No. 52.

No. 57.

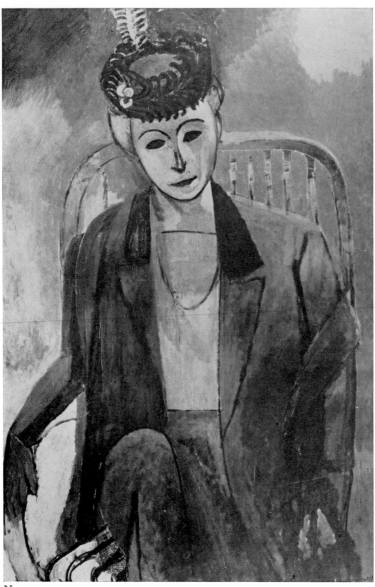

No. 55.

266

No. 56.

Analysis, page 387.

No. 68.

No. 67.

No. 61.

270

No. 346.   No. 369.

The Hindu-Persian miniature on the left and the Japanese print on the right show similar distortion of perspective, and similar equality of foreground and background, as in the Matisse reproduced on the opposite page.

No. 64.

Analysis, page 389.

272

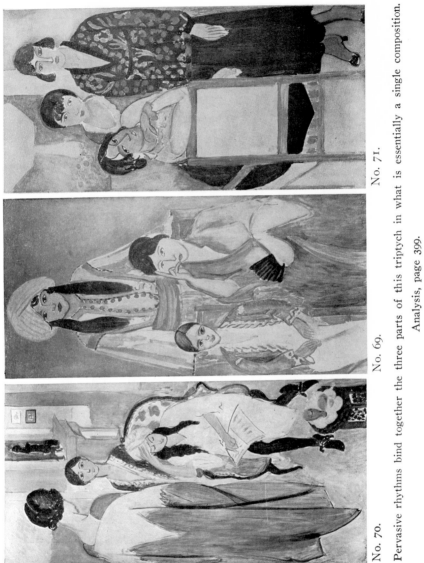

No. 70.

No. 69.

No. 71.

Pervasive rhythms bind together the three parts of this triptych in what is essentially a single composition.

Analysis, page 399.

No. 327.   No. 70.   (Detail.)

No. 389.   No. 71.   (Detail.)

In the upper pair of pictures the Matisse resembles the Negro head in its mask-like rigidity, its pattern of features in which line replaces the grooves in the statue, and the specific type of its distortions.

The lower pair make clearly apparent Matisse's debt to Manet's drawing.

274

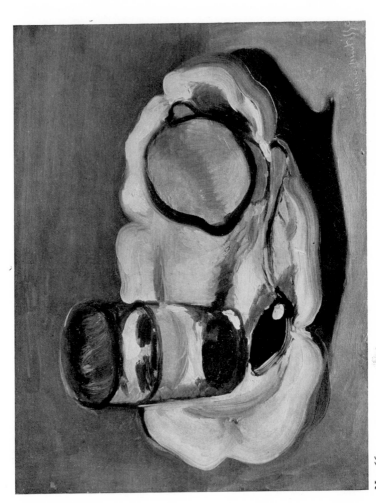

No. 66.

No. 72.

Analysis, page 404.

No. 76.

No. 79.

No. 73.

Analysis, page 407.

No. 80.

No. 74.

No. 84.

Analysis, page 409.

282

No. 344.

No. 381.

The use of a projecting plane as a screen to subdivide the space in a composition, as in the Japanese print on the left, and of a broad curvilinear pattern, as in the Syrian tile on the right, are combined in the Matisse below.

284

No. 90.

Analysis, page 412.

No. 86.

No. 94.

No. 97.

No. 98.

Analysis, page 415.

No. 88.

No. 91.

No. 95.

No. 99.

No. 106.

No. 105.

No. 104.

No. 109.

No. 110.

No. 108.

Analysis, page 417.

o. 108a.

No. 100.

No. 114.

No. 117.

No. 123.

No. 121.

No. 122.

No. 125.

No. 118.

No. 111.

No. 129.

310

No. 119.

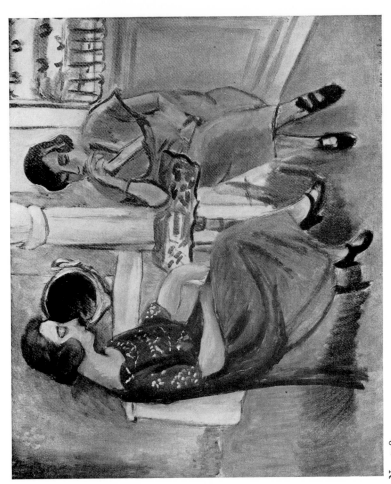

No. 128.

No. 135.

No. 131.

314

No. 375.

Matisse's occasional broad, loose drawing of foliage as in the landscape opposite, clearly has its origin in Japanese pictures of the type illustrated above.

No. 133.

No. 312.

No. 328.

Exaggeration of rounded volumes to the point at which they appear detached from the body to which they belong, is shown in the Hindu sculpture on the right and the Negro sculpture on the left. In the picture below, Matisse

317

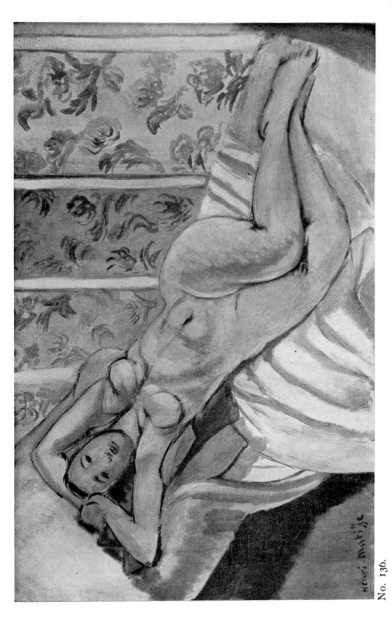

No. 136.

Analysis, page 421.

No. 134.

Analysis, page 419.

No. 132.

No. 144.

No. 146.

No. 148.

No. 140.

324

No. 348.

Extreme spatial compression of background, figures and intermediate objects, and alternation of highly patterned and relatively
unpatterned areas, are observable both in this Hindu-Persian miniature and in the Matisse opposite.

No. 141.

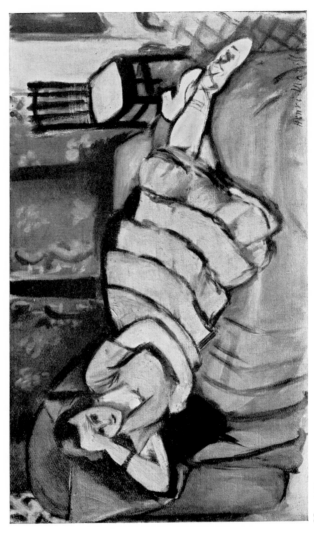

No. 145.

Analysis, page 425.

No. 152.

No. 380.

The plastic resemblance between this Japanese print and the
Matisse opposite is extremely close, both in their general organization by stripes and bands, and in the specific distribution of compositional units.

No. 156.

No. 155.

No. 150.

No. 153.

No. 158.

335

No. 160.

336

No. 379.

The interplay of motifs in this Japanese print, in which a
curvilinear theme is set against an angular pattern of which
the framework is formed by stripes and bands, is adapted by
Matisse with characteristic modifications, as illustrated on the
opposite page.

No. 157.

No. 162.

No. 168.

No. 167.

No. 172.

No. 173.

No. 175.

No. 448.

Modigliani's utilization of motifs from Negro sculpture, here illustrated, has been further employed and modified by Matisse, as shown
in the companion picture.

No. 176.

346

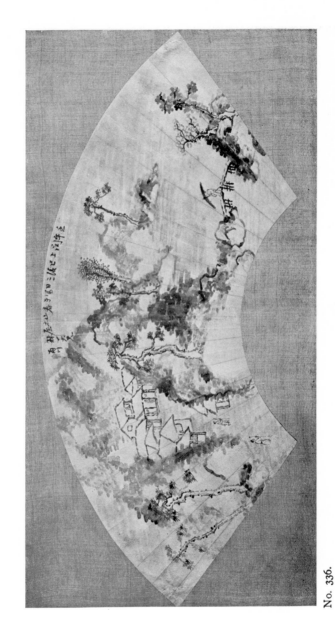

No. 336.

This Chinese painting shows the elaborate arabesques of which Matisse adapted the essential features to another medium, in his drawing below.

No. 200.

No. 202.

No. 203.

No. 204.

No. 206.

No. 209.

No. 212.

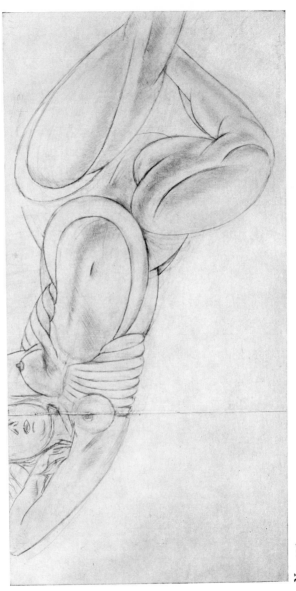

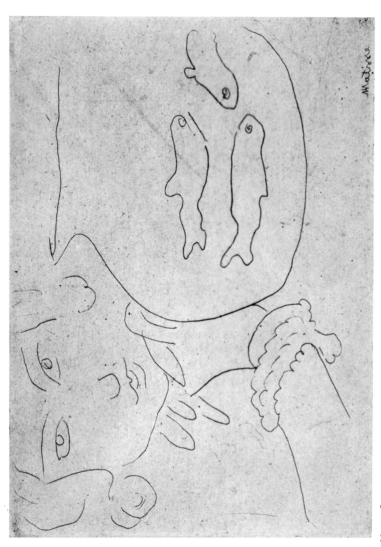

No. 218.

358

1931 Henri-Matisse

No. 219.

LE FAVNE

Ces nymphes, je les veux perpétuer.

Si clair,
Leur incarnat léger, qu'il voltige dans l'air
Assoupi de sommeils touffus.

Aimai-je un rêve?

No. 222.

No. 221.

No. 220.

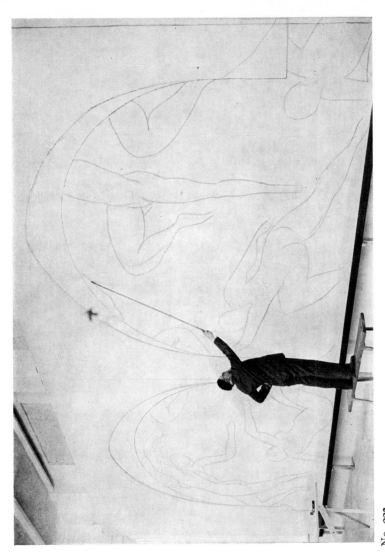

No. 223.

APPENDIX

BIOGRAPHICAL SKETCH*

HENRI-MATISSE was born on December 31, 1869, the son of a grain-merchant in Le Cateau, France. His father wished him to become a lawyer, but his legal studies were interrupted by a lengthy illness and convalescence. While awaiting the return of his strength he became interested in painting and, in spite of parental objections, he finally discarded the law and devoted himself entirely to art. Before the change was definitely made, in his moments of leisure, he took a course in "design" given to makers of embroidery, and began independent painting.

In 1892 he went to Paris to pursue a systematic study of art.† His first instructors were Bouguereau and Gabriel Ferrier, but their teaching was so unintelligible and unprofitable to him that after a month he withdrew from their classes and became a free student at the Ecole des Beaux-Arts. His time there was divided between drawing from the antique and copying old masters at the Louvre. He succeeded in impressing favorably Gustave Moreau, who was at that time criticizing the work of the Beaux-Arts students, and after a time was invited to study in Moreau's own studio where he worked for four years. Moreau's scrupulous respect for his pupils' individual bent and personality, and at the same time his insistence upon a firm grounding in the traditions, were both of the greatest assistance to Matisse; they confirmed his confidence in himself, and at the same time brought home to him the importance of learning the meaning of art by an objective study of the old masters.

During this period he eked out his income by making for sale copies of old masters in the Louvre (2, 9, et al.) The benefits of this copying were much more than financial, they were also an intimate knowledge of plastic traditions and a skill with the brush which were invaluable when he began to work in his individual vein. About a year after his arrival in Paris, when he was still at the Beaux-Arts, he exhibited seven pictures at the Exposition of the Société Nationale des Beaux-Arts, usually called the Salon du Champs-de-

*The events in the life of Henri-Matisse are very generally known, and this sketch is in the main a summary of the more important of them. It contains also a number of details communicated to the authors by the painter himself, which are of value for the light which they throw upon the development of his interest in art.

†In 1893 Matisse was married to Amélie Noëllie Parayre and has three children, Jean, Marguerite (now Madame Georges Duthuit), and Pierre.

365

Mars; one of the pictures, "Reader" (3), was bought by the French government. This Exposition was the occasion of a controversy between Puvis de Chavannes, the president, who recognized Matisse's ability even at that early period, and Jean Béraut, an influential member of the jury. The president's favorable view prevailed, and Matisse was made an associate member of the Société Nationale des Beaux-Arts, a dignity which assured recognition of his work without the formality of trial by jury. This success stimulated him to take stock of himself and the stage of accomplishment which by that time he had reached. "Reader" (3) was a picture dark in color, and so completely dominated by the old masters that Matisse felt that in it he had acted merely as an amanuensis for the painters of the past. He became acutely conscious of the two worlds in which he lived, the museum-world in which he had worked, and the living world as yet unreflected in his own painting. He was compelled to meet the problem of producing an expression of his own personal perception, and at the same time of overlooking nothing of value in the traditions. In his own words, "It seemed to me that on entering the Louvre I was losing the sensation of life which was of my time, and . . . that the pictures I was painting under the direct influence of the masters did not represent what I felt intimately in me. . . . But I have always maintained one foot in the Louvre so that, even when going forth adventurously, I have always had an anchor in the native land."

With this realization of conflict, Matisse's individual career in art may be said to begin. His quest for a pictorial expression of his own led him first to impressionism, and took him, physically, to Brittany, in company with the impressionist painter Emile Wéry. In the summer of 1896 and of 1897 he painted there, and during these years he also devoted serious attention to the canvases of the impressionists. In 1897 he met Pissarro, Bonnard, Vuillard, and Serusier, and in the same year he painted "Dinner Table" (6), the first picture in which he felt he had really expressed himself. Impressionism at the time was still under the ban of the academicians and the large part of the general public who took their critical cue from that quarter; but in the disapproval which greeted "Dinner Table" (6) Matisse found, not cause for discouragement, but testimony to the fact that he had discovered the way toward his own personal form of expression.

A period of rapid growth followed, growth both in knowledge

and in accomplishment. In 1898 he went to London to study Turner; in Paris he discovered Japanese art, and made the acquaintance of Laprade, Biette, and Derain. Soon after, he went to Corsica, where he remained for a year and painted. In 1899 he bought a Cézanne "Bathers," and shortly afterward his interest in massive form led him to work in sculpture. So definitely had his personal interest, his individual style, expressed itself by this time that his paintings were refused at the annual Beaux-Arts Salon. From 1900 until 1904, working in Toulouse and Paris, he continued to assimilate the influence of impressionism and neo-impressionism, always conscious, however, of the classical traditions of painting, and consequently on his guard against the submergence of design by technical preoccupations and concern for light-photography into which so many of the feebler impressionists fell. In 1903 he studied the exhibition of Mohammedan art in Munich. In 1904, the year of his friendship with Cross, the neo-impressionistic influence reached its height with him; but he was quick to discover its limitations. In that year he exhibited and sold what he considered his first entirely characteristic painting "Phlox" (18) —a picture which he feels represented him, not, like "Dinner Table" (6), as he was at a particular stage of development but as, in essentials, he has remained since. This picture appeared in his first one-man exhibition at Vollard's gallery in which forty-six of his works were hung. How far he was from general recognition is apparent, however, from the fact that "Phlox" (18) was sold for only one hundred and fifty francs.

In 1905 he went to Collioure and worked there at the same time as Derain; on his return to Paris he exhibited at the Salon d'Automne, in company with Marquet, Manguin, Vlaminck, Rouault and Derain, a number of pictures which gained for the painters the sobriquet of "Les Fauves," and provoked in academic circles a storm of hostile criticism. They were charged with wilful eccentricity, senseless disregard of nature, and a deliberate intent to scandalize the public and advertise themselves. Matisse's departure from color-division had alienated the impressionist critics no less than those of an earlier academicism, and for the moment the opinion prevailed generally that he was an anarchist who had completely cut himself off from the traditions of painting.

In 1906 was held an exhibition of fifty-five of his paintings at the Galerie Druet, and the turning of the tide began. The Steins, Gertrude, Leo and Michael, and the Misses Cone of Baltimore, were his first important patrons, and not only recognition from critics of discernment, but a measure of financial success followed, though pictures of the importance of his "Blue Still-Life" (33) and "Joy of Life" (31), now in the Barnes Foundation, brought, respectively, only eight hundred and twelve hundred francs. However, more general acclaim was quick to follow. In 1907 he opened his own school and continued it intermittently for two winters; though it attracted from sixty to a hundred students, he found the distraction from his own work irksome, and discontinued it finally in 1909. In 1908, at the Stieglitz Galleries, his first American exhibition was held, and in 1910, in Paris, at the Galerie Bernheim-Jeune a retrospective exhibition of his work from 1895 to 1910. Also in 1910, he painted the famous Stschoukin decorations and made a visit to Moscow. In 1911, 1912 and 1913 he spent the winter in Morocco, and added new Oriental motifs to his painting. In 1912 the Neue Staatsgalerie of Munich bought one of his paintings, a large still-life (49), and in 1915 he had a second American exhibition.

In 1917 he moved to Nice, and has resided there ever since, though he has returned each year to Paris for brief visits. In 1921 a recognition more conspicuous than any previous came to him in the purchase by the Luxembourg of an "Odalisque" (119), though by that time he was no longer in need of any official testimony to his standing. Other indications of universal esteem followed quickly. In 1927 his "Fruit and Flowers" (149) won first prize at the Carnegie International Exhibition, and the first retrospective exhibition of his work in America was held in New York. In 1928 the Luxembourg purchased a second picture of his, "Sideboard" (173), for which three hundred thousand francs had been bid, but after offering it to the Museum as a present, he accepted one franc in payment, in deference to the law prohibiting gifts to the gallery by artists. In 1930 he visited Tahiti, and also made three trips to the United States, during one of which he acted as judge in the Carnegie Exhibition. In the same year a comprehensive exhibition of his work was held in Berlin; similar exhibitions followed in 1931 at Paris, Basel and New York, as well as an exhibition of his sculpture in New York. In 1931, he was commissioned to paint a set of decorative murals for the Barnes Foundation, Merion, Pennsylvania; to these and to a set of eaux-fortes for a forthcoming edition of Mallarmé's poems, he has since devoted himself chiefly.

ANALYSES

THE purpose of the following analyses is twofold. First, to make more definite and concrete the method here employed as well as the general æsthetic principles which illuminate Matisse's work. Both the method and the principles have been extensively illustrated in the text by reference to particular pictures; but pictures are more than instances of principles: they are individual creations, relatively complete in themselves and demanding attention in their own right. The analyses attempt to focus upon each picture the relevant explanatory principles, and to indicate the unique purpose and set of qualities which make it what it is. It must be understood that the analyses are offered as *illustrations of method,* not as final conclusions about the particular pictures analyzed.

The second purpose is to survey the more important types of Matisse's forms. Only in the light of such a survey is it possible to realize how varied are his modes of organization, how extensive his knowledge of traditions, and how great his sagacity in selecting the particular effects and technical means best adapted to the execution of his plastic designs.

The analyses here published are a selection from a much larger number, which cover most of the pictures referred to in the text. The remainder of these analyses will be published subsequently for the guidance of students who wish to make a more intensive study of Matisse's work.

JOY OF LIFE* (31)

The outstanding feature of this striking painting is its extremely picturesque and gaily-colored pattern, the principal characteristic of which is an all-pervasive feeling of color-movement. This movement and pattern are appropriate to the subject-matter—an Arcadian scene of nudes dancing, playing music and reclining at ease in a landscape. The main theme is an arabesque-formation which appears in the design as a whole and in most of the component units, even in those figures which convey the feeling of repose. The development of this theme represents to the fullest extent Matisse's capacity to make rhythm and contrast pervade each unit of the organization: line, space and light, each coöperates with

*Illustration, p. 241.

color in forming the pervasive rhythms and contrasts. The organization is a triumph of the interaction of all these plastic factors in a decorative pattern which also expresses a great variety of universal human values.

The form of the picture, like that of a building, a steamship, or a symphony, harmoniously unites an indefinitely large number of elements, and the design as a whole is repeated in a number of areas, within each of which a corresponding compositional arrangement prevails. Four such areas form the main compositional units: a large triangular pattern in the center, and three other areas, also triangular, which enframe the first on all sides. The central triangle includes the large expanse of yellow ground, the groups of figures set against it, the strip of blue sea, and the pink-lavender sky. Two of the enframing triangles, those to the left and to the right, are sets of multicolored areas which fill the upper corners of the picture and sweep downward from the apex of the central triangle to the lower part of the green tree on the left and to the piper and goats on the right. Taken together these two enframing triangles seem like an open stage-curtain hanging from the top of the picture and drawn aside to reveal a vista of landscape. The third enclosing triangle is placed obliquely in the right foreground; it includes the patterned part of the ground against which three figures are set. In the central triangle there is a group of dancing nudes which form, plastically, a series of curvilinear vertical-oblique planes; these planes, with the enclosed bowl-shaped space, form the focus of the organization of colored planes of which the composition consists.

The intersection of these four principal areas results in a general arabesque-pattern, which is carried out, varied, and made extremely complex by the elaborate detail in the units contained in each area. The lines in the pattern are of all degrees of curvilinear quality, their arrangement is extraordinarily rhythmic, and in conjunction with equally varied bright colors they produce an effect of highly active color-movement, within which appear, by way of contrast, passages or episodes distinctly reposeful. The movement centers in the group of dancing nudes, and is there rapid and circular; in the enfolding lines and areas on either side it proceeds backward and forward, up and down, in a wide, comparatively deliberate sweep; in the figures of the foreground and middle ground it flows tranquilly and here and there halts in a poised equilibrium. It comes definitely to rest in the large triangular area of yellow, blue, and pink-lavender planes in the center, which serves as a setting for the dancers, and also for the two reclining figures in the middle distance. In this central part of the landscape, all degrees of movement and rest are thus brought together, and each, by contrast, sets the others into sharp relief.

What chiefly renders the movement is compositional interplay between the very numerous and variously shaped and placed lines and areas of color which constitute the pattern of the picture. The general linear flow is sometimes vertical, as in several of the figures and tree-trunks; sometimes horizontal, as in the horizon-line; most often oblique, as in the reclining nudes; but in most of the pattern the lines, with their conjoined area-lines, pass from one direction to another, and this change and alternation of direction pervades every part of the canvas. In conjunction with the diverse intervals between them, these compositionally active contour-lines lend a very great degree of variety to the space-motif, a variety which is augmented by differences in the sharpness of the outlines themselves, and the consequent differences in the movement suggested by them. As one plastic factor or another predominates, space becomes in turn shallow and deep, merely decorative or quite realistic, but always colorful, highly patterned, and full of compositional movement.

The pattern of color-areas of which the picture is composed is given its arabesque-form not only by the size, shape and position of the areas themselves, but also, and in scarcely less degree, by the lines of demarcation between them. These are sometimes formed by the direct contact of the areas, but more often they are themselves actual narrow strips of color, or of bare canvas which functions as color, and as such they make an important contribution to the movement and compositional function of the areas. They vary in width, sharpness of outline, and in their color; and the area-lines by which many of them are paralleled emphasize these variations and give to the lines a richer plastic content. Not only do the lines and area-lines all unite in the general network of pattern which covers the whole canvas, but they add specific relations of color-contrast, and contribute to the variety of movement and to the spatial ordering of volumes and planes. For example, in two groups of detail which balance each other, in the curtainlike area en-framing the central vista of landscape, most of the color-compart-ments on the right are separated by broad colored lines; most of those on the left are in immediate contact with each other, with only an occasional intermediate strip of color or of bare canvas. The surging movement which pervades this entire setting, in other words, is obtained on the right chiefly by accentuated lines of contour; on the left, mainly by the swirling color-areas themselves.

The incessant change, contrast and movement of space and line is further augmented by the color-scheme of very bright tones of yellow, red, pink, blue, green and lavender. The individual colors are not confined to any one area of the canvas, but each recurs throughout the surface, with constant tonal modification, so that every note of color is at the same time varied and balanced elsewhere. The repetition serves to unify the picture, the change to diversify it, and the ubiquitous effect of contrast is heightened by differences in degree of solidity of the color-areas, some of which are definitely, even though slightly, voluminous, while others are essentially flat.

The contribution of light to the pervasive active movement of the design is commensurate with that of color, line or space. The color is made what it is as much by its saturation by light as by its own intrinsic quality; the light adds also a pervasive luminosity by which the whole picture is flooded, and its focus back of the dancing nudes lends added weight to this general area as the compositional center of the whole organization.

The design, to sum up, is primarily a decorative color-pattern, in which all the plastic means are fused in the drawing and modeling of every element; background, middle ground and foreground are united on equal terms to yield a total effect not unlike that of a poster or brightly-patterned banner. Its frankly ornamental purpose necessitates non-realistic, highly generalized and distorted drawing: the figures, trees, and all other details of subject-matter are treated as patterns of color, line, space and light, and whatever features do not lend themselves to this reduction are ruthlessly pruned away. These patterned units are rhythmically repeated through the design, but always with differences in detail. A mass, for example, may be balanced by several color-areas fused in a shape similar to its own. Rhythm pervades everything, it harmonizes the contrasts and promotes the intense color-movement which sweeps uninterruptedly through the picture in a broad arabesque. The accentuated pattern of color-compartments is the setting for a plastic form that conveys a sense of joyous life in Arcadian surroundings. The feeling of lightness, of dance alternating with repose, of the surge of flames or of ocean waves—all

ANALYSES

are rendered by unceasing interplay of color, light and line in space.

The design as a whole represents an organic fusion of derivations from Greek and Hindu sculpture, mosaics, the forms of Andrea del Castagno, Giorgione, Tintoretto, El Greco, Rubens, Renoir, Gauguin and the impressionists, all of which, because of the exotic color and the decorative pattern of intertwining arabesques, are dominated by a quality fundamentally Oriental.*

BLUE STILL-LIFE† (33)

The general plan of this picture consists of three large horizontal sections placed one above the other, each in the form of a broad band, and each composed of rich and well-integrated decorative units. These three main sections or areas are: (a) the large expanse of tablecloth which forms almost the entire immediate foreground, (b) the table-cloth with its group of multicolored still-life objects, and (c) the total area of background. Each of these areas is treated in a different manner, and all three are woven harmoniously into an intricate and extraordinarily decorative color-pattern.

In the section of the immediate foreground—the tablecloth—the large deep-blue floral motifs alternate with almost equally large areas of the bluish-white ground of the cloth itself; these motifs appear detached from the cloth and are placed at such distance from each other that their broad spatial intervals are very active in the pattern. This ornamental foreground is brought in contact with the second area which forms the central section of the total composition. The constituents of this central band are more numerous than those of the foreground area; they are also smaller, more varied and contrasting in color, and are packed more closely to-

*It has been asserted by critics that Matisse's previous work is summed up in this painting. This implies that all that had gone before served as a preparation for the particular form embodied here, and that his subsequent work was in another direction and illustrative of different principles. As a matter of fact, the same principles of plastic organization which underlie this picture can be pointed out in his work of all subsequent periods. What gives this picture its individuality is the color-movement, the general arabesque-formation, and the use of line, light, space and color, varied and adapted to particular plastic ends Oriental in general character. All these traits are discernible in Matisse's work of all periods, even the latest.
†Illustration, p. 243.

gether, thus forming a contrast in space-composition with the widely separated units of the first area. The third main compositional section—the background-setting—consists of a drapery on the right, part of a wall-like screen in the center, and, to the left, a portion of the screen decorated with floral motifs. These motifs, like those on the tablecloth, appear as volumes in space, detached from the ground of the screen proper. The two sets of spatially isolated units counterbalance each other, since one is in the upper left of the picture and the other in the lower right. Space-composition from the upper left corner to the lower right is thus organized in a sweep of volumes and intervals, in which are included the floating volumes of detached floral units on the vertical screen, the more compactly arranged still-life on the oblique-horizontal plane of the table, and the detached decorative motifs on the vertical foreground tablecloth.

The relationship between the contrasting directions of the planes upon which these objects and decorative motifs are set, converts the three main horizontal bands of the pattern into a step-like formation of two vertical planes joined by a central oblique-horizontal one. The theme of space-composition is varied, in each of these main areas, by a shift of emphasis to either the volumes or the spatial intervals. The rhythmic contrasts between degrees in accentuation of volume and of space are paralleled by variations in the colors, which make both the volumes and the intervals function also as color-contrasts.

The general color-scheme includes practically all of Matisse's rich gamut. As the eye travels over the canvas it finds a unit of color-pattern which duplicates, with minor variations, a cognate unit in another part of the canvas; in each instance the components of the pattern are line, light and space rendered in color-contrasts which vary from the delicate and subtle to the extremely vivid and bright. But the picture is perceived mainly as a harmony in blue because that color, in tones varying from a deep dark blue to a bluish white, dominates the ensemble. More correctly speaking the picture appears as a series of multicolored jewel-like ornaments placed within a blue setting. Furthermore, the blue itself runs through so many shades that it contributes notably to the pervasive theme of contrasts; for example, in the tablecloth, a bluish white adjoins areas of very deep blue which in turn are juxtaposed to areas of lighter-toned blue; again, in the center of the background, two shades of blue, both extremely well lighted, are placed in juxtaposition. This pervasive blue, reappearing in areas which vary in size, tone, context and plastic activity, is a potent factor in establishing variety as well as unity in the design.

Whatever the colors employed, their areas function also as planes differing in size, shape and compositional purpose. Indeed, between the two extremes represented by the large plane of the tablecloth and the small planes which draw and model the floral motifs on the screen, there are planes of all size, color and degree of accentuation and contrast. These ubiquitous planes embrace all the plastic elements, and thus make of the design an active color-pattern of planes.

A large plane of color, representing the shadow cast upon the background by the table and large jar, starts from a point about half way up the left side of the canvas and ascends almost to the top, back of the large jar on the right. This broad expanse of colored shadow, in comparison with the elaborately patterned planes elsewhere in the picture, is a simple pattern formed by three flat areas, each of relatively uniform and subtly contrasting color. This large plane, by its obliquely ascending curvilinear sweep from the lower left toward the upper right, counterbalances the diagonal sequence of volumes and spatial intervals which, as already noted, moves from the left upper corner of the canvas to the lower right.

These two main diagonal rhythms, which largely balance each other, are more fully stabilized by a series of horizontal and vertical units that pervade the organization. Among this series is the horizontal band of the tablecloth in the foreground, in which the general tendency of the internal units is more toward the vertical than toward the horizontal or oblique. This vertical placing is repeated in the individual bands, broad areas, and stripes of contrasting color in the background, and occurs also in greater or less degree in the components of the horizontal area of still-life. In sum, the compositional unity of the picture is effected by the rhythmic contrasts of volumes and spatial intervals reinforced by an all-inclusive network of interwoven vertical, horizontal and oblique color-areas. These color-areas are extensively diversified in plastic content; for example, the vertical jar is more fully modeled than the semi-voluminous decorative motifs of the screen and tablecloth, while the bands and stripes of the drapery and screen are relatively flat.

The previously-noted sweep of volumes and spatial intervals from the upper left corner to the lower right is the keynote for a pervasive movement of color which is reflected in every section of the canvas, and is focalized in the still-life objects in the center of the table. This color-movement is participated in by the line, light and space as these enter into the drawing, modeling and compositional distribution of the objects. The degree and the character of the movement are abundantly varied: the large relatively heavy floral motifs on the tablecloth seem to swim in the free space of the foreground; the smaller ornaments of the screen are light delicate volumes that float and gently droop; in the objects on the table, the movement varies in degree of intensity between the precipitous rise of the large voluminous jar on the right, the lively, flamelike linear activity of the long thin multicolored twigs in the small vase, the small voluminous movement of the pieces of fruit near the edge of the table, and the quiet poised movement in the group of objects at the center, at which point the concerted movement of the total design comes to rest.

So far we have seen that the principle of contrast embraces the color of the objects, their degree of three-dimensional quality, their spatial intervals, their position and their movement. It involves also all the other components of their drawing and modeling, i.e., their line, light and technique. Some of the objects on the table, for instance, are drawn and modeled largely by color-hatchings like Cézanne's, others by a fusion of light and color either without much aid from linear contour, or with practically total subordination of the color to broad dark outlines. An active linear pattern is formed by the relations between the accentuated contour of the objects, the bands and stripes in the background and immediate foreground, and the linear elements of the motifs on the tablecloth and screen, of the twigs in the small vase, and of the handles and plate. All these linear factors vary greatly in degree of accentuation, and in breadth as well as in color; consequently, they make of the linear pattern a theme as diversified as that of the color and of the space-and-volume composition.

Similarly an intricate pattern of light is formed by the organization of few large, definitely-shaped areas and numerous small highlights. It contributes much to the decorative value of the design because the areas of light are rendered as variegated color—bluish white, pale rose, saturated bright green, blue, orange and yellow— repeated in different sections of the canvas. Thus light enhances the decorative and expressive values of the contrasting colors, just as did the volumes, the spatial intervals and the linear elements. Likewise the light-pattern also serves, through the rhythmic organization of its components, as a unifying factor in the total composition.

The structure of this picture is closely analogous to that of a symphony, that, let us say, of César Franck. The three main decorative sections or patterned areas of the design correspond to the separate movements of the symphony, each with its own pervasive pattern, the theme or melody which gives it character and identity. The themes of each part of the picture, like those of the individual movements in the symphony, are repeated or deployed in the other parts so that a series of rhythms, like the phrases and melodies in the symphony, serve to bring the main patterns into a harmonious total organization. In this picture the motifs of the main compositional divisions are echoed in their subsidiary patterns by forms generically similar in their fusion of the plastic elements. Each of these forms is diversified in its linear, luminous, colored and spatial content; and the relative emphasis upon each of these determines the specific identity of the form in question. In short, Matisse does with color what Beethoven and Franck do with orchestral tone: the musicians deploy sounds, intervals and beats in an indefinite number of variations which establish a widely different series of relationships and result in musical phrases or melodies which, by being repeated, varied, balanced and counterbalanced throughout the composition, effect the unity of the total organization. Similarly, Matisse so treats the plastic elements of the represented objects that the latter emerge as color-units variously coördinated in larger compositional factors which, by their different relationships, create an organized interplay of color within each of the decorative patterns as well as throughout the design as a whole. In other words, all of the elements—line, light, color and space— so affect each other that the individual themes intertwine not only within each separate pattern but within the totality of the three main patterns of the design. It is this interaction of the components which results in the series of contrasts as well as in the pervasive harmony characteristic of the design.

We perceive the picture as richly harmonic color with reverberations that grip and play upon the feelings like a symphony of Beethoven or César Franck. The effect in each case is similar because Matisse's color, like the orchestration in the work of many composers, is the dominating factor and is embedded in a complex, highly-organized and unified ensemble of secondary components. The organization moves us not only because of what it is in itself but by tapping the emotional content of innumerable experiences in other realms. We feel the color-organization as extraordinarily rich, deep, luscious, strong and powerful. In the contrasts of color we feel drama that extends from the shock and boldness of the unexpected to the charm of the delicate and subtle. As our attention centers on the tablecloth we relive the feelings and memories associated with the deep rich color and pattern of old Persian tile, or with the soft lusciousness of an ancient Chinese rug. The table, with its lemons, oranges, apples, seems like a cluster of sparkling gems of many colors resting upon a cushion of rich blue velvet. The detached floral ornaments of the screen look like a garland of bright and variegated flowers, or like two gaily-costumed dancing marionettes. The drapery at the right has the depth and richness of color that recall old velvet, or a Kermanshah rug. The single piece of fruit on the right corner of the table has the lightness of eggshell, the poise of a *danseuse de pas seul*, the effulgence of a jewel; in contrast, the apple and orange on the opposite corner have the solidity, weight, and textural quality of blocks of dull mineral ore impregnated with gold or copper. The large ornament on the left of the foreground-tablecloth becomes an eagle soaring with extended blue wings in a pale azure sky. The ornament at the right of this section of tablecloth is a real basket standing in front of the table, and filled to overflowing with solid, charming blue flowers that droop with a graceful fluid movement into a swimming pearly atmosphere. The color of the picture as a whole is reminiscent of an Oriental bazaar loaded with diversely-shaped, multicolored articles displayed to charm the eye and compel the beholder to covet them as personal possessions. The sweeping arabesques of bright, variegated, exotic colors reinforce the Oriental flavor and recall our emotional reactions to a lively dance or to the swift graceful flow of a sunlit river. Again, the picture is a mosaic, a carnival at Nice, a halloween party, a cornucopia of fruit, of precious stones. The color glows, shines, shimmers, scintillates, dances. All these associated memories are pervaded with the feeling that goes with rich, deep, luminous, powerful, juicy and variegated color, free from stridency or raucousness. Particularly charming is the surface-quality, due partly to small planes of contrasting color used in the modeling, but more particularly to the color-chords which result from the subtle interpenetration of several colors blended in a single color-area. These color-chords, as well as the structural use of color to build up solidity of objects, are derivations from Cézanne which Matisse has transformed by ingenious instrumental uses into new forms loaded with deeply moving effects of their own.

RED MADRAS HEADDRESS* (42)

This three-quarter length portrait is conceived primarily as a decorative design, not as a characterization or realistic presentation of the sitter. The figure with ornamented headdress and gown forms a pattern of color-patches and linear elements set off with dramatic emphasis by the comparatively uniform bright, intensely blue background. Color-contrasts range from the dramatic clash between bright and vivid colors, or between bright and dark colors, to the subtle relation of diverse dark tones. The compositional problem was to unite this patterned multicolored figure with the plain blue background while retaining the theme of color-contrast.

The major contrast-theme of the design, stated in the bold contrast of the multicolored patterned figure against the broad expanse of unpatterned background, is developed in the subsidiary sections of the figure: the variously-shaped orange ornaments of the robe are set off by large areas of a single dark blue tone, the linear pattern of the face is superposed upon a comparatively uniform expanse of contrasting color, and the same is true of the lines separating the fingers, and of the yellow serpentine decoration on the vermillion headdress. Each of these line-and-color patterns acquires its own distinctive character by its individual color, the color-relations into which it enters, and its shape. For instance, the linear element is thin, ragged and tortuous in the headdress and not unlike an irregular wall-of-Troy motif, it is rather broad and wing-like in the gown, and is made of parallel narrow strips in the hands. The accentuated linear pattern, with its numerous subsidiary units, exhibits constant variation not only in the color, shape, direction and character of the line, but also in its instrumental use in the composition. For example: the yellow serpentine line gives a lively sense of movement; the simple and broad linear contour of face, features, neck, yoke and forearms conveys the idea of repose; the short streaks and spots in the bands of embroidery or lace on the gown give a quick dancelike movement; and the pervasive curvilinear ornamental motifs on the gown unite to form the sweeping movement of a broad arabesque.

*Illustration, p. 253.

The rhythmic relationship between the color and the linear elements of the separate patterns is the principal factor that binds the figure into a unity. The uppermost of this series of patterns is the headdress, which is also the culminating point of the rhythm of yellows that pervade the figure. The yellow gives a different effect in each of the decorated areas in which it occurs, chiefly by actual change of tone and by its relationship with the area of color with which it is directly contrasted; for example, in the headdress the yellow is extremely bright and vivid in itself and is contrasted to an almost equally intense vermillion; in the gown the tone of the ornaments is a dull orange and so in less vivid contrast with the blackish blue of the dress proper; in the chair it is a bright orange and is set off by adjacent areas of light green, flesh color, blackish blue and dull orange. The previously-noted changes in the size and shape of the linear element of these yellow units provide further variety within the unity effected by the rhythms of both the linear and tonal quality of the yellow. In this theme of color-and-line contrasts, the space, as well as the drawing and modeling, are distorted and adapted to the specific compositional purpose.

The design as a whole is a rather flat pattern of areas and lines, subtly rendered in space by means of color-planes. The face, which seems at first like a flat mask, is composed of a compact series of very subtly-defined planes receding from the chin to the ear. They consist of the patch of pink on the cheeks, the varied brush strokes which draw and slightly model the eyelids, chin, nose, and the broad lines of color around the facial features, the chin, neck and jaw. These latter contours also form an accentuated linear pattern reminiscent of Byzantine mosaics and Egypto-Roman portraits but with more color-drama. Similar relationships between pattern and space prevail also in the other sections of the figure. In the headdress and gown, for instance, the decorative motifs are separated by subtle space from the fabrics, and function in the modeling of them much as highlights do in the conventional rendering of volume.

The pattern of the wall-of-Troy decoration on the headdress is echoed in the lower part of the picture by the interlocking planes of the crossed hands, with difference in color, size and especially in activity of space and volume. Indeed, the patterned unit made up of the hands, the front of the gown, and the chair, is an extraordinarily effective space-organization of quasi-voluminous planes of color and well-defined intervals. The foremost part of the figure's right hand is a plane of pink patterned by green lines defining the intervals between the fingers; the back of this hand is a flat, oblique, receding plane of light green; below and slightly back of this hand is the orange plane of the chair, slightly tilted toward the right; just back of this is an irregular pattern of planes formed by the dark blue areas of the gown and their superposed orange ornaments; above and in front of the planes of the gown, chair and right hand is the oblique plane of the left hand and wrist. This plane extends upward and slightly backward toward the right, and forms an angle with the plane of the figure's left forearm, an angle which encloses this unit of space-composition and emphasizes the contrasting position and direction of its constituents. The entire group made by hands and chair is set against the bodice of the gown and is separated from it by a definite interval of space. The compact organization of planes and of slightly three-dimensional color-volumes is concentrated, as just noted, in the unit made by the hands and chair; from this point it moves backward and upward through the sleeves, and downward, backward and forward through the lower part of the gown, until it comes to the extreme outlying border of the figure.

The pattern of light is also very active in the decorative ensemble. The accentuated light-area of face-and-neck increases the drama of contrast between the vermillion of the headdress and the blackish blue of the gown, and this light-unit is repeated in the unit of the hands. Another theme in the general pattern of light is the rhythmic duplication of the bands of embroidery on the yoke and cuffs, and across the front of the gown. These bands are related to the continuous bands of light in the headdress, but are formed by small brush strokes of dark green placed upon a background of greenish white; the bands run in different directions and are set in different planes, as are also the face, neck and hands. Minor constituents of the light-pattern occur in the floral elements on the gown and also in the subtle diffuse lighting of the blue background; the latter is varied in tone by modulations of light, and is darker on the right side than on the left.

The outline of the figure divides the background into three curvilinear triangles which, together with the dark blue-and-orange triangle made by the section of the gown in the lower left corner of the canvas, enframe the central and most active part of the composition, i.e., the hands, torso and head. These triangular sections of the setting become an integral part of the design by their similarity in general shape to the numerous multicolored patterns which make up the figure. Indeed, triangularity is all-pervasive in the total pattern and becomes one of its main themes. The triangular shape of the facial pattern is repeated in the V-shaped area of the neck, and, with a greater degree of variation in all the plastic means, in the yoke of embroidery and in most of the irregular ornamental motifs of the headdress and gown. In other words, the abstract character of triangularity, like color, light, line and space, is one of the means through which rhythm and contrast are carried out through the entire picture and in each of its units.

This picture, painted in 1908, only a year later than "Blue Still-Life" (33), shows few influences of impressionism, and those that there are, e.g., the technique of brush strokes in the decoration of the headdress and in the bands of embroidery, are given an Oriental flavor. The total plastic form is an original synthesis of Oriental decorative motifs and daring color-contrasts with the Egypto-Roman or Byzantine type of face, and a simplified rendering of Cézanne's compositional planes.

GOLDFISH* (51)

The plastic problem of this picture, that of making of a still-life in a room a design of space-composition, is one that has engrossed painters since time immemorial. Differences in the treatment have been generally in the degree of emphasis upon, and in the relationship between, the two principal constituents of space-composition: space and mass. For example, the Dutch painters of the seventeenth century, as well as Chardin and Courbet, make both space and mass function with approximately equal subtlety or forcefulness. In Cézanne, the emphasis is upon the throb of the masses; in Seurat, it is upon the spatial intervals; in Manet, there is a well-proportioned balance between the subtlety of space and the reduced voluminous quality of objects. In contrast to these various earlier interpretations of space-composition, the basic novelty in this Matisse composition consists in making of color and pattern two powerful rivals of space and mass. That is, the dynamic relationship between the still-life objects and their spatial intervals involves principally the rhythms and contrasts of bright and dark color-compartments, placed in dramatic juxtaposition and well defined in shape by broad and dark linear contour. For

*Illustration, p. 261.

example, the æsthetic appeal of the large expanse of space around the table and its objects lies as much in the sensuous quality of the color-constituents and in the quaint angular pattern of their inter-related shapes as in the subtlety of space and the pulsation of masses and planes within it. Similarly, the compactly-grouped objects on the table are primarily contrasts of colors and patterns.

The two main parts of the composition—the corner of the room, enclosed by the floor and walls and dominated by blue, and the group of the table and objects upon it, dominated by the brown of the table—are interrelated by the thrust and counterthrust of their respective color-patterns; that is, the mass of the table and still-life projects backward toward the right into the space enclosed by the floor and walls; also, the floor in the immediate foreground extends from left to right, but as it reaches the right corner it turns at a sharp angle and moves directly backward, upward and toward the left to a point back of the statue's head. Further, the wall to the right is a plane moving obliquely backward to form an angle with the upright plane of the background-wall containing the window. Similar counterthrust of planes prevails in the organization of the subsidiary units: the planes of the top, sides and legs of the table intersect at sharp angles and make, in the lower section of the picture, an intricately patterned space-organization of color-compartments, not unlike the familiar framework of cubistic pictures, but made more substantial and expressive by the color-power and by the drama of the contrasting colors, planes, spatial intervals and patterns.

This unit of interpenetrating planes in the foreground is balanced in the upper right by another complex unit which includes the panel of the door, the picture over the door, and the landscape with its variegated pattern of irregular shapes. All of these planes are also contrasted in color and placed at sharp angles to each other.

In accordance with the general plan of rhythmic contrast, the objects on the table are related to each other as compartments differing in color, shape and position in space. The statue is an arabesque of circular and elongated curvilinear areas of luminous pink irregularly outlined in deep lustrous black; the position of its base and legs parallels the receding horizontal-oblique planes of the brown table-top, tan cover and blue plate; its torso has the same vertical direction as the blue bowl and green vase; the elongated curvilinear shape of the statue's arms and legs is repeated in the green vase, in the orange-red fish, and in the blue upper section of the bowl outlined by the rim; the pink-and-black circular areas of the statue repeat in shape the blue plate, orange flowers and green leaves. The two principal parts of the total picture, noted above as projecting into each other in opposite directions in space, are further contrasted by concentration of curvilinear patterns in one of them, and of angular shapes in the other. However, a tendency to rigidity and angularity in the curvilinear elements in the objects just discussed converts the pattern made by the statue, bowl, plate, vase and flowers into an integral part of the preponderantly angular pattern made by the parallel and interpenetrating planes of the base of the statue, the various sections of the table, and the subdivisions of the floor and walls. Moreover, the angular pattern in the subdivisions of the floor and side-wall contains rhythmic echoes of the curvilinear element, notably in the pictures on the wall, in the large pink area of the landscape, and in the green drapery hanging over the easel. Unity is further maintained between the two contrasting main sections by their common band-like character, their participation in the in-and-out thrust and counterthrust of the total organization, the quality of their color, and the active part each plays in the dramatic rhythms of light-and-dark color-contrast.

The color throughout is deep, rich and translucent, and a glow like that of stained glass is attained by Matisse's familiar interplay of one set of colors against another. His usual procedure is varied here, however, in that the pinks, greens, tans and light blues function as relatively small bright and light units scattered upon large expanses of dark deep blue and dark reddish brown. All these colors are extraordinarily luminous in themselves, and their judicious placing in relation to each other makes each set of them serve as a foil and reinforcement to the other. Thus each brings out by contrast of tone the luminous brightness or the deep translucency of the adjacent color. This reciprocal effect is particularly noticeable in the background and side-wall: the window, the long band composed of the picture over the door and the landscape, the picture hanging on the wall to the right, and the green drapery below it, are all set into and surrounded by the continuous expanse of the deep dark blue. A similar reciprocal color-reinforcement occurs, but in a different color-scheme, in the bright and light pink, blue, green, orange and tan units on the table, which are set off by their deep black outlines and the relatively dark red-brown table. That is, this red-brown area serves as a sort of color-background to the differently colored objects upon it; it is itself, in turn, set off by the surrounding deep blue which forms a continuous sheet-like setting to the total picture. This setting, unlike similar settings in the traditional styles of painting, is made more complex and dramatically patterned by sharply angular projections into it of various areas abruptly contrasting in color and degree of illumination. That is, this deep blue area, while receding immediately from the lower right corner, branches off to the left and right into angular oblique, vertical and horizontal geometrical areas; these extend toward the left below the table, upward between the easel and door, toward the right above the easel, toward the left below the window, downward to the left of the bowl, and directly upward between the door and the window. This emphasis upon both space itself and its patterned arrangement is greater than that to be found in Matisse's other adaptations of the traditional sheetlike setting.*

The pattern made by the two contrasting sets of colors is, more than usually in Matisse, a direct and definite contrast of positive light and dark areas. Brightness in the color-ensemble is maintained in spite of the greater extent of relatively dark color-areas, and the effect of many colors is obtained by an active interplay of tones of only four main colors, blue, brown, green and pink. Both the interplay and activity of these colors are reinforced by their judicious repetition as tones in various parts of the canvas, and by broad outlines of contrasting color that make their shape predominantly either curvilinear or angular. Line, consequently, because of its accentuated width and its intensity of tone, functions as color, as a factor in the contrasts of light and dark, and as an agent in the formation of internal patterns in many of the objects. Line thus creates another element of contrast, that between broad definitely shaped areas and those with small internal patterns.

The design as a whole reveals an abstract strength and power probably never exceeded by Matisse. This is due primarily to the reinforcement of each of the plastic means by the others. Line is an active participant in the rhythms, contrasts and patterns of color and of light and dark; it contributes also to a perspective mainly conceived as a set of relations between planes of color, which in turn are parts of a well-knit bizarre pattern. Vice versa, narrow bands of color function as components of the linear patterns, as planes in space, and as determinants of spatial intervals. Color and light work in equally close coöperation: every area is a

*Cf., e.g., 66, 88.

part of the color-pattern and also of the pattern of light and dark; in other words, the relations between areas are at one and the same time relations of color and of degree of light.

Furthermore, not only does each of the plastic means contribute to the effect of the others, but the units that result from this reciprocal action all contribute to the pervasive rich, luminous color-power of a bizarre and strong pattern which is expressive as well as unusually decorative. Much of this expressive power is due to the creative use of many traditions. The design achieves the deep luminous richness of stained glass, partly by the intrinsic quality of the color and partly by the emphasis upon broad linear contour. The latter, in its varied use, is reminiscent of the Byzantines, the early Hindus, Cézanne, and the cubists; this is true likewise of the general pattern and its subsidiary units, and also of the varied adaptation of planes to decorative and expressive purposes. The tonguelike projection through the table-leg in the center foreground corresponds to the familiar projecting knife, spoon or other elongated object found in the work of Chardin and the Dutch still-life painters of the seventeenth century. This effect in Matisse becomes an integral part of a rhythmic pattern containing other abrupt thrusts into space, such as the corner of the table, the base of the easel, and the raised elbow of the statue.

The design represents a very original rendering of a quite familiar theme. The arrangement of volumes in space follows closely that found in a considerable number of traditions, but the means by which spatial organization is achieved, solidity rendered, and the individual units brought together in a unified form, are found in their combination nowhere except in Matisse. They consist of a highly rhythmic and colorful pattern, in which the colors have great intrinsic charm, relations of sensuous harmony and contrast which powerfully enhance this charm, and a reinforcement by varied, sensitive and rhythmic line which makes the pattern not only ornamental but expressive, i.e., capable of conveying the essential qualities of massiveness and roominess. Light is no less active, both as infusing an added richness and glow in color, and emphasizing the conviction of spatial intervals. The bizarre and exotic decorative design, in other words, reveals a substratum of solid reality which makes the picture as convincing and powerful as it is vivid and charming.*

*For comparison with another version of the same subject-matter see chapter on Thematic Variation, pp. 164–165.

RIFFIAN* (56)

A large seated figure, extending the total length of the canvas, is worked into a setting of background and floor by a bizarre and vivid patchwork-pattern of daringly contrasted bright color-areas. The background consists of large expanses of blue, cadmium yellow, emerald green, so related and contrasted that their ensemble forms a brightly patterned setting of stripes and bands, the direction of which is generally vertical. This upper half of the setting, the brightest and most luminous large section of the picture, emphasizes by contrast the shape, color and tone of the figure silhouetted against it, and also the large expanse of the magenta floor. The sharp line of contact of the floor with the background and figure makes an irregular angular pattern containing very unusual color-contrasts. The floor as a whole is broken up into oblongs, broad bands and bizarre angular areas by the vertical brown legs and oblique yellow sandals, and by the brown box upon which the figure sits. Thus unity between the two contrasting sections of the setting—the background and the floor—is established by rhythmic repetition of the varied geometrical shapes of their constituent areas.

The theme of bands and stripes is carried out also in the figure but in this they are arranged in a more complicated pattern, they extend in all directions, and tend to be curvilinear; they thus form a contrast with the preponderantly straight and vertical bands of the setting. Similarly with rhythmic contrasts of color: the green, yellow, blue and red of the setting reappear, with modification of tone, size, relationship and plastic function, in the internal color-pattern of the figure. The head, for instance, is a patchwork of green and yellow planes; the green coat is embellished by punctuation with clusters of red, blue and yellow dabs surrounded by spots of bare canvas, which form small sparkling starlike units resembling sunbursts.

The rosette or starlike shape of these small multicolored clusters is a motif repeated in various other parts of the figure: in the radiating pattern made by the intersection of the forearms with the stripe down the middle of the coat; at the junction of the lapels or sides of the cape; and in the shadows of the folds of the sleeve at the right as they meet the arm and the decorative horizontal band at the elbow. Also, the bell-shaped outline of the

*Illustration, p. 266.

388   APPENDIX

shoulders unites with the bands of shadow and light in the green undergarment to form a fanlike pattern radiating from the collar. The star-motif occurs again in the facial features, but in a minor degree of completeness.

The patchwork-pattern of the total picture is the framework for a set of dynamic relationships of color-planes and volumes in deep space. Viewed from a distance of about forty feet, the whole figure thrusts itself as a large volume in the foreground and is entirely surrounded by roomy space. This spaciousness, in addition to its independent appeal, emphasizes the drama of the colors: i.e., the contrasts are no longer merely between juxtaposed areas but, because of the introduction of deep space, between areas in front of and behind each other.

The figure, perceived as a planelike volume in space, constitutes the focus of a set of large interpenetrating planes that move in all directions. The figure as a whole is an upright plane placed at a slightly oblique angle to the plane of the picture, with its right side more remote than its left. The striped draperies or screens on either side of the background are also upright planes placed at oblique angles to the plane of the picture; they contrast in direction to each other and to the plane of the figure, and they converge toward the large blue and yellow planes in the extreme background. The latter are more or less parallel to the plane of the picture, as is also the plane of the box upon which the figure sits. Counterbalancing this series of upright planes, the plane of the floor moves upward in horizontal-oblique perspective and closes up the box-like arrangement of planes and space which surround the bulk of the figure and set it off. Like the large units, the subsidiary sections—the feet, legs, box, parts of floor, arms, light and dark areas of coat, cape, undergarment and face—all are planes set in deep space and contrasting in direction. The face, an original combination of traits from the Byzantines and Cézanne, is drawn and modeled by broad planes of contrasting colors arranged in a highly decorative pattern; its wedgelike planes come forward and counterbalance the receding and converging main planes of the background. The theme of subdivided large planes is developed also in the background: its green and yellow stripes are planes set close together, and the broad areas of blue and yellow are also distinguishable planes.

None of the areas is in reality uniform in color: each is mottled with light that intensifies the tone and creates subtle internal patterns. Technique is an important aid to these effects: brush strokes of thin and thick paint, and small spots of bare canvas modulate the tone within the individual areas of color and avoid surface-monotony. Almost everywhere the contrasting color-areas meet through the intermediation of a linear contour of bare canvas that functions also as light and contributes greatly to the liveliness of the pattern and of the entire composition. Each area here, in contrast for example to "Music Lesson" (64), is a positive color in itself; i.e., there are no blacks, grays, nor neutral tones. In this sense it is akin to "Joy of Life" (31); but in contrast to the large swirling movement of the latter, this picture conveys the idea of the rigidity generally connected with inanimate things. This static rigidity, however, is made to live by the activity of color, line, light and space, worked into themes of areas, bands, stars, all integrated in a form in itself expressive of character and individuality. The composite effect of the figure and setting is that of a highly decorative patchwork of patterns resulting from the interplay of color-contrasts and linear elements. This type of organization requires extensive distortion for the sake of a form which, though primarily decorative, also expresses the values of simplicity, bigness, exotic quality, vivid plastic drama, static pose, and the character of the sitter.

MUSIC LESSON* (64)

This large canvas represents a Matisse version of familiar Oriental effects of compartmental color-pattern, in which the drama of color-contrasts results from the alternation of areas of relatively neutral tones with areas of bright colors few in number and large in expanse. It differs from his other interpretations of Oriental traditions† in that most of the large areas are decorated with accentuated linear patterns which break up their uniformity and diminish the degree of color-contrast. The color-scheme is light but not particularly bright. The few bright colors used—green, magenta-pink and brownish yellow—are toned down by their interplay with numerous grays—brownish gray, bluish gray, pearly gray-white and grayish black. The color-contrasts are positive, but are less daring and exotic than is usual in Matisse's pictures of Oriental character.

*Illustration, p. 271.   †Cf., e.g., 31, 51, 56.

The organization of the design results in a rhythmic movement of color-areas and linear patterns, which ascends directly from the lower foreground to the top of the composition and slightly recedes through the successive planes in objects, figures and vista of landscape. A continuous succession of colored bands and stripes, appearing in the landscape and the objects and figures in the room, leads the eye back and forth from one part of the picture to another, and so unites in one plastic design the two contrasting elements—the interior and the outdoor scene. In this unity, background and foreground are equally active, much as in Fra Filippo Lippi's "Virgin Adoring Child" (326a).

An outstanding feature of the design is its sharp division into vertical and horizontal elements, the constant interrelation of which makes of the total pattern an irregular checkerboard, decoratively varied and enhanced by numerous curvilinear and arabesque motifs. In its width, the picture is divided into three broad vertical sections that extend from the top to the bottom. The central section, comprising landscape, balcony and floor, is enframed to the left by the long shutter and the seated man, to the right by the picture hanging on the wall, the two figures, and the piano. This vertical movement of line and mass is one of the major themes of the organization and it counterbalances the horizontality of numerous oblongs, which constitutes another main motif. Indeed, this interplay of vertical and horizontal pervades practically all areas of the canvas; stress upon one or the other of the two, and the proportion in which they are combined, determine the individual character of each unit. For instance, the oblong brownish-yellow floor in the middle of the foreground is of decidedly vertical position, but because of the lines, slightly darker than the floor itself, which divide it into oblique-horizontal bands, it assumes a horizontal aspect also, and enters into relations of sequence and rhythm with the other units and areas scattered everywhere, in which the same combination of aspects appears. The rhythmic horizontal bands in the floor are only one set of the numerous horizontal units which are repeated throughout the entire composition in relation to vertical units. Both types, horizontal and vertical, occur as lines, bands and oblongs, and they vary in length, width, color and relationship to each other. Further examples of this characteristic of the design will illustrate its importance as a fundamental principle of the organization.

The radiator, separated from and related to the area of the

floor by a gray-green horizontal band of shadow, is a horizontally-placed oblong cube divided in its upright surface by a pattern of vertical stripes alternately green, white and bluish gray. Thus the horizontal and the vertical, present in both floor and radiator, are in each contrasted with one another in direction, color and function. That is, the floor, a brown oblong plane, is a vertical arrangement of horizontal units which, vaguely suggestive of steps or rungs of a ladder, move collectively in the same upward-backward direction; on the other hand, the radiator is a white-green volume with its upright plane a horizontal succession of vertical stripes. The pattern of these stripes is more pronounced than the corresponding pattern in the floor, and they are contrasted with each other in color, in light and dark, and particularly in the spatial relation of their component narrow planes that move in and out, at an oblique angle to each other, like the folds of an accordion. The bluish-gray upper plane of the radiator is again a narrow horizontal band of color, but through the medium of its faintly-patterned oblique stripes, it becomes an oblique-horizontal plane. The latter recedes from the top of the upright plane of the radiator, and connects the latter with the upright plane of the balcony-railing, in the manner of the tread and upright of a step, i.e., of planes placed at right angles to each other.

At the junction of the radiator and balcony, a set of parallel horizontal stripes of grayish tones function as receding narrow planes immediately back of the radiator. They also, by their spatial distribution, form a series of horizontal folds which may be perceived either as coming forward, wedgelike, or as receding at the line of contact of the stripes. Consequently, they are related in color and plastic effect to the foldlike rhythms noted in the upright section of the radiator, to which they are also contrasted in direction and degree of clean-cutness. At the same time, by their direction and linear character, these stripes participate in the horizontal rhythms which move upward from the plane of the floor to the top of the canvas, through the successive oblongs of balcony-railing, ground, pond and upper parts of the landscape; they also extend to right and left through the numerous horizontal stripes, bands and oblongs in the area of the piano, the picture hanging on the wall, the figure in the foreground, and the shutter.

In accordance with the general theme—the interrelation of vertical and horizontal elements—all the horizontal oblongs just mentioned acquire in various ways a certain degree of vertical quality also: by their position in space, as with the upright planes of balcony-railing and music-rack; by their internal pattern, as in the green book on the piano; or by being placed on top of one another to build up a large vertical area, as in the components of the floor and also of the landscape as a whole.

Another sort of relationship between vertical and horizontal elements makes of the central vertical portion of the composition, from the bottom of the canvas to the top, an organization of planes moving in and out as they ascend in steplike or foldlike formation. Thus in the landscape the successive horizontal oblongs of gray ground, brown pond and upper section of green foliage are related in a manner somewhat similar to that of the folds in the radiator, but to which they are placed at right angles. Immediately above the railing, the horizontal oblong made up of the gray ground, the brown-red-and-tan upper part of the woman's body, and the bright green patch to the right of her chair, is an upright plane which forms an angle with an adjoining horizontal band, the brown surface of the pond; the latter, a curvilinear oblong, recedes in horizontal-oblique direction from its line of contact with the gray ground. Above the pond, the upper section of the landscape is so modulated in tone that the area appears divided, at the level of the statue's raised elbow, into two horizontal oblongs, one of which includes the statue and the bunch of large leaves, and the other the bush of foliage above the statue and the slightly indicated palms. The lower of these oblongs moves directly upward from the level of the pond; and the upper, containing the bush and palms, tends to recede.

Most of these broad planes are subdivided into subsidiary planes which have their own plastic functions. In the upright plane made by the horizontal-oblong area of the balcony, the arabesque of the railing proper is in a plane in front of that occupied by the black-and-brown garment of the woman, and this latter plane is in turn in front of that of the gray ground. These three planes, closely packed together, contrast with each other in pattern, shape and color. Similarly, the area of the pond is internally varied by patterns of horizontal and vertical elements which include the falling water at the upper left, the green plant at the lower right, the modulations of light in the area of the water, and the curvilinear horizontal broad lines made by the ripples in the center and by the leaves at the lower edge. Thus patterned, the deep brown area of the pond stands out in sharp contrast to the relatively uniform

light gray area below it and to the complex bright green section
above. Furthermore, this brown area is made an integral part of
the design by the rhythmic duplication of its constituents in the
pattern of other compositional units: its horizontal and vertical elements, for instance, are a particular variation of the all-pervasive
motif of stripes; the curvilinear-horizontal lines of the ripples
form a flowerlike arrangement that recurs with greater emphasis
in the bushes and statue; the general color of the area is repeated in
the woman's blouse, in the floor and, in lighter or darker tones, in
the frame of the picture hanging on the wall, in the violin, in the
chair on the lower left, and in the color of the flesh. Still further,
the curvilinear shape of the pond is one of the units in the rhythm
of decorative arabesques present in the balcony, the music-rack,
the violin, the bushes and the statue, and these arabesques are
echoed in the side of the piano, the legs of the man, and the figure
in the picture hanging on the wall. In each instance this curvilinear
pattern establishes a contrast with adjacent rectilinear patterns.

The variety of movement of interpenetrating planes culminates
in the organization of the green upper part of the landscape. This
section is made of five main units: the statue, the greenish-blue
bush above it, the group of large green leaves to the right of the
statue, and the two palmlike linear units at the upper right and
upper center of the landscape. The bizarre composition of this
total green section is so intricate that a detailed description is necessary to elucidate its plastic kinship with the parts of the picture
already analyzed.

The lower of the two bands, previously referred to, which form
this green section of landscape, is arranged in four main areas
or planes which extend in and out, from side to side, and therefore repeat, on a larger scale and in different color-scheme, the
folds of the radiator. Two of these planes form a pocket which
encloses and walls-in the statue; these two planes are in turn subdivided into narrow stripes by linear modulations of light and by
the pattern of brush strokes. The rhythm of the vertical stripes on
the plane to the left of the statue is continued in the pattern of
parallel vertical bands in the plane of the blue-gray shutter. In the
plane to the right of the statue, the modulations of color, effected
by elongated brush strokes, result in a series of narrow strips of
light and dark green, arranged in a fanlike pattern of triangles
radiating from a focus of shadow back of the statue. The outer
contour of this fanlike pattern meets the plane made by the large

leaves, itself a series of closely superposed parallel planes arranged in a rosette-pattern. The composite plane of these leaves recedes from the center of the entire green oblong toward the right and narrower part of the rosette, and forms a sort of vertical wedge with the fanlike unit. At the right of this rosette of leaves, the landscape seems to come forward again toward the plane of the window in an encircling movement which partly enframes the area of the pond, and is continued around the lower edge of the pond by several small units of foliage which carry on the enframing effect. In this latter section of the landscape between the rosette of leaves and the window, the irregular ribbonlike brush strokes make a pattern of small ill-defined triangles or pyramids that stand in space like a series of tents back of each other. This triangular motif is echoed in the fanlike plane to the right of the statue, and also, with greater linear emphasis, in the pattern of the palms in the topmost section of the landscape. In brief, the total horizontal green oblong which includes the statue and rosette of leaves carries out the general design of stripes and bands functioning as planes in a foldlike space-composition.

Furthermore, the above-described rosette made by the group of large leaves repeats, in the upper part of the picture, the element of curvilinear decoration, noted in the pond, the balcony, the piano-rack, the violin, and so on. Various other forms of the rosette occur again in the statue, the bush and the palms. In each of these, the rosette-pattern is differently constituted; in the statue, for instance, it is formed by the head, shoulder, breasts and arms, all radiating from the neck in a compact composition of quasi-voluminous planes. The curvilinear rhythms of this rosette are repeated in the blue-green bush above the statue, but in the bush the formation of the rosette is less complete and its chief constituents are a series of short, interrupted curves and superposed planes which radiate and are organized in a patterned rounded volume. In the large leaves to the right of the statue, the rosette is more definitely shaped, and, as already noted, is constituted by a set of large parallel planes. In the palms at the center and on the right, curvilinear contours rather than masses or planes are pronounced. Their pattern, however, is organized also in sets of superposed planes, which, when seen in relation to the group of leaves, the bush and the statue, acquire a sufficiently voluminous character to function, together with these more pronounced masses, in a rhythmic beat of volumes in space. This rhythm of volumes in space, in contrast to the rhythm of planes in the lower part of the picture, characterizes the entire green section of the landscape. In other words, while Matisse repeats in the upper part of the canvas the steplike plan noted in the lower, he transfers the emphasis from planes to volumes: the foreground is made chiefly of planes with only a tendency toward organization in volumes, while the landscape proper is constituted mainly by volumes subdivided into planes.

Foreground and landscape—indeed, all sections of the picture—are organically integrated in a single plastic composition by all-pervasive rhythms of patterns and planes. These rhythms are responsible also for the extensive, intricate and extremely varied series of plastic relationships. For example, the accentuated lines in the broadly drawn figure in the picture hanging on the wall form a pattern of stripes and bands and repeat also the angular curvilinear pattern of the palms and the rosettes in several other units of the composition. The statue is an arabesque-formation of volumes which counterbalances a similar pattern of the planes of the figure on the balcony. Again, the areas of color in the seated figure on the left constitute not only a steplike arrangement of planes but also a rosette-pattern focalized in the hands, and in which the linear elements are accentuated. A further instance of the pervasive rhythmic organization is found in the man's hands, in his coat, shirt and tie, and in the light and shade in the modeling of his face and hair, all of which are stripes, lines and bands of color.

This pervasive repetition of decorative motifs is perhaps even more noticeable in the part of the picture occupied by the piano and the objects upon it. This entire unit is a series of successive horizontal oblongs placed one above the other, which contrast in color, size and treatment, but are related in shape and pattern to units in various other parts of the canvas. For example, the accentuated linear arabesque of the music-rack, repeated with slight variations in the violin and its cloth and case, is, in effect, continued by the pattern of the balcony, and is echoed in the statue, palms, bushes. The green music-book, sharply contrasting with the magenta-pink top of the piano, is a rhythmic note in relation to the color of the landscape; the horizontal and vertical stripes and bands in its subdivisions carry out the pattern which pervades the entire design, as do also the vertical bandlike subtle modulations of light in the horizontal magenta oblong below the violin. Again, the leg of the piano together with the long curvilinear sweep of the side of the piano balances a similar unit formed on the left by the arm and leg of the seated man. Also, the violin and its cloth and case form a series of closely-packed horizontal planes parallel to the plane of the piano-top, the green music-book, the pond, the top of the radiator and the floor. Moreover, the closely-superposed planes on the piano form collectively the tread of a step of which the piano-rack is the riser. This rack, the blue cover of the sheet of music, and the two figures at the piano, form another group of compact parallel vertical planes which repeat the already-noted unit of planes in the balcony, seated woman and gray ground.

This interrelation of the various sections of the picture is made more interesting by the intricate and bizarre treatment of space. Deep space is distorted in the familiar manner of the Persian miniatures so that foreground and background are brought to a more uniform level, and distant units function in the pattern as actively as do those in the foreground. As Matisse carries out this Oriental treatment of space, he maintains more adequate representation of distance than do the Persians, at the same time achieving a more effective pattern by the activity of the units in the space-organization.*

This original treatment of space, in conjunction with the decorative organization already described, makes of the total composition an enormous rosette radiating in space from the figure on the balcony diagonally downward and forward to the man on the left; upward and backward to the statue and bushes; upward and forward to the head of the girl at the piano and the reproduced picture at the upper right corner; and downward and forward to the right to the unit of violin and case. In turn, each of these radiating units may be conceived as the apex of a pyramid of which the right and left points of the base are two of the other principal masses. Whichever of these masses is selected as the focus of the space-organization, a zigzag movement leads from one mass to the other through three-dimensional space. For instance, the observer may start at the lower left corner—the figure of the man—then move to the woman on the balcony, then to the girl at the piano, and to the picture on the wall; or, from the man at the left to the woman on the balcony, the statue, the rosette of large leaves and the mass of the bush. Or else, starting with the statue, the movement may lead to the figure on the balcony, then to the girl at the piano, the boy at the piano and end at the picture on the wall. Inasmuch as each of these focal units or landmarks is com-

*Cf., e.g., 346.

posed of more or less accentuated planes, the latter participate also in this complex organization in space, and, by their differences in color, shape, size and direction, they contribute much to the rhythmic contrasts which are all-pervasive in the design.

Another factor in unification is the disposition and interrelation of the large component planes of the total organization. An inverted triangle of striped and relatively simple oblong planes is formed by the picture on the wall in the upper right, the area of the floor and radiator in the lower center, and the shutter in the upper left. This large triangular formation interlocks with another formed by three complex units patterned with curvilinear arabesques—the landscape at the apex, the man at the left, and the piano and figures at the right. These two triangular organizations, by virtue of the different location in space of their respective apex and base, make of background and foreground a unified pattern of contrasting elements.

The whole picture is flooded with light in the manner of the impressionists: so pervasive, indeed, is the union of light with color that in the general luminosity the particular areas in which light falls are not immediately obvious, and really dramatic contrasts of light and dark scarcely appear at all. The all-embracing light-pattern, as active as any other unifying factor in the composition and inextricably bound up with the color, line and space, is also impressionistic in some degree, but is modified by the influence of Japanese prints in that the areas, unlike those of the impressionists, are well defined in contour. Aside from making a pattern of its own, light also makes specific contributions to the compositional functions of the other elements. Adjacent compartmental color-areas are illuminated in different degree, so that a light-shadow contrast, rarely vivid but quite definite, aids in their differentiation. Several of the horizontal areas, e.g., the book of music, the pond, and the part of the piano-top which occupies the extreme lower left corner, are subtly patterned by vertical bands of light and shadow; and similar bands, beside carrying out the general linear pattern, contribute to the modeling of the radiator and the face of the seated figure on the left. Small irregular spots of bare canvas which function as light, placed around the contour of the music-rack and the railing of the balcony, in the green foliage at the edge of the pond, about the arms of the chair near the lower left corner, and in several other units of the composition, by their contact with comparatively positive color, add a sparkling quality to these areas of the canvas, at the same time as they also carry out the general rosette-motif.

The study of this picture in comparison with the traditions upon which Matisse has drawn reveals his status as a creative artist. What he took from the main sources of his inspiration, Persian miniatures and Japanese prints, is modified by borrowings from the early Egyptians and Hindus, from the impressionists and Cézanne. The Persian derivations, noted in the treatment of space, have been altered by the steplike arrangement of the planes, which yields an effect of dynamic movement of volumes in space. From the Japanese prints is drawn the color-scheme of bright, exotic, light colors set off by large units of neutral grays; also the decorative patterns of bands and stripes contrasted with patterns of arabesques, and the decorative use of actual script. Each of these traits has been significantly modified. The colors, for example, are more mottled with light and more luminous than in the prints; the framework of stripes, bands and arabesques is more varied, less mechanically executed; the linear patterns are broader and more emphatic in their movements and rhythms; and the miniature-quality of the prints is replaced by a looser, broader treatment derived from Manet.

Manet's influence pervades the whole of the drawing and modeling, but simplification is carried further, and wherever it occurs it is combined with elements taken from other traditions. The statue, for example, is an organic synthesis of adaptations from Manet, the Byzantines, and Hindu and Negro sculpture; the bush and leaves are treated by elements reminiscent of Manet, the other impressionists, and Cézanne; in the woman on the balcony the drawing is a merging of the silhouette-effect of Egyptian and early Greek figures with Manet's broad and epigrammatic rendering of essentials. The important fact about these traditional derivations is that they are not mechanical or isolated replicas of the originals: the modifications introduced are invariably directed to bringing each unit into harmony with the general principle of the design. In other words, Matisse has created a new form out of the raw materials of the traditional elements above mentioned; and his ability to effect an infinite variety in the proportions of the traditional forms used, together with his sensitiveness to contextual relationships and his ability to weave diversified units into an integrated design, make of this picture something new in the tradition of painting.

THREE SISTERS* (69–70–71)

These three pictures, into each of which enter three figures approximately the same, form a single composition unified by a continuous rhythmic sequence of the constituent units. Its framework is formed by two intertwining triangles which extend through the triptych as a whole. The first has its apex in the turban of the standing figure in the central panel, and its base extends between the extreme lower right and left corners of the other two panels; the second triangle, inverted, has its apex in the smallest figure in the central panel, and its other angles in the tall standing figures on the right and left of the side-panels. The two triangles interlock in space with a combined lateral, up-and-down and in-and-out movement; considered in relation to depth, the organization as a whole, starting from the two small figures in the central panel, recedes to left and right, and forms a horizontal ellipse by which the large central standing figure is encircled as though by a belt. This ellipse extends most definitely through the heads of the figures, as shown in the accompanying diagram; the heads are ovals, roughly vertical or vertical-oblique in direction, and from them the figures seem to hang like suspended masses. The general movement 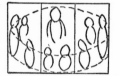 of the ellipse has variations of which that in the left panel is typical: here the ascending line through the heads, instead of receding steadily, comes forward in the standing figure; this alternation of advance and regression adds activity and rhythm to the movement as a whole. The variety is increased by vivid contrasts in color, tone and size between the heads and the bodies to which they belong; but unity within each figure is maintained by the oval shape common to the head and the remainder of the mass, and also by the repetition in each, as regards both constituent parts and general form of organization, of the abstract triangularity of the general framework.

In each separate canvas, the three figures form a pyramidal composition of semi-voluminous masses in compact space, with variations between the figures in size, color, and position. Each of the three pyramids is differently placed upon the canvas; in the left panel, the apex of the pyramid is in the left in the foreground; in the central panel, it is in the middle in the background; in the right panel, it is on the right in an intermediate plane. These dif-

*Illustrations, pp. 272, 273.

ferences, however, taken in their ensemble, are the very factors which establish a balance between the two contrasting side-panels, and give to their masses a harmonious relationship with those in the central canvas. The composition, which as a whole is comparatively simple and close to conventional types, is extensively varied by differences in the position of the units, in their coloring, and in the rendering of their detail. The tall standing figures at the left and right of the triptych, for example, which in general balance each other, are quite similar in the patterns formed by their oval heads, curved shoulders, oval-oblong bodies, and the pointed projections below. Conjoined with these points of resemblance, there are numerous points of contrast: one figure is viewed from the front, the other from the rear; the projections are folds of drapery in one, feet in the other; the V-shaped pattern of the neck in the figure on the right is replaced, in the corresponding figure in the left panel, by a similarly shaped portion of garment; the figure on the left is in front of its companions, that on the right midway between them. The sharpest point of contrast between these two is in color and in the relation of their color to that of their background. The figure on the left is chiefly of vivid green and canary-yellow against a background of reddish brown, gray-green yellow, rose-lavender, tan, purple, and white; that on the right, of prevailingly dark magenta, black, blue, and bluish gray, on a background of grayish blue-green, light green, and yellow.

The color of these two figures also has a distinctive relationship to the color-design of the triptych as a whole. This color-design has three outstanding motifs: green, purple, and tan-brown in a progressive increase in extent of employment and intensity of hue. The green, pale and of subsidiary importance in the right panel, appears more extensively with greater vividness in the central picture, and reaches its maximum of intensity in the left panel; the prominence of the purple and the direction of its movement are exactly reversed; and the brown-and-tan, concentrated in the central picture, is diffused throughout the side-panels. A fourth motif, less pronounced and chiefly important as a quiet note counterbalancing the drama of the other three, is provided by the large expanse of comparatively uniform gray which fills the entire undecorated background of the central panel. This gray does not reappear in the side-panels, but the comparatively quiet tones of grayish blue and green in the right panel, grayish blue in the left,

and, to a lesser degree, grayish notes of pearly-white tone throughout the triptych, are allied to it in sensuous quality and compositional function. These four separate motifs in the color-design are
interwoven to give a pervasive sense of color-movement and
color-contrast to the picture as a whole, and also to unify the
three separate panels.

The throbbing beat of color-rhythm which results from the
action of intertwined color-themes is heightened by a series of
relatively small black areas which are judiciously distributed through
the three panels. The black is extraordinarily rich, deep, and luminous, it is varied in tone from a black proper to a warm brown,
and occasionally set off by interspersed dots or flashes of white.
Within the general black areas the light-shadow contrast is usually
between lighter and darker shades of black, and these contrasts
echo those between the areas as a whole and adjacent areas of
bright color. Sometimes, however, it is spots of bare canvas that
give the effect of light, and the consequently heightened contrast
results in a glitter or sparkle, as in the star-shaped motif in the
shoes, the tabouret, and the statuette in the left panel, in virtually
all the eyes, and in the magenta-and-black blouse on the extreme
right. The areas of black are varied also in shape: in the hair, for
example, their predominantly ovoid form relates them to the oval
motif in the design as a whole, which reappears in many other
details; in the left panel, the two long undulating bands of uniformly rich black hair are rhythmically related in shape to the
stockings and shoes, the piece of Negro sculpture, and the arms and
frame of the chair. In general, the compositional effect of the black
passages depends both upon their individual activity and the
reinforcement which they bring to the other factors in the organization.

The color-areas, in the main, are large, broad and compartmental, with internal patterns of brush strokes or variations in
thickness of pigment to produce light-effects, though scattered
among them are occasional quite elaborately decorated areas, of
which the blouses in some of the figures, and the tabouret and
armchair in the left panel are examples. These make a note of contrast with more uniform areas, partly by forming a patterned
organization of their own, but chiefly by their directly perceptible
difference from the adjacent compartments. The chief contribution to the drama of the triptych, however, is made by the differences between the hue or tint of the areas, and by their placing in

space. Characteristic contrasts in direction are those between the vertical figures, chair, statuette, pictures and walls, and the oblique-horizontal mantlepiece, book, plate, etc., in the left panel; in the right panel there is a balancing drama in the intersecting planes and lines of the floor and chair, and of the figures and the reproduced picture in the background. To provide contrast to both individual space-compositions, and to furnish the element of stability essential to the space-organization of the group of pictures as a whole, the central panel is organized with comparative simplicity, in large parallel vertical planes; the smaller planes at different angles, such as those formed by the fan, arms and hands, make only a minor note of contrast. Thus in spatial arrangement, as in color, this panel is relatively tranquil.

Throughout the triptych, linear effects are distinctly accentuated and widely varied. To bring the linear pattern as a whole to a commensurate degree of compositional activity with those of color and space, the contours of objects and areas are made clearly per-ceptible, either by broad dark actual lines or by such means as areas of bare canvas, or contact of contrasting color-compartments. Many whole areas, the statuette, for example, or strands of hair, folds of drapery, arms and legs, are so drawn as to function compositionally no less as bands than as compartments of color.

This simplified and distorted drawing bridges the gap between illustration and decorative design: while giving enough information to make the figures interesting as human beings, it reshapes them in a form suitable for inclusion in a highly ornamental ordering of color-planes. In the hands, for example, each distortion serves a definite compositional end: in the central canvas, one hand with six fingers makes a rhythm with the many-lined pattern of a fan; the hand holding the fan resembles a fin, but in shape it is related to the sleeve and various sections of the gown, together with which it forms a rosette-pattern radiating from the wrist; in the panel on the right, the hand with only two fingers looks more like a lobster's claw than a human hand, but the pattern made by this distortion harmonizes with the adjacent linear patterns of the cuff, collar, face and arm; likewise, the right hand of the seated figure in the picture on the left is an integral part of the pattern of the turban. No detail is rendered literally or without reference to the form as a whole, but in none are the liberties taken so great that the rendering sinks to the status of meaningless abstract pattern.

The influences most apparent in this triptych are the Japanese, the Byzantine, and Manet's. From the Japanese prints come the strident exotic colors in flat compartmental areas, alternating with dull neutral areas, and making accentuated linear patterns; the universal drama of vivid contrasts, to which contribute the positive notes of black and the difference between patterned and unpatterned areas; and the compositional fluidity which makes of the three panels a single unified picture. However, here as usual, Matisse's treatment of color and line is less mechanical than the Japanese, and his modification of color-areas by brush strokes and different thicknesses of pigment avoids their comparative monotony, as do his looser, more varied and more expressive linear contours. The composition as a whole is more close-knit and the movement more active and forcible, so that instead of the daintiness of the prints the picture shows a pulsating rhythmic sweep of color-areas in comparatively deep space, reminiscent of that in the mosaics of San Vitale at Ravenna. Japanese miniature drawing is entirely discarded, and the broad lines and generalized forms represent an extensive interfusion of elements from the mosaics in general and from Manet. However, the elements taken from Manet are not simply added to the others, but are themselves modified: the simplified masses are more definitely constituents in a compartmental pattern, the areas of bare canvas have a more precise shape, and there is more vividness and drama in their contrast with areas of black. The blacks themselves add to the lustre of Manet's the decorative and compositional function exercised in Japanese prints by a dull and monotonous black.*

Each unit in the triptych is thus a fusion of elements derived from different traditions; all are reworked in Matisse's own distinctive manner, with specific provision made, as noted above, for their compositional unification; but in each the traditional ingredients are mixed in different proportions, so that variety as well as unity is assured. The heads, for example, in spite of their common derivation from Manet and the Byzantines, are clearly differentiated from one another. Accentuated linear patterns in the facial features of the seated figure in the right panel testify to the predominance of the Byzantine element, but the face next to it is more nearly pure Manet;† in the left panel, the face of the central figure contains a version of the pattern which in Negro sculpture is formed by grooves,‡ but which here is simplified as in Manet,

*Cf., e.g., 358a. †Cf. illustrations, p. 273.
‡Cf. illustrations, p. 273.

404 APPENDIX

and rendered by a linear drawing like the Byzantine. The resemblance to Negro sculpture reappears in the masklike face in the left of the central composition, though it is less pronounced; the other two heads in the same panel are a combination of Manet and the Byzantines, though again in different proportions. In this panel, the silhouetted setting of the large figure in Oriental garb against a flat background of uniform neutral tone, is vaguely reminiscent of the effect frequently obtained by a similar practice in Mughal-Persian or Indian miniatures.*

From the foregoing survey, it will be seen that though these panels say things plastically different about substantially the same subject-matter, the plastic statement of each is a continuation of that of the other two, just as the later movements of a symphony or acts of a drama continue the general theme and spirit of the earlier. In other words, each part in this triptych makes its distinctive but harmonious contribution to the form of the total design, which is a novel and individual expression of the abstract values of bigness, simplicity, drama, rhythm and color-power.

BLUE VILLA† (72)

A villa set in the midst of a landscape is in this picture the focus of a compact organization of color-rhythms in space. Masses of foliage, bushes, branches, hill, clouds and sky, arranged as balancing units at the right, left, top and bottom, participate in a continuous undulatory movement of contrasting color-units. They enframe and set off by contrast the central group of relatively rigid geometrical planes, which make up the mass of the building. Contrast is as pronounced between these divisions of the framelike landscape as it is between them collectively and the villa: each division, that is to say, has in addition to its specific illustrative force, a distinctive plastic identity. The bushes in the lower foreground, dominated by green and light brown, are a mass of irregular circular planes grouped in a few horizontal rows that recede in compact space. The tree to the left of the villa is a large undulating dark gray plane which emerges from among the planes of the bushes in the foreground, and sweeps precipitously upward through the rhythmic movement of its irregularly shaped curvilinear areas. These areas move to right and left of each other as well as upward; their composite pattern is more like that of a large leaf or feather on a single plane parallel to that of the picture than, as in the

*Cf., e.g., 351. †Illustration, p. 275.

bushes, a pattern of planes receding in space. A number of small superposed brush strokes, however, convert each area of this tree into a slightly three-dimensioned mass of closely-packed planes differentiated in space by their degree of light or variety of tone. The two elements—juxtaposition and recession of planes—occur in both the tree and the bushes, but with a difference in emphasis designed to heighten contrast: the tree is primarily a two-dimensional pattern, the bushes a group of masses composed in deep space.

The area of the tree as a whole is rhythmically contrasted in color, light and direction with the area of the sky and distant hill which forms the upper part, the horizontal band, of the total enframing landscape. In this upper part of the composition, the pattern of elongated irregular areas is as pronounced as is the receding movement of planes; but its distinctive character, in contrast to that of the tree and bushes, arises from the dramatic contrasts of light and dark, due to the alternation of deep blue, light lavender-gray, light blue, grayish white, dark lavender-gray and dark grayish-blue areas. The general direction of these individual areas is horizontal like that of the total upper section, but in their relations to each other in three-dimensional space they are vertical parallel planes slightly oblique and with zigzag movement from side to side. This zigzag rhythm involves the blue and gray units taken as a whole, and also the organization of the long ribbon-like brush strokes which subdivide the areas into smaller planes.

The chief characteristic of the fourth enframing unit, the tree and part of the background-hill, which form the upright area on the right of the picture, is its rhythmic curvilinear pattern of oblique narrow strips of color or broad lines. These lines, formed chiefly by the branches of the tree, together with the irregularly shaped areas between them, repeat, with marked variations, the general pattern of the large tree to the left of the villa, and also counterbalance the direction of its curvilinear movement. The linear pattern of the unit at the right is chiefly a succession of small irregular dabs of white and bright green, strips of deep slate and small spots of the bare gray ground of the panel. This arrangement results in a curvilinear pattern of bright broken-up strips of color that move in and out in space as well as upward and toward the left, and stand out in front of the dark intervals which they outline. In contrast, in the tree to the left, the individual characteristics and the relationships of the same factors—areas, lines and brush strokes—

result, as already seen, in an emphasis upon the curvilinear sweep of a large area or plane of dark color.

The above survey shows that the contrasts between the four segments of the enframing landscape are due to the emphasis laid upon one or another of their plastic constituents: receding circular planes of contrasting color in the bushes, sweep of a large dark plane in the tree on the left, dramatic contrast of light and dark zigzag planes in the sky, and brightly colored linear pattern in the tree on the right. The movement and pattern of curvilinear units which prevail in all four sections bind together the contrasting aspects in an uninterrupted flow of color-rhythms which encompass the central building. At each corner of this undulatory frame, the contrasts are greatly reduced by the intermediary transitional relationships. The two large planes in the left of the immediate foreground partake of the circular-plane character of the bushes, as well as of the dark tone, flat expanse and general upward swing of the large tree immediately above them. In the upper left corner, the dark projection of the tree against and into the light area of the sky is rhythmically related in shape, tone and movement to the adjacent deep blue patch of sky which carries the oblique-vertical sweep of the tree over into the oblique-horizontal rhythms of the clouds and sky. Again, a connecting link, in the upper right corner, is the kinship between the broken-up pattern of the deep blue horizontal area of sky and that of the green vertical and oblique upper branches of the tree. This tying together is aided by the rhythmic relations between the shape of the dark gray-blue plane of the distant hill, that of the light and dark areas in the sky, and that of the pattern of irregularly shaped intervals between the branches of the tree. The transition from the linear tree on the right to the planes of the bushes in the foreground is effected chiefly by color-rhythm: the green, dominant in the linear units of the tree, is repeated as a minor color-note in the bushes, where it parallels the oblique-curvilinear rhythm of the branches; vice versa, the brown of the bushes is echoed in some of the dark intervals between the branches of the tree.

The villa, enframed by the wavy contrasting color-rhythms of the landscape, establishes a series of further contrasts in color, shape of areas, and space-composition; it also stabilizes the organization as a whole. The contrasts between the villa and its landscape-setting involve practically all the plastic characteristics of the building: its position in space as the central pivot around which the

ANALYSES

enframing units revolve; its color-scheme which is different from
that of any other part of the picture; the character and relationship
of its component planes, which are placed at various and preponderantly clear-cut angles to each other, in contrast to the
groups of chiefly curvilinear and parallel planes in the landscape-
setting; its linear pattern, relatively rigid and related to strips and
bands of color; and its light, which is the large focus in the light-
pattern of the total picture. The general movement of each part of
the landscape leads to the central mass of the villa and there comes
to rest through the intermediation of the planes of the building.
For instance, the sections projecting from three sides of the central tower duplicate, but in static form, the enframing organization of the landscape; the general direction of trees, bushes, clouds
and hill toward the center of the composition, is continued by the
planes and linear patterns of the roofs; the central dome of the
villa echoes and lends stability to the varied curvilinear rhythms
of the landscape.

The curvilinear flow and semi-diffuse contours in the landscape,
reminiscent of the Chinese and Japanese, are replaced in the
planes of the villa by an angularity and a rigidity suggestive of
Cézanne's. Cézanne's influence is also perceptible in the organization of the landscape in planes, and in the technique of superposed
hatchings in some of its parts.* On the other hand, the building
acquires an Oriental flavor by its color-scheme, black-and-white
effect, black brush-point linear pattern, extensive areas of unpainted panel and generally light and crisp drawing. The areas of
light green which form the roofs of the various parts of the villa,
and the area of rose in the left middle ground of the landscape,
relieve the monochrome tendency of the entire color-scheme.

The total form of the picture represents an integrated ensemble
of elements derived chiefly from Cézanne and the Chinese, and
rendered in Matisse's own idiom of rhythmic movement of color-
contrasts which he adapts to one of his varied experiments with
a green-gray-tan color-scheme of landscape.†

GIRL IN BLACK ON BALCONY‡ (73)

This painting, a superlative achievement of Matisse's Nice
period, is based upon three fundamental motifs: a set of rich deep

*Cf., e.g., the foreground in this picture with that in Cézanne's "Mt. Ste.
Victoire" (408).
†For thematic variations of this color-scheme see pp. 109–111.
‡Illustration, p. 278.

colors to which an intimate fusion with light lends a striking glow and sparkle; a bizarre criss-cross pattern; and an organization of subtly rendered full and free spatial relations.

Blue dominates the color-scheme, in spite of the presence of large areas of black, tan and ivory; the blue is so intense and so pervasive that its overtones extend through the other colors. It varies in shade and quality: it is deep, opaque and toned with purple in the shadows of the floor; in the upper left corner and in the area above the balustrade it is an intense, bright, luminous ultramarine; in the sea showing through the railing to the right of the figure it changes to a translucent turquoise; in the lighted part of the floor it assumes a greenish tinge; and it is a bluish cast over the pearly white of the railing itself. This distribution of color is so closely paralleled by one of light that the color-relations are also relations of light and dark, and the organized patterns of color and light largely coincide: the focus of each is in the pink hands. So intimate is the interaction of the two patterns, and so strongly do the rhythms of each reinforce those of the other, that the gemlike quality of the painting is due as much to the effect of light upon color as it is to the intrinsic quality of the color itself.

The pattern of the picture is chiefly one of stripes and bands. Three broad areas, quite definitely marked off from each other, extend across the canvas from left to right: the area of the sea, the beach, and the floor of the balcony; a fourth, considerably smaller and less well defined in direction, is constituted by the large dark shadow in the left foreground. These generally horizontal broad areas or bands are intersected by a much larger number of stripes, made up of the upright posts of the railing and the shadows on the floor; the stripes, whether vertical or oblique, form sharp angles with the broad horizontal bands and so make up a pattern very markedly criss-cross. The intervals between the stripes automatically become themselves stripes or narrow bands parallel to those of the railing and the shadows, and reinforce both the rhythmic effect and that of angularity. This patterned setting is more definitely organized by the unit of figure and chair, itself highly patterned, but with much greater variety in detail. The stripes and bands in it are more curvilinear, they intersect at very diverse angles, and extend in constantly changing directions. Hence they both contrast with and repeat the linear pattern of the setting, and at the same time they add an additional note of color-contrast.

No less important in the unification of the picture and the establishment of its characteristic identity, are the spatial relations between figure and setting. Space in general is free, full and luminous, clearly perceptible around and between all the masses and their component parts, and suggestive of infinite distance in the background. Its formal organization in the figure, chair and balcony presents a very novel and striking design. The receding oblique-horizontal plane of the balcony-floor forms with the upright plane of the railing a right angle opening toward the left, in which the chair and figure are set. In these masses, vertical and oblique-horizontal planes form what amounts to another right angle, opening this time to the right; and the unit made by the figure and chair is set at an angle to the balcony. The rhythmic sequence of figure, chair and balcony, with the balcony enframing the chair and figure, sets up a general gyratory movement in space from right to left.

In spite of great activity in the pattern of lines, stripes and bands, the general effect of the composition, because of the simplicity of the color-scheme and the subtlety of space, is peaceful and quiet.

RED RUG* (84)

The extraordinary appeal of this picture is due chiefly to two distinctive qualities: its bright, rich, delicate and cheerful color-ensemble of rose and gray sharply punctuated by notes of blue, black and brown, and the picturesque distribution and organization of the subject-matter. Abundant distortions, not only of realistic values but also of traditional forms, all conspire to achieve the novelty and bizarreness characteristic of this charming version of the Nice type of picture. Practically all phases of the design—color-scheme, pattern, space, planes and composition—are dominated by the emphatic part played in each by the large decorated expanse of the rose-red rug. Extending from the immediate foreground to about three-quarters of the total height of the picture, this large area of rich juicy color with its superposed tan-and-black arabesques is a precipitously rising plane which functions as a background to the main part of the subject-matter and sets it off, much as does the similarly distorted perspective in Persian miniatures.

*Illustration, p. 281.

This rapidly rising oblique rug is brought into compositional equilibrium by its sharp contact with the vertical plane of the background proper, which occupies the uppermost part of the canvas. The latter is a small, generally horizontal, oblong area of pearly shades of gray relieved only by a few vertical and horizontal lines of slightly deeper tone and by small areas of black, blue and brown. This background, by contrast of tone, quality of color, size, and type and amount of internal patterns, brings the area of the rug into striking relief, and helps to establish it as the keynote of the organization. The set of pearly grays, while concentrated and extending to right and left in the upper part of the picture, penetrate through the light color-scheme of figure and chair into the large rose-red lower section of the canvas. This interpenetration of foreground and background, by means of color, illustrates one of Matisse's many ways of so adapting color-organization to composition that the two become practically one and the same thing. Both contrast and plastic integration are achieved by the familiar interplay of two distinct sets of color, the pearly grays and flesh tones, and the positive rich, juicy and lush rose-red. Complexity and movement of pattern in the rose-red section and relative simplicity in the pearly gray, lend further emphasis to the dramatic contrast. These lively contrasts, however, occur within a tightly-knit set of compositional relationships which encompass all parts of foreground and background and blend them into a harmonious composite whole. Drawing, modeling and compositional distribution of subject-matter are the most active contributing agents to this total plastic integration.

Drawing of the figure as well as of the decorative motifs on the rug and the various other units in foreground and background, is accomplished by the simplifications characteristic of Manet, but with greater emphasis upon decorative shapes or pattern. Within this general decorative type of drawing, definite contrasts and rhythms are established between the various sections: the large arabesque or rosette-like pattern made by the areas and lines that build up the figure, is echoed in the small floral ornaments on the rug and in the decorative motifs on the armchair. No less effective compositionally is repetition, in various units of the foreground—fringes of armchairs, row of paint-brushes, arms, fingers, toes, shoulder straps, shaded and lighted areas in the garment—of the series of parallel vertical, horizontal and oblique lines and stripes which dominate the pattern in the background. The principle of interpenetration of two distinct sets of contrasting factors, already illustrated by the color-organization, is here developed in the general linear framework of curvilinear arabesques and relatively straight lines.

Unification of the various decorative themes is obtained not only by the shape, color or linear character of their constituents, but also by the slanting position of the objects in relation to each other, which causes an effect of awryness to pervade the composition. Perspective and three-dimensional quality are distorted in practically all parts of the picture. The single unit constituted by the figure and armchair is a large radiating organization of relatively flat areas silhouetted against the rising plane of the floor. Around it as a focus are distributed the other units of the subject-matter, also simplified. The distorted perspective in these is such as to yield a centripetal effect to the whole organization, so that the scattered objects in the room—table with brushes, bed with cover and violin, door, chair, wardrobe, armchair—seem at one and the same time to revolve around and to lead toward the large central unit of figure and armchair. In other words, the sequence of these objects both enframes the figure and extends the rosette or wheel-like rhythm of the latter to the entire organization. In this ingenious and novel adaptation of the traditional enframing device, the feet of the figure, while part of the central rosette-arabesque, are so distorted in shape and position that each becomes also an active constituent of the outer encircling rhythms. The large expanse of rug with its all-over pattern of curvilinear motifs serves as an intermediary frame within the outer ring made by the objects. The revolving theme of the organization as a whole is carried out in this intermediary frame by the curvilinear shape of the individual floral motifs, and by their relations to each other and to the plane of the rug itself. These decorative motifs seem to be detached from the fabric of the rug and to be set in separate planes at varying angles to the rug proper; thus they participate in both the revolving curvilinear rhythm and the general feeling of awryness. This arrangement of the decorative motifs as planes is in conformity with the general plan of the design as an organization of planes.

The individuality of the design consists in the preservation of Oriental, especially Persian, character in a novel decorative version in which the linear patterns, arabesques, spatial relationships and color-ensemble are all more alive and moving than in the originals.

FRENCH WINDOW AT NICE* (90)

The subject of this picture, a seated figure near a window through which a landscape is visible, has been utilized by painters from time immemorial, and often by Matisse himself. What is novel and striking is the comparatively slight illustrative rôle assigned to the figure itself, which occupies a very small proportion of the area of the canvas, and is rendered almost if not quite as broadly as the setting. So nearly are the two on the same footing that the window as a whole may be regarded as the subject; the figure, though it is plastically the most active unit in the composition, is so far from dominating the picture that it is essentially only one element among others. It is this departure from conventional allocation of emphasis that establishes an effect of bizarreness, of dramatic contrast, which is carried out in the detailed employment of space, color, light and line.

A shaft or voluminous area of deep space extends from top to bottom through the center of the picture and seems to enclose the figure, which is placed in its lower left and extends up little more than a third of its height. The shuttered window at the back forms the rear wall of this shaft; its walls on the right and left are constituted by sets of planes organized in column-like units which include the doors, opened inward, and the curtains. Even the plane which encloses this alcove in front, though of course it is left unoccupied by any material object, may be supplied imaginatively by an extension downward of the folds of the curtains which are drawn together at the top of the picture. The extreme right foreground is occupied by a couch which is compositionally a part of the adjacent column-like curtain; the left foreground is simply part of the space of the room. This asymmetrical balance is only one of the series of contrasts upon which the drama of the picture depends. The figure, decentered to the left, is balanced a little higher up by the view disclosed by the partly raised shutter on the right; and the generally deep space of the lower part of the picture is replaced in the upper by compressed space. Subsidiary contrasts appear within each of the broadly contrasting areas. The two column-like units, though their general effect is voluminous, are largely drawn by planes set close together, with little continuously rounded solidity, and there is even a contrast between them: on the right the planes are broader and flatter; on the left, the planes are more numerous, the modeling is more definitely

*Illustration, p. 284.

rounded, and there are more positive though as unrealistically rendered areas of deep space between the folds and between the curtain and the door and floor.

In the vista the distance extends away to infinity, but this distance is again indicated rather than realized, and though the figures in it are far apart they are set each in a single plane. In the uppermost part of the window, though the number of planes is small and they are parallel to each other, the essential reality of space is not lost: each plane stands at an appreciable interval from every other. The general plane of the shutter is flat, but the planes on which the slats are set form an angle to it, and this accordion-like organization is repeated in the curtains and elsewhere in the picture. The contrasts are thus harmoniously related by rhythms: instead of flat opposition of characteristics there is interpenetration of qualities and plastic relationships in all the units of the design.

The contrasts and rhythms of space are merely the skeleton of the picture, which the color, light and line clothe with flesh and blood. The color is of the general Nice type, light, cool and delicate, with rather subdued contrasts; however, a note of striking contrast is struck in the figure by the vivid vermillion of the pantaloons. This color, the brightest and most weighty in the whole picture, does much to make of the figure the focal point in the organization. The color-contrast between the vermillion and the blues, grays and lavenders is softened by shades of rose in the bed-cover and floor. This contrast of color-relations between the figure and adjacent areas on one hand, and the much less emphatic pearly tones in the relatively flat areas on the other hand, reinforces the spatial contrasts.

The dominant plastic part played by the figure is due also to the bright light which falls upon the blouse, sets it clearly in space, and forms the focus of the light-design, the other elements of which are the numerous and variously placed strips of light in the curtains, bed-cover, shutters, window-sill and vista. It is the light too which gives prominence to the vista and, in conjunction with the deep space, endows it with the plastic weight needed to make it balance the figure. In addition to its accentuation of the chief compositional features, light plays a large number of other plastic rôles. It pervades and vivifies the color, and is largely responsible for its delicate pearly quality; in the curtain, in contrast with darker areas, it provides the effect of solidity, and of the in-and-out movement of the folds; it performs the same function in the slats of the shutters, and also conveys the sense of sunlight filtering in from the out-of-doors; it renders direct sunlight very vividly in the vista; the sill at the bottom of the window is an area of unpainted canvas, the light value of which is the chief factor in the convincing solidity of the unit.

In addition to these fairly specific rôles, both color and light play an extremely important part in the compositional pattern. As usual, the color is applied chiefly in compartments, in which light is also always active. These compartments, and the lines formed by their intersection, are extended over the whole surface in the widest variety of size and position. The pattern as a whole is divided into three vertical areas, the central shaft and the columns on each side, within which are numerous horizontal and vertical lines and compartments; balancing both are the curvilinear and oblique folds of the curtains, stripes on the couch, and frame of the chair, and also the patch of zigzag brushwork on the floor. At the top of the central shaft is a half of a rosette-pattern, in which elements of the vertical, horizontal and oblique, both straight and curvilinear, are all united, as they are also in the quasi-rosette pattern of the figure, and in the vaguely suggested rosette-organization in the vista. These three rosette-motifs are the nodal points of the general pattern, and their elements of line, light and color, are repeated and varied in all parts of the picture, even in the comparatively isolated vertical stripe of color, with curlicue ornaments, at the extreme right and left. Within the vista itself, the figures are vertical, the beach horizontal; the line of transition from the vista as a whole to the figure is oblique and comes forward in space from the remote right to the much nearer center; it passes across the vertical and horizontal lines in the shutter, and its movement in the third dimension is echoed by the much less extensive in-and-out rhythm of the slats. These motions, relationships, and contrasts are not merely of line: light, color and space participate actively in them, so that the pattern not only weaves into a single fabric every area of the surface but fuses, in each area and in the form as a whole, all the plastic means. The interplay of rhythms and contrasts of light, line, space and color, explains the variety, activity, and constantly renewed interest of the whole picture.

The elements taken from the traditions are many, but they are completely reworked and given a characteristic Matisse form. The beach in the vista recalls Manet; the drawing of the figure Manet, Degas, Toulouse-Lautrec, and the Orientals; the subtle space-composition is like Carpaccio's, especially in the foreground; and the delicate play of light upon color is akin to Vermeer's. The decorative stripes and bands go back to the Orientals; the light, bright and delicate color has a quality like that of Egyptian textiles of the third century; and the line of dots in the curtain to the left is slightly reminiscent of mosaics. The pervasive lavender in the color-scheme has Oriental antecedents, but all the derivations alike are transformed by Matisse's individual feeling for color, in its sensuous quality, dramatic contrast, and characteristic relationships.

WOMAN AT DRESSING TABLE* (98)

Matisse has here made of the familiar Nice color-scheme an intricate series of subtle relationships between delicate volumes and accentuated, highly illuminated spatial intervals. A gamut of light lavender shades and tints is so predominant that the ensemble forms a delicate lavender color-pattern with pearly silver tone, and something of a water-color or gouache quality. The pervasive delicacy is relieved of monotony and given color-power by adequate punctuation with dark or positive colors which establish focal points in the delicate and luminous color-organization. Such are the brown of the hair, the reddish-brown shadow to the right of the mirror, the yellow bottle, the black chair, the blackish-gray tray, the green trees, and the dabs of dark color indicating small figures on the beach. Moreover, the distant blue sea, the magenta floor and the yellow area of the mirror, by their tonal quality, form also a set of positive colors, and, by their position in relation to each other, make a triangular pattern which enters into subtly dramatic contrasts with the delicate lavenders and grays. This pattern also promotes the integration of the total color-composition by the location of its constituents at the upper center, lower left and lower right.

Subtle contrasts appear everywhere, not only between areas little varied in hue or tone, but also between areas of color and of light, and between objects, i.e., volumes or planes, and their spatial intervals. This union of subtle relationships and delicate color-scheme results in a form combining the charm of an intime interior-scene and the clear luminosity of a view of the distant sea.

Attention is compellingly directed to the varied and unified movement of the space-composition. A receding obliquely upward movement extends from the lower right to the upper central por-

*Illustration, p. 288.

tion, and embraces three main units contrasting with each other in the general character of their respective space-organizations: the table with still-life, the actual plane of the window, and the view through the window. The table is a large oblique-horizontal plane, patterned by broad areas of light and shade, upon which plane, as a base, the upright objects are distributed at accentuated intervals of space; these objects are organized in a definite composition of slight masses in clean-cut space. This rhythm of upright units in space is continued to right and left by the figure and the mirror, which partly enclose the table and still-life.

The second element in the total space-organization includes the window-frame, the shutters and the curtains. This area, unlike the first in which volumes and spatial intervals are equal in compositional activity, is a compact organization of planes in relatively diminished space. These planes, differing in size and shape, are preponderantly upright but their subdivisions are oblique, vertical or horizontal as the composition may require. For example, the horizontal oblong between the transparent curtain and the top of the table, from the representative point of view, should be a flat vertical plane but it has been converted into a voluminous oblique unit resembling a pillow; this unit carries the perspective directly from the plane of the foreground-table to that of the distant sea.

The vista of beach and sea which forms the third main division of the space-composition contrasts with the other two in that its relatively uninterrupted space recedes into infinity.

Rhythmic relations between such factors as pattern, line, light, color and direction of the constituent units of each of the areas establish a set of plastic connections which unite all the parts in a definite compositional entity. The area of the sky is a large focus of light which balances in the upper portion of the canvas the equally extensive and luminous unit at the lower right of the table; the plane of the sea is parallel to that of the table, which in turn parallels the floor and the book; the diaphanous curtain, the plane of the window itself, and the planes made by the dark trees on the beach, are rhythmic repetitions, in reverse direction, of the compact group of parallel light and dark planes made by the table, shadow on the table, tray and shadow on the tray; the beach with its figures and trees echoes rhythmically the space-composition of the still-life; and the ripples on the sea continue with variations the horizontal linear rhythm made by the pattern of the closely-packed bands in the shutter.

Variety and balance within the linear framework of the total design are effected by contrasts of long verticals and obliques with short horizontals which are often broad brush strokes. The lines vary also in their function in the design: they represent planes and spatial intervals in the shutters, pattern of ripples in the water, and volumes in the band which ties the curtain on the right. Linear patterns, by their repetition in various parts of the composition, further contribute to the rhythmic ensemble: the curvilinear folds of the curtains are related to the back of the chair, to the braid on the woman's gown, to her left arm, to the carafe, to the frame of the mirror, to the horizontal band holding the curtain on the right, to the branches of the trees, and to the patterned edge of the small transparent curtain. Line, ranging from obviousness to subtlety, contributes also to both the dramatic and the subtle color-contrasts, and, by its plastic quality, draws out the three-dimensional value of objects, with little or no support from modeling by light and shade, or from color. Drawing is so simplified that in certain instances its function is exercised by linear contour alone. The glass and carafe, for instance, are rendered with so little detail that their drawing seems like a trifling linear sketch; but their essential identity and their particular position in space are adequately and convincingly conveyed.

In sum, Matisse has converted a conventional genre subject into an intricate design in which varying aspects of space are organized in a pattern of areas, bands and stripes, of light and delicate color, characterized by both subtle and vivid contrasts. In spite of the complexity of the space-composition and the variety in the character and function of the plastic constituents, the design as a whole conveys a sense of simplicity, due chiefly to the large units of space and the relatively monochrome color-ensemble. This simplicity is accompanied by a feeling of tranquility and of luminous, airy delicacy.

ODALISQUE* (108)

The two distinctive features of this picture are first, an interlocking organization of two contrasting groups of colors, and second, a compositional use of the rosette-motif.

One of the groups of colors consists of delicate, light and pearly tones of blue, lavender, ivory and gray, with lavender tones dominating the set, and placed chiefly at the left side of the picture. The

*Illustration, p. 298.

group on the right, balancing the first, is composed of a series of vivid, intense, exotic tones of brown, red and magenta. Starting from the lower left corner, the colors of the first set move directly upward, then around to the right within the angle of the upper left corner, and then downward to the pearly-gray drapery in the center of the picture. The colors of the second group move downward from the upper right corner, then around toward the left within the angle of the lower right corner, and then upward to the left of the central gray drapery. The pattern thus formed by the vivid colors is so related to that of the delicate ones that, together, they consolidate the total color-composition in a sequence of units which interlock much as do the branches of a Greek-fret motif. Tones of lavender and purple pervade the total color-scheme, but each of the two contrasting sets of colors is in itself a subsidiary organization of contrasts which involve the shape of the areas, their direction, size, internal linear decoration, degree of solidity, position in space, as well as their actual color and intensity of tone.

The relation between the two main groups of colors coincides with the contrasting interplay of light and dark, of angular and curvilinear decorations, of planes and volumes, and of space and mass. For instance, the pearly blue-lavender-gray section as a whole forms a large unit of light set into the brown-red-magenta pattern which functions as the counterbalancing area of dark. These two main sections include areas which are relatively uniform, and others which are internally ornamented with curved or with straight linear patterns: the decorations are preponderantly straight in the blue-lavender-gray section, and curvilinear in its brown-red-magenta counterpart. The merging of color, light and line in the latter yields the large rounded volumes of the legs and couch, which project in various directions through three-dimensional space, while most of the delicately-colored areas on the left are drawn essentially in flat planes. These planes are compactly arranged so as to form an angular enclosure around the space in which is set the oblique mass of the couch and figure.

Equilibrium between the numerous contrasting factors is maintained by well-established plastic interrelationships. The central light area, representing the drapery, head, arm and hand of the figure, and belonging to the pearly-toned theme, is also part of a composition of volumes and spatial intervals compactly distributed in a rhythmic organization, of which the other factors are supplied by the vivid red trousers, the exotic magenta couch, the dark pillows and book, and the small areas of shadow cast upon the couch. The pearly gray masses of this central group are thus units in both contrasting color-schemes.

The masses in the center of the composition radiate into space from just below the middle of the gray drapery, around which point they are organized in a three-dimensional rosette. The red trousers move upward, downward, forward and backward in space, one leg toward the left, the other toward the right; the book, the arm and the folds of the gray drapery on one side of the figure balance the large folds of the drapery on the other side; the neck and head balance the lower area of the gray drapery, and the volumes of the pillows duplicate those of the legs. This rosette of volumes makes of the diagonal pattern constituted by the figure and couch the focus of a decorative space-composition. The rosette-motif is carried over from this focus into all parts of the picture with great variety in color, plastic function and degree of completeness. It recurs in the large sweeping lines and planes which build up the three-dimensional mass of the couch; it is repeated in the two-dimensional floral and arabesque linear decorations in the background; it occurs again in the angular linear pattern on the floor, and also at the meeting place of the planes of the wall, window, shutter and curtain. The small flash of irregular highlights on the red trousers and on the jeweled rings are minor echoes of it.

This picture belongs definitely to the Nice period, because of its color-gamut and its highly-illuminated, clear and limpid atmosphere.

MOORISH WOMAN* (134)

The very pronounced Oriental feeling in this picture arises from both its representative and its plastic qualities. The model's headdress and transparent draperies, her nudity and her position in the chair, are literal reminders of the voluptuousness and sensuality associated with the inhabitants of the seraglio. The illustrative factors are, however, outweighed by the complex decorative and expressive qualities of the plastic constituents.

The general plan of the design is an arrangement of contrasting planes with especial attention to their patterns and to their movement in space. The three main compositional units—figure, armchair and background—form a compact succession of semi-

*Illustration, p. 318.

voluminous areas placed one in front of the other and contrasted in most of their elements. The colors in the setting are strongly reminiscent of Japanese prints in their bright, exotic sensuous quality, their daring contrasts, and their arrangement in bands decorated with floral motifs not unlike Oriental script in effect. The color-contrasts in the figure and armchair are softened, and they yield a pervasive mellow tone-quality relieved of monotony by the vivid green of the headdress and the actively moving curvilinear patterns. The figure as a whole forms a large arabesque of semi-voluminous planes, organized in an irregular rosette-motif, with subsidiary arabesques and rosettes in the pattern of the brushwork, the light-and-shadow modeling, and the linear drawing. This activity and sweep of movement contrasts with the relative rigidity and the definitely vertical position of the planes of the setting; but, when perceived in its relation to the semi-rigid area of the armchair, the rosette made by the figure repeats, on a larger scale and with more pronounced three-dimensional quality, the floral-motif set against the geometrically-shaped areas of the background.

Further kinship between figure and background is provided by the pattern of the technique in the lower part of the transparent garment, which duplicates the effect of Oriental script, and also by a set of variations upon a motif of ovals in all parts of the picture. The diaphanous drapery in the foreground is a series of concentric oval planes which impart a swirling movement to that area; shoulders, arms, hand, thighs, legs, breasts and abdomen are all slight, graceful volumes of curvilinear quasi-oval shape; the face is a definite oval enframed by the green oval headdress; even details such as facial features, rings and beads are drawn with an oval contour. In the background the oval motif, perhaps not so easily discerned, is nevertheless constantly repeated in the individual dabs of color, in their grouping into patterns, and also in the intervals between the motifs. A compositional purpose is served also by the tilted position and relative simplicity of the torso, which placed between the vertical planes of the background and the oval planes of the foreground-drapery, links these two factors into a unit. This general direction of the torso is paralleled by that of the floor, seen on either side of the armchair and extending into comparatively deep space. Movement varies greatly in the different parts of the picture: swirling in the immediate foreground, and angular in the planes of the background, it partakes of the quality of graceful repose in the figure.

The interaction of the decorative and expressive elements in figure and background tie these two parts together in a compact, finely-integrated design greatly varied in pattern, color and degree of movement.*

RECLINING NUDE† (136)

The distribution of the subject-matter in this picture, a large figure placed diagonally against a contrasting setting, is of a familiar type: Giorgione, Titian, Tintoretto, Goya, Manet, Renoir, each has at times adapted it to his individual form. Matisse has treated it frequently in compositions very different in total form but akin in plastic qualities characteristic of the artist.‡ This composition is allied with those of the earlier men in distribution of subject-matter upon the canvas, not in total plastic form.

The diagonal figure is the compositional focus of a compactly-organized set of audacious, dramatic contrasts of planes and volumes of exotic colors, in a pattern of stripes, bands and rosettes. The color-scheme forms an odd and striking ensemble: extraordinarily vivid and exotic colors, delicate pearly tones and dark or dull unappealing ones are irregularly distributed around a large transverse area of flesh-color bizarrely patterned by the various tones of the modeling-planes and by dark linear contour. The color-contrasts are clashing throughout most of the picture. They vary in degree of intensity according as the areas in contact are all bright and vivid, or include also dark or dull, or light and delicate tones. Matisse here again, as in numerous other pictures, succeeds in harmoniously incorporating, in a generally bright and vivid color-scheme, a color unappealing in sensuous quality, the heavy, dark and dull reddish-brown immediately below the couch in the lower left. This uninteresting brown is enclosed by a vermillion at the bottom, a yellow above and a pearly gray on the right; the unit resulting from the violent contrast of these four colors is an integral part of the appealing and unusual total color-ensemble, and contributes to its startling sensuous quality. As in many Japanese prints, the dull area here serves as a foil; it emphasizes the vividness, the brightness, the lightness of the adjacent areas; it lends variety to the contrast between the colors separated by it, which elsewhere are in direct contact with each other. In short, this

*For comparative data with another version of the subject-matter, see chapter on Thematic Variation, p. 166.
†Illustration, p. 317.   ‡Cf., e.g., 94, 108, 119, 145.

brown area adds to the exotic and bizarre quality of the bright color-organization without disrupting its unity. The actual color of the area occurs nowhere else in the composition, but it partakes of both the red just below it and of the brown shadow on the yellow area above it; moreover, its pattern of brushwork is consistent with the decorative use of technique elsewhere in the picture; and its shape—an oblong band and a broad stripe—repeated throughout the picture, is a characteristic of the entire pattern.

The general plan of the color-organization is a pattern composed of three large sections. The central section, solidly painted and intricately patterned, is the large transverse oblong occupied by the couch and figure, and terminated by triangular planes of yellow and red. Flanking this at the upper right is a large triangular plane representing a screen divided into vertical bands and stripes. The third section of the pattern is a triangle at the lower left, also made up of juxtaposed flat oblongs and geometrical shapes, which balances the screen. Thus the figure, drapery and pillows form a roughly oblong organization of volumes set within four triangular planes.

The large transverse mass of the figure is made up of a sequence of well-defined small volumes—cylinders, cones, pyramids, spheres —which cause the various parts of the body to seem detached from the trunk, yet to fit into each other like the parts of a jointed doll or mannequin. These volumes are arranged in patterns: the arms around the oval masklike head form a three-dimensional triangle; the small spherical and pyramidal volumes radiating from the lower point of the neck appear as a rosette; the sections of the cylindrical trunk are a concentric arrangement of receding and protruding rings; the thighs and legs, shaped somewhat like Indian clubs, form a quasi-rosette pattern of superposed elongated masses radiating from the knees.

These semi-detached volumes are modeled by patterns of light and shadow in a technique of hatchings, small patches and irregularly accentuated black, gray or dark brown linear contour. The component volumes, in other words, which make of the total figure an interrelated series of voluminous geometric patterns, are themselves treated decoratively with internal patterns of light-and-dark contrasts, of brush strokes, and of linear accents. These internal patterns form a series of relatively parallel bands or stripes which function as planes and emphasize the general shape, direction and three-dimensional quality of each particular volume. Long

ANALYSES 423

strips of light and shadow, for instance, form the cylindrical arms and legs; curvilinear patches of contrasting tone model the breasts in a pattern of facets; irregular small areas and curvilinear stripes make up the planes of the trunk. It is this subdivision into planes, and the use of accentuated linear contour, which give rise to that type of distortion frequently encountered in early Byzantine paintings* and mosaics† and in Hindu‡ and Negro¶ sculpture: the breasts, portions of the abdomen, etc., seem to be detached from the body.

The figure as a whole is in sharp contrast with the rest of the picture by virtue not only of its diagonal position, but also of its three-dimensional quality, its accentuated linear contour, and the tonal color-contrasts of its internal patterns. The obliquely-placed figure is dramatically set against the vertical screen and drapery, the yellow and red areas at the foot of the couch, and the yellow portion of the couch in the upper left corner, all of which are on a slant at right angles to that of the figure. The interrelation of these contrasting factors brings about the unity of the picture and the equilibrium of all its parts. For example, the components of the screen—parallel bands and stripes, and curvilinear floral motifs—are echoes, with striking variations in color, size and direction, of the rosette and stripe patterns in the modeling of the figure. The junction-line of the screen and couch follows the oblique slant of the figure. In relation to this, the pattern of purple flowers and green leaves which decorates the oblong sections of the screen, may be perceived as a set of undulating bands parallel to the nude; these bands may also be regarded both as a continuation of the obliquely-placed folds of the drapery, and as rhythmic repetitions of the vertical bands and stripes of the screen. The curvilinear floral motifs, with their contrast to the rigid oblong bands which they ornament, repeat, in different color-scheme and in varying degrees of solidity, the curvilinear pattern of volumes and planes in the oblong trunk. The narrow vertical stripes separating the decorated sections of the screen form a pattern which reflects that of the long, narrow planes modeling the component volumes of the figure. Some of these stripes in the screen also continue the pattern of the figure: those on the thigh are continued by the stripe of gray-blue just above in the screen, and the uppermost, shortest blue stripe of the screen is an extension of the vertical stripe of light on the highlighted sections of the breast and ribs.

*E.g., 324. †E.g., 317. ‡E.g., 312. ¶E.g., 328.

The plastic bonds established between the figure and the diversely colored units of the couch, drapery and pillows solve a compositional problem treated in many different ways by Matisse.* It is that of tying together a unit relatively continuous in one direction and its setting of contrasting color-bands running in the opposite direction. This particular solution is the work of three main factors. First, the relatively single color of the figure establishes a color-element common to all the relations between the figure and the contrasting yellow, red, gray and lavender; second, the individual subdivisions of the couch and drapery run obliquely from the lower left toward the upper right and counterbalance the slant of the figure, but, by their juxtaposition, they build up the large slanting oblong mass of the total couch which underlines the diagonal movement of the figure from the lower right to the upper left; third, distinctive plastic characteristics are rhythmically duplicated in the contrasting areas of figure and couch. For example, the couch, drapery and pillows are all, like the figure, made up of broad bands of color; these bands are divided into narrow stripes by means of broad lines of contrasting color and tone, or by variation of color within the area, or by light-and-dark modulations accompanied by active pattern of brush strokes.

None of the bands, stripes, triangles or oblongs in the entire picture is rigid or sharply angular. A pervasive curvilinear quality, which reaches its height in the figure and couch, tempers the angularity of the composition throughout. The figure is an arabesque of semi-rigid volumes, the couch suggests the sweeping curve of a hammock, the drapery rhythmically repeats and balances the broken curves of the legs, and the arabesque of the total figure is echoed in the floral decoration on the screen.

This semi-fluid movement of the volumes, planes and decorative motifs takes place in the reduced space required by the decorative form of the design, and this involves distortion of perspective. The plane of the couch, for instance, is only slightly inclined from that of the screen; the color-planes of the floor and of the shadow below the couch produce the distortion of perspective necessary to make the floor, the shadow and the arm of the couch function together as an upright composite plane parallel to the general vertical plane of the screen. This vertical plane in the lower left is partly continued from the left to the center of the foreground by the cascade-like fall of the drapery over the side of the couch. Between

*Cf., e.g., 19, 34, 48.

the two spatial boundaries constituted by the screen in the background and the drapery, floor, shadow and arm of couch in the foreground, is sandwiched a cluster of small closely-packed volumes which include the two rounded corners of the arms of the couch, the pillows, the head and the immediately adjacent parts of the body. This distribution of objects in space is repeated in the treatment of the screen, the floral ornaments of which appear detached from the fabric, as though floating in free space. Thus treated, the screen serves both as a relatively flat background-plane and as an expanse of space in which flattened decorative volumes are suspended.

This extremely complicated design is highly typical of Matisse's form. It is a decorative pattern of bright, exotic, vivid colors in daring contrasts; and this dominant principle of contrast is carried out consistently in line, space, color and light. The strong Oriental flavor of the ensemble is derived chiefly from the sensuous quality of the color and from the accentuated pattern constructed by adaptation of forms from Hindu sculpture, Japanese prints and Persian miniatures. These Oriental features are fused with others from Negro sculpture, Manet and Cézanne.

REPOSE* (145)

In this picture Matisse attains an expressive power and depth of color perhaps greater than in any of his other work; he also obtains a form as decorative as any rendered in his familiar gamut of bright and vivid hues. The lush red, the solid blue and tan, and the luminous white are characteristically contrasted to each other, and organized in a Matisse type of patterned framework which includes bands, stripes and geometrical areas; but the intrinsic color-quality of the ensemble represents a new version of color-values contributed by the Venetians, by Rubens, Renoir, Cézanne and Manet. In the reds, for instance, Matisse merges the fiery fulness of Rubens with the mellowness of Titian and the juicy richness of Renoir. But while Matisse's red recalls all of these, it is not repetitive of any of them: it is not so lively or so crude as it is usually in Rubens, it is not so deep or so dramatically patterned with light as in Tintoretto, it is not so subtly nuanced as in Titian, nor is it internally enriched by color-chords as in Renoir. Again, the large area of blue approaches very nearly the structural solidity, expressiveness, sensuous appeal and power of

*Illustration, p. 326.

Cézanne's color, but is not applied in the same manner. All these traditional expressive and decorative uses of color have gone into solution, and the result has characteristics more typically those of Matisse than of anyone else. The colors are used in broad areas; they are applied with a technique derived from Manet but carried to a further degree of simplification; they are subdivided by subtle brush strokes and accentuated dark lines into a pattern of bands and stripes; their contrasts yield an exotic flavor; and they are organized in a decorative space-composition in which rhythmic contrast of patterns plays the most effective rôle. For instance, balance is established in space between the small mosaic-like pattern of the wall in the upper left corner and the checkered floor in the lower right; between the two opposite angles made by the elbows; and between these, the pillows and the flounces of the dress.

The sequential procession of color-areas across the picture is strongly emphasized and reinforced by the linear pattern. These color-areas and lines move downward and forward from the upper left corner of the background through the couch, pillows, figure to the lowermost point of the skirt; then the movement changes its direction and recedes upward and toward the right corner of the background through the legs of the figure, the floor, chair and wardrobe. This oblique forward and backward movement, taking place in both deep and lateral space, is counterbalanced, in the immediate foreground, by the horizontal section of the couch; at the sides, by the vertical areas and lines in couch, wall, chair and wardrobe; and by the lateral or horizontal succession of vertical bands from the left to the extreme right of the background.

The composition as a whole falls into three main divisions: the left part of the picture, including one arm of the figure; a central unit of couch, dress and curtain; and a unit on the right containing the legs of the figure, the chair, floor and part of a wardrobe. In the central unit, a large expanse of blue is sandwiched between the vertical planes of the red couch and reddish-brown curtains, and enveloped by uninterrupted receding space, to which emphasis is lent by the accentuated perspective of the couch. The blue robe is a solid volume of color, and the figure covered by it is convincingly three-dimensional and real. This plastic realization of solidity arises less from the conventional use of light and shade than from the interaction of the structural color itself, the linear patterns, and the compactly piled-up parallel curvilinear planes made by the individual overlapping flounces. In contrast to this relatively simple organization, the right and left areas contain complex groups of volumes, planes and spatial intervals, with more varied color. The head and arms of the figure, the pillows, the head of the couch and the wall on the left are arranged in receding layers varying in size, color, shape and direction, and grouped in a rosette of volumes around the neck and shoulders of the figure. This rosette-motif is repeated more vaguely on the right in the intersecting lines of the patterned floor, and still more vaguely in the semicircle formed by the volumes and planes of the wardrobe, the chair and the legs of the figure.

Space is subtly rendered in all three parts of the picture, particularly between the wardrobe and the floor; around the rungs and legs of the chair; around and between the volumes forming the rosette on the left; and in the suggestion of deep distance conveyed by the black strip separating the two reddish-brown curtains in the center.

The quality of the color, as above noted, links this picture definitely to the Venetian tradition, not only by direct Venetian affiliations, but through the other painters, Rubens, Renoir, Cézanne, whose forms are based upon that tradition. The picture, without losing any of Matisse's characteristic decorative charm, attains also a degree of richness, depth, glow, structural quality and expressiveness of color that is perhaps unique in his work. Here, as usual, he has invoked the aid of the impressionists, especially Manet's simplified drawing and luminous quality of paint. Matisse's emphasis upon the luminosity is animated by his usual decorative intent: it makes the areas so treated accentuated points in a light-pattern which is also a constituent of the general pattern of color-contrast.

The totality of the relations between the color, the pattern and the rhythmic flow of the space-composition, embodies, in plastic equivalents, the expressive and decorative values of the subject-matter: a graceful figure in repose.

DATA ON WORKS OF ART MENTIONED

DATA ON WORKS OF ART MENTIONED

In the following lists are given the titles of the pictures and other works of art corresponding to the numbers used in the text to document the particular points made.* The paintings by Matisse are arranged in chronological order as regards years, and the works belonging to each year are alphabetically listed. The same rule is followed with his drawings, lithographs and black-and-white work in general, but the two lists are separate: the enumeration of the black-and-white work, commencing with No. 200, begins after that of the paintings is complete. To assist in identification, such descriptive details are added as the size of the pictures and the collections in which they are to be found. Unless otherwise specified, the pictures listed are painted in oil on canvas. The first enumerated dimension is the height of the picture. The Matisse exhibitions referred to are those held at Galerien Thannhauser, Berlin, in 1930, at Galeries Georges Petit, Paris, in 1931, and at the Museum of Modern Art, New York, in 1931.

Following the enumeration of Matisse's work, a third list, "Miscellaneous Works of Art," commencing with No. 300, includes data on such paintings, prints, mosaics, etc., referred to in the text as having a bearing on Matisse's work. Works referred to in this list are classified as to traditions, and the order of the traditions is roughly chronological.

(A) PAINTINGS BY MATISSE

1890

NO.

1. **Books.** 8⅝" x 10⅝". Collection Henri-Matisse, Paris–Nice. Page 191.

1892

2. **Still-Life.** (Copied from a painting by David de Heim in the Louvre.) 39" x 57⅞". Collection Henri-Matisse, Paris–Nice. Exhibition 1931 Paris, No. 1. Pages 191, 365.

*The inclusion of page references converts this data into a supplementary index.

1893

3. **Reader.** Wood. 17⅝″ x 13¾″. Castle, Rambouillet, France. Page 366.

1895

4. **Still-Life with Tumbler.** 17¾″ x 13⅛″. Collection Cone, Baltimore. Exhibition 1931 New York, No. 2. Page 191.

1897

5. **Bouquet.** 18⅛″ x 15″. Collection Félix Fénéon, Paris. Exhibition 1931 Paris, No. 2. Pages 50, 103, 191.
6. **Dinner Table.** 39½″ x 51½″. Collection Dr. Curt Friedmann, Berlin. Exhibition 1931 New York, No. 6. Pages 191, 366, 367. Illustration, page 227.

1898

7. **Houses at Fenouillet.** Cardboard. 9¼″ x 13¾″. Barnes Foundation No. 358. Pages 46, 53, 90, 91, 93, 104, 105, 106, 135, 138, 192, 194, 209. Illustration, page 228.
8. **In the Luxembourg Gardens.** 16⅛″ x 13″. Collection Félix Fénéon, Paris. Exhibition 1931 Paris, No. 10. Pages 36, 192.
9. **Seascape.** (Copied from a painting by Jacob Ruysdael in the Louvre.) 21⅛″ x 28¾″. Collection Hans Purrmann, Berlin. Exhibition 1931 Paris, No. 3. Pages 191, 365.
10. **Small Jar.** (Painted in the autumn at Fenouillet.) Cardboard. 5½″ x 7½″. Barnes Foundation No. 133. Pages 26, 32, 46, 68, 92, 106, 120, 129, 139, 192, 193. Illustration, page 229.

1899

11. **Academy Figure (blue).** 28⅜″ x 21¼″. Collection Frank Stoop, London. Exhibition 1931 Paris, No. 5. Pages 44, 54, 90, 127, 128, 191, 197, 210. Illustration, page 230.
12. **Landscape.** (Corsica.) 15″ x 18″. Collection Madame Desjardins, Paris. Exhibition 1931 Paris, No. 4. Pages 47, 103, 191.

1900

13. **Ray.** (Copied from a painting by Chardin in the Louvre.) 44⅛″ x 55½″. Collection Henri-Matisse, Paris–Nice. Exhibition 1931 Paris, No. 6. Exhibition 1931 New York, No. 3. Page 191.

1901

NO.

14. **Carmelina.** $31\frac{1}{2}'' \times 25\frac{1}{8}''$. Collection in Boston. Exhibition 1931 Paris, No. 7bis. Exhibition 1931 New York, No. 8. Pages 26, 37, 44, 69, 84, 91, 105, 119, 120, 128, 129, 138, 139, 150, 197. Illustration, page 231.

15. **Woman Dressing her Hair.** $36\frac{5}{8}'' \times 27\frac{1}{2}''$. Collection Stephen C. Clark, New York. Exhibition 1931 Paris, No. 7. Pages 67, 129, 138, 197.

1902

16. **Notre-Dame.** $19\frac{3}{4}'' \times 25\frac{5}{8}''$. Collection Jean Biette, Le Havre, France. Exhibition 1931 New York, No. 9. Pages 38, 146.

1904

17. **Notre-Dame.** $18\frac{1}{8}'' \times 21\frac{3}{4}''$. Collection Bernheim-Jeune & Cie., Paris. Exhibition 1931 New York, No. 10. Page 193.

18. **Phlox.** Cardboard. $13\frac{3}{4}'' \times 11\frac{3}{4}''$. Collection Madame Olivier Saincère, Paris. Page 367.

1905

19. **Standing Figure.** Wood. $12\frac{3}{4}'' \times 7\frac{1}{2}''$. Barnes Foundation No. 84. Pages 32, 46, 48, 66, 82, 91, 93, 104, 108, 117, 118, 139, 144, 424. Illustration, page 233.

20. **Still-Life with Melon.** (Collioure.) $26'' \times 32''$. Barnes Foundation No. 64. Pages 37, 44, 51, 52, 53, 62, 91, 105, 118, 119, 128, 133, 135, 143, 150, 194. Illustration, page 236.

21. **Woman with Hat.** $31\frac{7}{8}'' \times 25\frac{1}{2}''$. Collection Michael Stein, Vaucresson, France. Exhibition 1931 Paris, No. 9. Pages 46, 47, 50, 51, 52, 57, 69, 71, 81, 87, 89, 90, 92, 103, 105, 111, 114, 120, 129, 132, 139, 157, 159, 174, 179, 180, 181, 182, 192, 193, 197. Illustration, page 235.

1906

22. **Bridge of Saint-Michel.** $25\frac{5}{8}'' \times 31\frac{7}{8}''$. Collection Messrs. M. Knoedler & Co., New York. Exhibition 1931 Paris, No. 15. Exhibition 1931 New York, No. 7. Pages 38, 62, 89, 108, 146, 179.

23. **Girl Reading.** $25\frac{1}{8}'' \times 31\frac{1}{2}''$. Art Museum, Grenoble. Exhibition 1931 Paris, No. 12. Exhibition 1931 New York, No. 12. Pages 23, 53, 105, 182.

NO.
24. **Idol.** 28¼″ x 23⅝″. Collection Ellissen, Paris. Exhibition 1931 Paris, No. 11. Pages 103, 174, 180, 209.
25. **Joy of Life.** (Study.) Wood. 4¾″ x 7½″. Barnes Foundation No. 35. Pages 56, 102, 104, 144, 156, 193. Illustration, page 240.
26. **Landscape.** (Collioure.) (About 1906.) 15″ x 18″. Barnes Foundation No. 73. Pages 45, 46, 51, 53, 54, 63, 64, 65, 66, 89, 103, 108, 135, 138, 140, 194. Illustration, page 242.
27. **Oriental Rugs.** (Collioure.) 35″ x 45¾″. Art Museum, Grenoble. Exhibition 1931 New York, No. 13. Pages 67, 72, 192, 209. Illustration, page 237.
28. **Sailor.** 39⅜″ x 32⅝″. Collection Krag, Paris. Exhibition 1931 Paris, No. 14. Pages 132, 179.
29. **Seated Nude.** Wood. 13″ x 16″. Barnes Foundation No. 212. Pages 37, 46, 62, 69, 70, 90, 91, 92, 93, 105, 116, 117, 127, 128, 129, 132, 135, 156. Illustration, page 239.
30. **Still-Life with Potted Plant.** (Collioure.) 38½″ x 31½″. Collection Frederic C. Bartlett, Chicago. Page 73. Illustration, page 244.

1906–1907

31. **Joy of Life.** 68½″ x 93¾″. Barnes Foundation No. 719. Pages 33, 45, 46, 49, 57, 63, 70, 71, 87, 89, 90, 91, 105, 106, 107, 116, 117, 118, 120, 132, 133, 134, 135, 138, 139, 147, 149, 155, 168, 170, 173, 192, 196, 197, 203, 368, 369–373, 389. Illustration, page 241.

1907

32. **Blue Nude‾(Souvenir of Biskra).** 36¼″ x 55⅛″. Collection late Dr. Claribel Cone, Baltimore. Exhibition 1931 Paris, No. 17. Exhibition 1931 New York, No. 15. Pages 65, 70, 73, 86, 91, 116, 120, 132, 133, 134, 135, 159, 170, 181. Illustration, page 249.
33. **Blue Still-Life.** 35″ x 45¾″. Barnes Foundation No. 185. Pages 36, 44, 46, 47, 51, 52, 53, 54, 67, 89, 92, 94, 103, 106, 109, 118, 120, 127, 139, 143, 149, 150, 154, 155, 156, 168, 171, 173, 194, 196, 197, 206, 210, 368, 373–379, 382. Illustration, page 243.
34. **Boy with Butterfly Net.** 70″ x 45¼″. Barnes Foundation No. 899. Pages 33, 39, 44, 53, 54, 115, 127, 145, 146, 167, 179, 182, 210, 424. Illustration, page 245.
35. **Madras Headdress and Oranges.** (Collioure.) Wood. 13″ x 16″. Barnes Foundation No. 878. Pages 48, 56, 89, 126. Illustration, page 250.

NO.
36. **River with Aloes.** 28¾" x 23⅝". Collection Alphonse Kann, Saint-Germain-en-Laye, France. Exhibition 1931 Paris, No. 18. Pages 47, 48, 56, 60, 64, 66, 93, 101, 103, 138, 140, 144, 207. Illustration, page 247.

1908

37. **Dinner Table.** 69⅝" x 85¾". Museum of Modern Western Art, Moscow. Page 197. Illustration, page 251.
38. **Eggplants.** 45¾" x 35". Collection Dr. Gold, Berlin. Exhibition 1931 Paris, No. 20. Page 33.
39. **Family.** 56¼" x 76⅜". Museum of Modern Western Art, Moscow. Page 72.
40. **Flowers in Pitcher.** 21½" x 18". Barnes Foundation No. 205. Pages 46, 47, 81, 90, 92, 93, 103, 104, 108, 112, 132, 139, 155, 209. Illustration, page 252.
41. **Fontainebleau: Entrance to the Forest.** 24" x 29⅛". Collection Krag, Paris. Exhibition 1931 Paris, No. 19. Pages 47, 49, 50, 54, 63, 87, 140.
42. **Red Madras Headdress.** 39¼" x 31¾". Barnes Foundation No. 448. Pages 46, 47, 48, 49, 52, 57, 67, 71, 87, 90, 105, 117, 118, 132, 157, 179, 180, 181, 182, 196, 379–382. Illustration, page 253.

1909

43. **Dance.** 101½" x 153½". Museum of Modern Western Art, Moscow. Page 197. Illustration, page 254.
44. **Flowers.** (Cavalaire.) 23⅝" x 28¾". Collection the Duchess of Roxburghe, London. Exhibition 1931 Paris, No. 21. Pages 44, 73, 138, 139.

1910

45. **Bathers.** 23⅝" x 28¾". Collection Georges Bernheim et Cie., Paris. Exhibition 1931 Paris, No. 145. (Not listed in catalogue.) Pages 53, 89, 90.
46. **Manila Shawl.** 44⅛" x 27½". Collection Gaston Bernheim de Villers, Paris. Exhibition 1931 Paris, No. 22. Exhibition 1931 New York, No. 21. Pages 44, 61, 106, 208.
47. **Music.** 101½" x 153½". Museum of Modern Western Art, Moscow. Page 63. Illustration, page 255.

NO.
48. Portrait of Girl with Cat. $37'' \times 25\frac{1}{4}''$. Collection Henri-Matisse, Paris–Nice. Exhibition 1931 Paris, No. 23. Exhibition 1931 New York, No. 20. Pages 26, 46, 49, 50, 69, 71, 81, 85, 87, 88, 89, 90, 92, 101, 105, 106, 107, 118, 120, 126, 132, 157, 168, 174, 179, 180, 181, 182, 424. Illustration, page 257.

49. Still-Life. $28\frac{3}{4}'' \times 36\frac{1}{4}''$. Neue Staatsgalerie, Munich, No. 8669. Exhibition 1931 Paris, No. 16. Pages 38, 61, 62, 93, 132, 155, 171, 209, 368. Illustration, page 259.

1911

50. Goldfish. $45\frac{3}{4}'' \times 39\frac{3}{8}''$. Collection Hans Purrmann, Berlin. Exhibition 1931 Paris, No. 24. Exhibition 1931 New York, No. 23. Pages 33, 46, 65, 89, 91, 93, 94, 106, 112, 133, 139, 147, 164, 196. Illustration, page 260.

1912

51. Goldfish. $46'' \times 39\frac{3}{4}''$. Barnes Foundation No. 569. Pages 33, 39, 46, 48, 72, 73, 87, 89, 90, 91, 92, 104, 107, 109, 112, 116, 118, 134, 139, 143, 145, 157, 158, 164, 165, 168, 174, 197, 382–386, 389. Illustration, page 261.

52. Still-Life with Bust. $39\frac{1}{2}'' \times 31\frac{3}{4}''$. Barnes Foundation No. 313. Pages 72, 103, 104, 107, 108, 116, 132, 134, 144, 168, 197. Illustration, page 263.

53. Still-Life with Oranges. (Tangier.) $37'' \times 32\frac{5}{8}''$. Collection Frau Thea-Sternheim, Berlin. Exhibition 1931 Paris, No. 13. Pages 37, 48, 49, 50, 51, 54, 82, 91, 106, 108, 109, 139, 140, 156, 173, 209.

54. Zorah on the Terrace. $44\frac{7}{8}'' \times 39\frac{3}{8}''$. Museum of Modern Western Art, Moscow. Page 197. Illustration, page 262.

1913

55. Portrait of Mrs. Henri-Matisse. $57\frac{7}{8}'' \times 38\frac{1}{8}''$. Museum of Modern Western Art, Moscow. Page 197. Illustration, page 265.

56. Riffian. $79'' \times 62\frac{3}{4}''$. Barnes Foundation No. 264. Pages 25, 26, 32, 33, 34, 48, 55, 66, 69, 87, 89, 91, 92, 93, 103, 104, 106, 107, 108, 111, 117, 118, 119, 127, 139, 148, 156, 159, 167, 168, 173, 179, 180, 182, 196, 387–389, 389. Illustration, page 266.

57. Woman on a High Stool. 57½″ x 36⅝″. Collection Henri-Matisse, Paris–Nice. Exhibition 1931 Paris, No. 26. Exhibition 1931 New York, No. 25. Pages 48, 53, 72, 90, 107, 118, 134, 145, 174, 197. Illustration, page 264.

1914

58. Interior with Goldfish. 56¾″ x 38⅝″. Collection Baron Napoléon Gourgaud, Paris. Exhibition 1931 Paris, No. 27. Exhibition 1931 New York, No. 26. Pages 54, 90, 112.

59. Yellow Curtain. 61″ x 37⅜″. Collection Alphonse Kann, Saint-Germain-en-Laye, France. Exhibition 1931 Paris, No. 28. Page 33.

1915

60. Gray Nude with Bracelet. 29¾″ x 24¼″. Collection Joseph Müller, Soleure, Switzerland. Exhibition 1931 Paris, No. 30. Pages 111, 134.

1916

61. Interior. 57½″ x 45¾″. Institute of Arts, Detroit. Exhibition 1931 New York, No. 37. Pages 38, 39, 62, 117, 132. Illustration, page 269.

62. Lorette. Wood. 13⅝″ x 10¼″. Kunsthalle, Bremen. Exhibition 1931 Paris, No. 32. Page 179.

62a. Lorette. 21⅝″ x 17¾″. Collection Adolph Lewisohn, New York. Exhibition 1931 Paris, No. 33. Exhibition 1931 New York, No. 32. Page 71.

63. Moroccans. 70¾″ x 110½″. Collection Henri-Matisse, Paris–Nice. Exhibition 1931 New York, No. 31. Page 156.

64. Music Lesson. 96″ x 82½″. Barnes Foundation No. 717. Pages 38, 56, 61, 62, 66, 67, 71, 91, 92, 103, 106, 107, 115, 117, 127, 128, 132, 133, 134, 145, 148, 158, 174, 181, 197, 389, 389–398. Illustration, page 271.

65. Portrait of Mrs. Greta Prozor. 57⅞″ x 25¼″. Collection Henri-Matisse, Paris–Nice. Exhibition 1931 Paris, No. 35. Exhibition 1931 New York, No. 33. Pages 132, 179.

66. Still-Life with Lemon. Wood. 10¼″ x 13¼″. Barnes Foundation No. 460. Pages 44, 48, 49, 91, 101, 103, 145, 146, 157, 158, 174, 194, 385. Illustration, page 274.

NO.
67. **Studio on the Quay Saint-Michel.** 57½″ x 45¾″. Collection David Tennant, London. Exhibition 1931 Paris, No. 36. Exhibition 1931 New York, No. 35. Pages 73, 90, 103, 107, 132, 134. Illustration, page 268.

68. **Woman Seated in Armchair.** 16⅛″ x 13″. Collection Baron Fukushima, Paris. Exhibition 1931 Paris, not catalogued. Pages 44, 71, 181. Illustration, page 267.

1910-1917

69. **Three Sisters, Gray Background.** (Central section of triptych.) 77″ x 38″. Barnes Foundation No. 888. Pages 48, 49, 57, 61, 62, 67, 71, 72, 87, 89, 90, 104, 107, 114, 116, 118, 119, 135, 154, 157, 174, 179, 180, 181, 197, 399-404. Illustration, page 272.

70. **Three Sisters, with Negro Sculpture.** (Left section of triptych.) 77″ x 38″. Barnes Foundation No. 363. Pages 34, 48, 49, 57, 61, 62, 71, 72, 87, 89, 90, 104, 107, 114, 116, 119, 135, 139, 154, 157, 174, 179, 180, 181, 197, 399-404. Illustrations, pages 272, 273.

71. **Three Sisters, with "Pink Marble Table."** (Right section of triptych.) 77″ x 38″. Barnes Foundation No. 25. Pages 48, 49, 61, 62, 71, 87, 89, 90, 104, 107, 114, 116, 119, 135, 154, 157, 174, 179, 180, 181, 197, 399-404. Illustrations, pages 272, 273.

1917

72. **Blue Villa.** Wood. 13″ x 16″. Barnes Foundation No. 196. Pages 47, 63, 89, 91, 108, 138, 404-407. Illustration, page 275.

73. **Girl in Black on Balcony.** 16″ x 13″. Barnes Foundation No. 882. Pages 39, 62, 118, 132, 144, 172, 195, 197, 407-409. Illustration, page 278.

74. **Head of Girl.** Wood. 13¾″ x 10½″. Barnes Foundation No. 905. Pages 112, 129, 179, 194. Illustration, page 280.

75. **Interior at Nice.** 25⅝″ x 21¼″. Collection Follmüller, Zurich. Exhibition 1931 Paris, not catalogued. Page 209.

76. **Painter in his Studio.** 57½″ x 38¼″. Collection Henri-Matisse, Paris-Nice. Exhibition 1931 Paris, No. 37. Pages 44, 48, 54, 101, 103, 120, 138, 139, 169. Illustration, page 276.

77. **Pink Marble Table.** 59″ x 39⅜″. Collection Alphonse Kann, Saint-Germain-en-Laye, France. Exhibition 1931 Paris, No. 39. Pages 34, 47, 65, 72, 93, 138, 139, 194.

78. **Pond at Triviaux.** 36¼″ x 29⅛″. Collection Frank Stoop, London. Exhibition 1931 Paris, No. 141bis. Pages 65, 111.

NO.

79. Seated Nude, Back Turned. 24⅜″ x 18½″. Collection Samuel S. White, 3d, Ardmore, Pa., U. S. A. Exhibition 1931 Paris, No. 40. Exhibition 1931 New York, No. 39. Pages 36, 63, 66, 208. Illustration, page 277.

80. Seated Nude in Tan Room. 16″ x 13″. Barnes Foundation No. 880. Pages 62, 90, 94, 117, 118, 139, 144, 168, 172. Illustration, page 279.

1918

81. Balcony. 12⅝″ x 15¾″. Collection Dr. Hahnloser, Winterthur, Switzerland. Exhibition 1931 Paris, No. 43. Pages 36, 48, 62, 66, 102, 103, 104, 112, 115, 145, 148, 195, 208. Illustration, page 283.

82. Black Scarf. 26″ x 51⅝″. Collection Lucien Demotte, Paris. Exhibition 1931 Paris, No. 45. Page 181.

83. Portrait of Mr. Demotte. 21⅝″ x 18⅛″. Collection Lucien Demotte, Paris. Exhibition 1931 Paris, No. 44. Page 207.

84. Red Rug. 18″ x 15″. Barnes Foundation No. 881. Pages 39, 47, 48, 67, 85, 92, 115, 116, 118, 133, 146, 172, 174, 195, 197, 222, 409-411. Illustration, page 281.

85. Still-Life with Peaches. 8⅝″ x 10⅝″. Collection Sacha Guitry, Paris. Exhibition 1931 Paris, No. 41. Pages 44, 47, 51, 52, 54, 92, 126, 127, 143, 194, 207, 208, 210, 221.

1919

86. Balcony at Nice. 25½″ x 18⅛″. Collection Paul Rosenberg, Paris. Exhibition 1931 Paris, No. 53. Pages 62, 90, 93, 112, 134, 195, 209. Illustration, page 285.

87. Bridge of Sèvres. 18⅛″ x 21⅝″. Collection Renand, Paris. Exhibition 1931 Paris, No. 55. Pages 112, 144.

88. Flowers in Glass Vase. 24″ x 18″. Barnes Foundation No. 548. Pages 46, 48, 89, 91, 92, 93, 145, 147, 157, 158, 174, 195, 385. Illustration, page 289.

89. Flowerpiece. 45¾″ x 35″. Collection Gaston Bernheim de Villers, Paris. Exhibition 1931 Paris, No. 51. Pages 63, 91, 93, 138, 139, 144, 147, 196, 197, 209.

90. French Window at Nice. 51¼″ x 35″. Barnes Foundation No. 897. Exhibition 1931 Paris, No. 52. Exhibition 1931 New York, No. 49. Pages 38, 39, 44, 62, 72, 90, 93, 112, 113, 120, 132, 134, 138, 144, 145, 146, 147, 195, 197, 412-415. Illustration, page 284.

91. Girl and Screen. 13″ x 16″. Barnes Foundation No. 879. Pages 39, 62, 87, 112, 127, 132, 155. Illustration, page 290.

NO.

92. Illustrated Book. 28¾″ x 36¼″. Collection Paul Rosenberg, Paris. Exhibition 1931 Paris, No. 54. Pages 47, 48, 62, 87, 128, 194.

93. Plumed Hat. 18¾″ x 15″. Private collection, New York. Exhibition 1931 Paris, No. 57. Pages 61, 63, 89, 92, 93, 113, 179, 181.

94. Reclining Figure in Landscape. 12¼″ x 16″. Barnes Foundation No. 204. Pages 47, 48, 64, 65, 70, 88, 89, 104, 107, 116, 138, 148, 155, 156, 157, 171, 421. Illustration, page 286.

95. Red Couch. 13¾″ x 22″. Barnes Foundation No. 892. Exhibition 1931 Paris, No. 112. Pages 50, 57, 67, 89, 91, 93, 104, 106, 107, 112, 118, 119, 165, 173, 195. Illustration, page 291.

96. Small Odalisque with Red Trousers. 13″ x 18⅛″. Collection Gaston Bernheim de Villers, Paris. Exhibition 1931 Paris, No. 50. Page 116.

97. Striped Gown. 13″ x 21⅝″. Barnes Foundation No. 914. Pages 88, 132, 165. Illustration, page 287.

98. Woman at Dressing Table. 28½″ x 23¼″. Barnes Foundation No. 394. Pages 39, 48, 65, 87, 89, 90, 92, 93, 103, 112, 113, 114, 118, 134, 147, 148, 172, 195, 415–417. Illustration, page 288.

99. Woman Seated in Interior. 25⅝″ x 19⅝″. Collection Dr. Hahnloser, Winterthur, Switzerland. Exhibition 1931 Paris, No. 56. Page 147. Illustration, page 292.

1920

100. Beach at Etretat. 13″ x 16″. Barnes Foundation No. 904. Pages 47, 49, 88, 91, 101, 107, 139, 174, 207. Illustration, page 300.

101. Country House. 13″ x 16½″. Collection Renand, Paris. Exhibition 1931 Paris, No. 64. Pages 37, 47, 51, 53, 54, 69, 110, 111, 113, 120, 138, 140, 208.

102. Etretat: the Tunneled Rock. 15″ x 18⅛″. Collection Lord Berners, London. Exhibition 1931 Paris, No. 67. Exhibition 1931 New York, No. 55. Pages 47, 48, 49, 83, 88, 92, 194, 207.

103. Girl on Balcony. 37¼″ x 29⅜″. Collection Joseph Müller, Soleure, Switzerland. Exhibition 1931 Paris, No. 58. Pages 38, 47, 48, 51, 70, 71, 103, 140, 179.

104. Green Dress. 16¼″ x 13⅛″. Barnes Foundation No. 891. Exhibition 1931 Paris, No. 61. Pages 36, 66, 67, 89, 91, 102, 104, 107, 118, 119, 174, 197, 208. Illustration, page 295.

NO.
105. **Interior with Seated Figure.** 18″ x 15″. Barnes Foundation
No. 549. Pages 34, 112, 115, 195. Illustration, page 294.
106. **Meditation.** 28⅜″ x 21¼″. Collection Gaston Bernheim de Villers, Paris. Exhibition 1931 Paris, No. 60. Exhibition 1931 New
York, No. 53. Pages 34, 120, 132, 166, 195, 197. Illustration,
page 293.
107. **Nude with Elbow on Dressing Table.** 36¼″ x 28⅜″. Collection
Josse Bernheim-Jeune, Paris. Exhibition 1931 Paris, No. 59.
Pages 48, 91, 139, 140, 195, 209.
108. **Odalisque.** 22″ x 26″. Barnes Foundation No. 195. Pages 34,
39, 47, 57, 67, 91, 104, 112, 113, 118, 119, 138, 139, 148, 155, 159,
195, 197, 417–419, 421. Illustration, page 298.
108a. **Reader in Landscape.** 18½″ x 24″. Collection Contemporary
Art Society, London. Pages 49, 195. Illustration, page 299.
109. **Standing Nude Near Window.** 18″ x 15″. Barnes Foundation
No. 184. Pages 39, 50, 57, 62, 85, 89, 90, 92, 103, 104, 107, 111,
112, 113, 119, 127, 169, 173, 195. Illustration, page 296.
110. **Two Rays, Etretat.** 36¼″ x 28¾″. Collection Lord Ivor Spencer
Churchill, London. Exhibition 1931 Paris, No. 66. Exhibition
1931 New York, No. 54. Pages 26, 47, 50, 92, 119, 132. Illustration, page 297.

1921

111. **Alhambra.** 18″ x 15″. Collection Berthold Nothmann, Düssel-
dorf. Exhibition 1931 Paris, No. 71. Pages 46, 68, 91, 93, 110,
111, 115, 120, 147, 149, 195. Illustration, page 308.
112. **Boats at Etretat.** 15″ x 17¾″. Collection de la Chapelle, Paris.
Exhibition 1931 Paris, No. 78. Pages 47, 113.
113. **Etretat.** 25½″ x 21¼″. Collection Paul Rosenberg, Paris. Exhibition 1931 Paris, No. 80. Pages 47, 88, 139.
114. **Etretat, the Sea.** 15⅜″ x 17⅞″. Barnes Foundation No. 894.
Pages 46, 47, 48, 49, 83, 88, 89, 140, 147, 174, 195. Illustration,
page 301.
115. **Figure in an Interior.** 21¼″ x 16½″. Collection Madame Hirsch,
Paris. Exhibition 1931 Paris, No. 68. Pages 50, 51, 92, 93, 144,
166.
116. **Figure with a Fan.** 21⅞″ x 18″. Collection Paul Rosenberg,
Paris. Exhibition 1931 Paris, No. 79. Page 36.
117. **Girl at Window.** 13″ x 21⅝″. Collection Madame Pichard,
Paris. Exhibition 1931 Paris, No. 84. Pages 38, 146, 155. Illustration, page 302.

NO.
118. **Interior at Nice.** 51¼″ x 35″. Collection Pierre Matisse, New York. Exhibition 1931 Paris, No. 85. Pages 195, 196, 197. Illustration, page 307.
119. **Odalisque.** 26⅜″ x 33⅛″. Luxembourg Museum, Paris. Pages 62, 113, 119, 145, 197, 368, 421. Illustration, page 310.
120. **Odalisque with Red Trousers.** 18⅛″ x 25½″. Collection Josse Bernheim-Jeune, Paris. Exhibition 1931 Paris, No. 69. Pages 26, 159.
121. **Shrimps.** 23¼″ x 28¾″. Collection Stephen C. Clark, New York. Exhibition 1931 Paris, No. 76. Exhibition 1931 New York, No. 58. Pages 49, 52, 92, 174, 195, 197. Illustration, page 304.
122. **Still-Life with Fish.** 23¾″ x 28¾″. Collection J. W. Freshfield, London. Page 103. Illustration, page 305.
123. **Two Figures Reclining in Landscape.** 15″ x 18⅜″. Barnes Foundation No. 893. Pages 26, 47, 48, 50, 64, 83, 87, 92, 116, 118, 119, 144, 172. Illustration, page 303.
124. **Violinist in Repose.** 36¼″ x 25½″. Collection Gaston Bernheim de Villers, Paris. Exhibition 1931 Paris, No. 72. Pages 57, 62.
125. **Waiting.** 24″ x 19⅝″. Collection Stephen C. Clark, New York. Exhibition 1931 Paris, No. 82. Pages 35, 39, 44, 113, 120, 195. Illustration, page 306.
126. **Window at Etretat.** 18⅛″ x 15″. Collection Henry Bernheim-Jeune, Paris. Exhibition 1931 Paris, No. 75. Exhibition 1931 New York, No. 56. Page 47.
127. **Woman with Green Parasol.** 28¾″ x 23⅝″. Collection Josse Bernheim-Jeune, Paris. Exhibition 1931 Paris, No. 74. Pages 46, 195.

1921–1922

128. **Domino Players.** 23¼″ x 28½″. Barnes Foundation No. 889. Pages 44, 47, 57, 62, 104, 118. Illustration, page 311.
129. **Woman in an Interior at Nice.** 25½″ x 20⅞″. Barnes Foundation No. 915. Pages 57, 103. Illustration, page 309.

1922

130. **Carnival at Nice.** 25⅝″ x 36¼″. Collection Cone, Baltimore. Exhibition 1931 Paris, No. 95. Exhibition 1931 New York, No. 61. Pages 92, 196.

131. Chinese Casket. 23⅝″ x 28¾″. Collection Charles Pacquement, Paris. Exhibition 1931 Paris, No. 91. Pages 26, 33, 34, 35, 49, 56, 89, 119, 148, 156, 168, 170, 197. Illustration, page 313.

132. Confidences. 21⅝″ x 18⅛″. Barnes Foundation No. 913. Exhibition 1931 Paris, No. 90. Pages 47, 48, 72, 87, 114, 195, 197. Illustration, page 319.

133. Conversation under Olive Trees. 39⅜″ x 31⅞″. Collection Josse Bernheim-Jeune, Paris. Exhibition 1931 Paris, No. 88. Pages 63, 64, 83, 110, 111, 140, 144, 157. Illustration, page 315.

134. Moorish Woman. 18¼″ x 15″. Barnes Foundation No. 890. Exhibition 1931 Paris, No. 89. Pages 34, 57, 62, 67, 84, 92, 102, 103, 112, 118, 126, 133, 146, 166, 197, 419–421. Illustration, page 318.

135. Reading. 9⅜″ x 13″. Collection Mrs. Morton, Glasgow, Scotland. Exhibition 1931 Paris, No. 92. Pages 44, 48, 50, 51, 83, 120, 170. Illustration, page 312.

136. Reclining Nude. 23¼″ x 36″. Barnes Foundation No. 199. Pages 39, 48, 50, 60, 69, 70, 72, 92, 105, 112, 127, 128, 129, 132, 138, 148, 155, 171, 196, 197, 421–425. Illustration, page 317.

137. Road through the Woods. 24″ x 19¾″. Collection the Duchess of Roxburghe, London. Exhibition 1931 Paris, No. 93. Exhibition 1931 New York, No. 60. Pages 46, 110, 111, 116, 120, 140, 195.

138. Under the Trees. 24″ x 19⅝″. Collection Gaston Bernheim de Villers, Paris. Exhibition 1931 Paris, No. 87. Pages 45, 46, 47, 50, 83, 110, 111, 195.

139. Woman with Cross. 14″ x 9½″. Private collection, New York. Exhibition 1931 Paris, No. 94. Page 57.

1923

140. Anemones in Chinese Vase. 29⅞″ x 23⅝″. Collection William Averell Harriman, New York. Exhibition 1931 Paris, No. 104. Pages 32, 33, 39, 50, 61, 65, 82, 86, 87, 91, 93, 94, 112, 118, 173, 195, 196, 197. Illustration, page 323.

141. Hindu Pose. 28½″ x 23⅜″. Collection Stephen C. Clark, New York. Exhibition 1931 Paris, No. 98. Pages 32, 33, 39, 45, 56, 57, 60, 62, 67, 68, 86, 87, 89, 102, 106, 107, 108, 113, 126, 138, 156, 158, 167, 168, 196, 197. Illustration, page 325.

142. Nude, Blue Background. 19⅝″ x 24″. Collection Brissac, Paris. Exhibition 1931 Paris, No. 101. Pages 89, 118.

NO

143. Odalisque with Raised Arms. 25½" x 19¾". Private collection, New York. Exhibition 1931 Paris, No. 103. Pages 34, 62, 63, 103, 120, 126, 133, 166.

144. Piano Lesson. 25½" x 31⅞". Collection Royan Middleton, Dundee, Scotland. Exhibition 1931 Paris, No. 102. Pages 34, 51, 57, 62, 71, 104, 112, 117, 159, 196. Illustration, page 320.

145. Repose. 10¾" x 18½". Barnes Foundation No. 898. Pages 36, 38, 66, 103, 112, 115, 119, 194, 195, 197, 207, 421, 425–427. Illustration, page 326.

146. Sketching on the River Bank. 23⅝" x 28¾". Collection Henri Canonne, Paris. Exhibition 1931 Paris, No. 100. Pages 45, 46, 47, 50, 195. Illustration, page 321.

147. Spanish Girl (Harmony in Blue). 18⅞" x 14⅛". Collection Gaston Bernheim de Villers, Paris. Exhibition 1931 Paris, No. 96. Pages 146, 149, 156, 165, 196.

148. Spanish Girl with Flowers (Harmony in White). 23⅝" x 19¼". Collection Josse Bernheim-Jeune, Paris. Exhibition 1931 Paris, No. 99. Pages 26, 32, 34, 37, 39, 50, 51, 56, 63, 68, 92, 103, 106, 113, 119, 127, 134, 146, 149, 156, 158, 165, 167, 182, 196. Illustration, page 322.

1924

149. Fruit and Flowers. 28¾" x 36¼". Collection Josse Bernheim-Jeune, Paris. Exhibition 1931 Paris, No. 106. Exhibition 1931 New York, No. 66. Page 368.

150. Moroccan Tray. 19⅝" x 24". Collection Marie Harriman Gallery, Inc., New York. Exhibition 1931 Paris, No. 115. Pages 38, 39, 44, 50, 51, 53, 105, 119, 127, 139, 143, 146, 149, 156, 168, 194, 196. Illustration, page 332.

151. Nude in Armchair. 22¼" x 13½". Collection Samuel A. Lewisohn, New York. Exhibition 1931 Paris, No. 113. Pages 50, 57, 65, 138, 210.

152. Odalisque with Magnolias. 23⅝" x 31⅞". Collection Gaston Bernheim de Villers, Paris. Exhibition 1931 Paris, No. 105. Pages 26, 34, 50, 53, 63, 91, 113, 127, 139, 145, 149, 156, 159, 164, 170, 173, 196, 197. Illustration, page 327.

153. Pink Blouse. 21⅝" x 18⅛". Collection Mrs. Walter Hochschild, New York. Exhibition 1931 Paris, No. 144. Exhibition 1931 New York, No. 52. Pages 63, 71, 180. Illustration, page 333.

NO.
154. **Still-Life, "Histoires Juives."** 31⅞″ x 39⅜″. Collection Samuel
S. White, 3d, Ardmore, Pa., U. S. A. Exhibition 1931 Paris, No.
114. Exhibition 1931 New York, No. 65. Pages 26, 32, 34, 36, 56,
57, 67, 87, 92, 93, 103, 108, 119, 134, 146, 149, 156, 167, 196.
Illustration, page 330.

155. **Still-Life, "Les Pensées de Pascal."** 19⅝″ x 25½″. Collection
Henri Canonne, Paris. Exhibition 1931 Paris, No. 111. Pages
44, 47, 86, 109, 112, 127, 144, 169. Illustration, page 331.

156. **Studio at Nice.** 36⅛″ x 28¾″. Collection Stephen C. Clark,
New York. Exhibition 1931 Paris, No. 107. Pages 32, 34, 39,
62, 63, 69, 101, 103, 105, 120, 127, 128, 140, 145, 147, 169, 196,
197. Illustration, page 329.

1925

157. **Lemons and Anemones.** 25⅝″ x 31⅞″. Collection Samuel A.
Lewisohn, New York. Exhibition 1931 Paris, No. 120. Exhibition 1931 New York, No. 67. Pages 39, 57, 60, 61, 62, 106, 126,
132, 146, 168, 194, 197. Illustration, page 337.

158. **Piano.** 23⅝″ x 29½″. Collection Stephen C. Clark, New York.
Exhibition 1931 Paris, No. 116. Pages 33, 38, 57, 60, 62, 63, 128,
146. Illustration, page 334.

159. **Pink Tablecloth.** 23⅝″ x 31½″. Collection McInnes, Glasgow,
Scotland. Exhibition 1931 Paris, No. 121. Pages 106, 115.

160. **Red Pantaloons.** 23⅝″ x 28¾″. Collection Messrs. M. Knoedler & Co., New York. Exhibition 1931 Paris, No. 122. Exhibition 1931 New York, No. 68. Pages 63, 89, 91, 92, 93, 195. Illustration, page 335.

161. **Rocks of the Valley of the Loup.** 15″ x 18½″. Collection Charles
Pacquement, Paris. Exhibition 1931 Paris, No. 119. Pages 54,
110, 111, 194.

162. **Yellow Dress.** 26″ x 20″. Collection Baron Fukushima, Paris.
Pages 60, 62, 63. Illustration, page 338.

1926

163. **Draped Nude Reclining.** 14½″ x 23⅝″. Private collection,
Paris. Exhibition 1931 Paris, No. 130. Page 39.

164. **Odalisque with Red Trousers.** 19⅝″ x 24″. Private collection,
Paris. Exhibition 1931 Paris, No. 129. Pages 82, 87, 89, 108,
126, 144, 156, 164.

1927

165. Ballet Dancer. 31⅞″ x 23⅝″. Collection Henri-Matisse, Paris–Nice. Exhibition 1931 Paris, No. 132. Exhibition 1931 New York, No. 72. Pages 33, 140, 156, 196, 209, 210.

166. Decorative Figure (Flowered Background). 51⅝″ x 38⅝″. Collection Henri-Matisse, Paris–Nice. Exhibition 1931 Paris, No. 118. Exhibition 1931 New York, No. 70. Pages 32, 70, 72, 102, 104, 156, 159, 185, 196, 208, 209.

167. Reclining Nude, Back Turned. 26″ x 36¼″. Collection Henri-Matisse, Paris–Nice. Exhibition 1931 Paris, No. 133. Exhibition 1931 New York, No. 73. Pages 32, 37, 38, 57, 89, 104, 108, 119, 120, 133, 144, 146, 156, 158, 159, 170, 173, 196, 197. Illustration, page 340.

168. Woman with Veil. 24″ x 19¾″. Collection Henri-Matisse, Paris–Nice. Exhibition 1931 Paris, No. 131. Exhibition 1931 New York, No. 71. Pages 49, 50, 64, 71, 83, 101, 120, 132, 133, 179, 182, 197. Illustration, page 339.

1928

169. Game of Checkers. 21″ x 28¾″. Collection Stephen C. Clark, New York. Exhibition 1931 Paris, No. 135. Pages 84, 104.

170. Gladioli. 61″ x 39⅜″. Collection Alphonse Kann, Saint-Germain-en-Laye, France. Exhibition 1931 Paris, No. 137. Page 139.

171. Harmony in Yellow. 34⅝″ x 34⅝″. Collection Henri-Matisse, Paris–Nice. Exhibition 1931 Paris, No. 136. Exhibition 1931 New York, No. 74. Pages 49, 103, 115, 126, 196.

172. Odalisque with Armchair. 25½″ x 31⅞″. Collection Henri-Matisse, Paris–Nice. Exhibition 1931 Paris, No. 134. Pages 26, 67, 84, 148, 196, 197. Illustration, page 341.

173. Sideboard. 28¾″ x 36¼″. Luxembourg Museum, Paris. Exhibition 1931 Paris, No. 138. Exhibition 1931 New York, No. 75. Pages 49, 50, 51, 52, 86, 94, 103, 126, 132, 146, 154, 173, 194, 368. Illustration, page 342.

1929

174. Odalisque with Gray Trousers. 21¼″ x 25½″. Private collection, Paris. Exhibition 1931 Paris, No. 139. Pages 33, 39, 57, 62, 72, 93, 118, 127, 138, 155, 164, 173, 196.

NO.

175. Tattooed Odalisque. 22" x 18⅛". Collection Henri-Matisse, Paris–Nice. Exhibition 1931 Paris, No. 140. Exhibition 1931 New York, No. 77. Pages 32, 33, 35, 36, 67, 108, 109, 113, 119, 144, 146, 174, 196, 197. Illustration, page 343.

176. Yellow Hat. 25⅝" x 17¾". Collection Henri-Matisse, Paris–Nice. Exhibition 1931 Paris, No. 141. Exhibition 1931 New York, No. 78. Pages 72, 157, 179, 182. Illustration, page 345.

(B) BLACK–AND–WHITE WORK BY MATISSE

1905

200. Landscape. (Collioure.) Pen-and-ink. 12" x 18". Barnes Foundation No. 757. Page 65. Illustration, page 347.

1914

201. Portrait of Miss Landsberg. Pencil. 20¼" x 16¾". Collection Henri-Matisse, Paris–Nice. Exhibition 1931 New York, No. 86. Page 187.

1923

202. Arabesque. Lithograph, plate No. 58. 21⅝" x 13". Collection Henri-Matisse, Paris–Nice. Pages 65, 187. Illustration, page 348.

203. Figure (Torso Nude) Reflected in Mirror. Lithograph, plate No. 43. 15½" x 11⅜". Collection Henri-Matisse, Paris–Nice. Page 186. Illustration, page 349.

1924

204. Interior, Woman and Still-Life. Lithograph, plate No. 60. 20⅞" x 13⅜". Collection Henri-Matisse, Paris–Nice. Page 187. Illustration, page 350.

205. Veiled Odalisque. Lithograph, plate No. 70. 24¾" x 18½". Collection Henri-Matisse, Paris–Nice. Exhibition 1930 Berlin, No. 214. Exhibition 1931 New York, No. 139. Pages 185, 186.

1925

206. Seated Nude. Stumping chalk. 24⅝″ x 18⅞″. Collection Henri-Matisse, Paris–Nice. Page 185. Illustration, page 351.

1927

207. Decorative Figure (Flowered Background). Sketch for No. 166. Charcoal. 24¾″ x 18½″. Collection Henri-Matisse, Paris–Nice. Page 185.

1928

208. French Window. Charcoal. 24¾″ x 18¾″. Collection Henri-Matisse, Paris–Nice. Exhibition 1931 New York, No. 104. Page 185.

209. Persian Woman with Cross. Lithograph, plate No. 130. 21⅝″ x 13″. Collection Henri-Matisse, Paris–Nice. Pages 61, 187. Illustration, page 352.

210. Reclining Nude. Lithograph, plate No. 120. 21⅝″ x 17¾″. Collection Henri-Matisse, Paris–Nice. Pages 185, 186, 187.

1929

211. Sleeping Girl. Etching, plate No. 89. 9⅝″ x 6⅞″. Collection Henri-Matisse, Paris–Nice. Exhibition 1930 Berlin, No. 171. Page 187.

212. Girl with Draped Headdress. Pencil. 22″ x 15″. Collection Henri-Matisse, Paris–Nice. Exhibition 1931 New York, No. 108. Page 187. Illustration, page 353.

213. Woman with Dog. Etching, plate No. 85. 6⅞″ x 9⅝″. Collection Henri-Matisse, Paris–Nice. Exhibition 1930 Berlin, No. 170. Page 187.

214. Woman with Parrots. Etching, plate No. 180. 6⅞″ x 9½″. Collection Burton Emmett, New York. Exhibition 1931 New York, No. 129. Page 187.

1930

215. Reclining Figure. Pencil. 10¾″ x 21″. Collection Henri-Matisse, Paris–Nice. Exhibition 1931 New York, No. 111. Page 186. Illustration, page 354.

1931

216. **Figure on Divan.** Pen-and-ink. 11⅛" x 15". Collection Henri-Matisse, Paris–Nice. Exhibition 1931 New York, No. 112. Pages 61, 67, 186. Illustration, page 356.
217. **Figure on Divan (Front View).** Pen-and-ink. 11" x 15⅜". Collection Henri-Matisse, Paris–Nice. Pages 186, 187. Illustration, page 357.
218. **Girl with Goldfish.** Etching. 3½" x 4¾". Collection Albert Nulty, Narberth, Pa., U. S. A. Page 187. Illustration, page 355.
219. **Nude.** Pencil. 18⅞" x 13". Collection Henri-Matisse, Paris–Nice. Page 186. Illustration, page 358.

1932

220. **Afternoon of a Faun.** Engraving. 13" x 9⅞". (From "Stéphane Mallarmé—Poésies," Albert Skira & Co., Lausanne.) Barnes Foundation No. 1092. Page 187. Illustration, page 361.
221. **Two Figures.** Engraving. 13" x 9⅞". (From "Stéphane Mallarmé—Poésies," Albert Skira & Co., Lausanne.) Barnes Foundation No. 1093. Pages 61, 187. Illustration, page 360.
222. **Two Nymphs.** Engraving. 13" x 9⅞". (Page from "Stéphane Mallarmé—Poésies," Albert Skira & Co., Lausanne.) Barnes Foundation No. 1094. Page 61. Illustration, page 359.
223. **Decorations.** Preliminary sketch for Barnes Foundation murals. 11' 8½" x 45' 2¾". Illustration, page 362.

(C) MISCELLANEOUS WORKS OF ART

300. **Greek Sculpture,** Elgin Marbles, circa Vth century B.C. "Ilissos(?)" from West pediment of Parthenon, "Theseus" (so called) or "Dionysos" from East pediment of Parthenon, "Three Fates (?)" from East pediment of Parthenon. British Museum A, D, K, L, M. Pages 71, 132.
301. **Greek Vases,** IVth and Vth centuries B.C., numerous examples in Metropolitan Museum of Art, New York; British Museum; and Barnes Foundation. Pages 71, 132.
302. **Egyptian Frescoes,** numerous examples in Metropolitan Museum of Art, New York; and British Museum. Pages 71, 132.

NO.

303. Egypto-Roman Funeral Painting "Portrait of a Woman," IId century, A.D. Collection Sambon, Paris. Byzantine Exhibition 1931 Paris, No. 684bis. Page 72.

304. Egypto-Roman Funeral Painting "Portrait of a Young Man," IId–IIId centuries A.D., from mummy discovered in a cemetery at Hawara in the Fayum, Egypt. National Gallery, London, No. 1264. Page 71. Illustration, page 256.

305. Egypto-Roman Funeral Painting "Portrait of a Young Woman," IId–IIId centuries A.D., from mummy discovered in a cemetery at Hawara in the Fayum, Egypt. National Gallery, London, No. 1260. Page 71. Illustration, page 234.

306. Egyptian Textile, IVth century A.D. Collection Forrer, Strassburg. Page 70.

307. Egyptian Textile "Fragment of linen embroidered," IVth–Vth centuries A.D. Metropolitan Museum of Art, New York, Acc. No. 10.130.1076 (8345G). Page 70. Illustration, page 238.

308. Egyptian Textile "Linen hanging, with tapestry inserts," Vth century A.D. Metropolitan Museum of Art, New York, Acc. No. 12.182.45 (14137G). Page 70. Illustration, page 248.

309. Egyptian Textiles "Mythological Scenes," polychrome tapestry medallions. IVth and Vth centuries A.D. Louvre. Byzantine Exhibition 1931 Paris, No. 173. Page 71.

309a. Egyptian Textiles, VIIIth century A.D. Bourse Museum, Lyons, Nos. 248, 250. Page 72.

310. Egyptian Textiles. Collection Forrer, Strassburg. Page 56.

311. Egyptian Textiles. Collection Sambon, Paris. Pages 56, 71.

312. Hindu Sculpture "Figure" (Kushan Empire) IIId–IVth centuries. Barnes Foundation. Pages 70, 423. Illustration, page 316.

313. Mosaic fragment "Bust of Spring," from pavement of Roman Villa at Halicarnassos (Room B). British Museum No. 39 (new catalogue No. 51C*). Pages 69, 70, 129. Illustration, page 234.

314. Mosaic fragment "Fish," rosette from corridor of Roman Villa at Halicarnassos. British Museum new catalogue No. 54F. Page 129.

315. Mosaic fragment "Dionysos with Panther," late Roman, from Halicarnassos. British Museum No. 48 (new catalogue No. 54C). Page 128.

* The new numbers given in this and other references are those which will appear in the forthcoming catalogue of the British Museum. They were obtained from the galley-proof through the courtesy of the officials of that institution.

316. Mosaic fragment "Head," IXth century, from the Abside of St. Ambrose, Milan. Castello Sforzesco Museum, Milan. Byzantine Exhibition 1931 Paris, No. 634. Page 69.

317. Mosaic fragments, Byzantine, from Kabr-Hiram near Tyre, Phœnicia (from the church of St. Christopher). Louvre No. 2230. Pages 70, 423.

318. Mosaic fragments "Hunting Scenes," from late Roman pavement, Carthage, VIth century A.D. British Museum Nos. 1, 3, 6 (new catalogue Nos. 57A, 57C, 57F). Page 69.

319. Mosaic fragments "Hunting Scenes," from late Roman pavement, Carthage, VIth century A.D. British Museum Nos. 3, 5 (new catalogue Nos. 57C, 57E). Pages 69, 129.

320. Mosaic fragment "Meleager," from pavement of Roman Villa at Halicarnassos (Room B) IIId century A.D. British Museum No. 35 (new catalogue No. 51A). Pages 70, 128. Illustration, page 238.

321. Mosaic fragment "Atalanta," from pavement of Roman Villa at Halicarnassos (Room B) IIId century A.D. British Museum No. 36 (new catalogue No. 51B). Pages 70, 128.

322. Mosaic Murals, VIth century. Basilica of S. Vitale, Ravenna. Page 56.

323. Mosaic "Lady in Waiting to the Empress Theodora," detail from VIth century mosaic murals of the Basilica of S. Vitale, Ravenna. Illustration, page 256.

324. Byzantine Paintings, XIIIth and XIVth centuries. Siena Academy and Barcelona Museum. Pages 70, 128, 423.

325. Byzantine Medal "Heads," date unknown. Collection Henri-Matisse, Paris–Nice. Page 70. Illustration, page 256.

326. Florentine Painting "The Magdalen," detail from altarpiece "The Magdalen and Scenes from her Life," unknown Italian master, XIIIth century. Florence Academy No. 8466. Page 71. Illustration, page 256.

326a. Fra Filippo Lippi (circa 1406–1469) "Virgin Adoring Child." Uffizi No. 8353. Page 390.

327. Negro Sculpture "Head," Gabun, Pahouins, Xth century. Barnes Foundation. Page 70. Illustration, page 273.

328. Negro Sculpture "Figure," Ivory Coast, XIIIth–XIVth centuries. Barnes Foundation. Pages 70, 423. Illustration, page 316.

329. Negro Sculpture "Figure," Guinea, XVth century. Barnes Foundation. Page 70.

452 DATA ON WORKS OF ART MENTIONED

NO.

330. Chinese Fresco "Portrait of a Priest," XIVth century (?). British Museum. Page 56.

331. Chinese Painting "Flock of Waterfowls by a Fall," by Chen-Tzuho (Chinshikwa), Ming dynasty, "Masterpieces Selected from the Fine Arts of the Far East," edited by Mikio Wada, plate CXLIV, volume X. British Museum. Page 64.

332. Chinese Painting "Musa Basho" by Ko-Shihhuang (Kashiko), Ming dynasty, "Masterpieces Selected from the Fine Arts of the Far East," edited by Mikio Wada, plate CXLVIII, volume X. British Museum. Page 65.

333. Chinese Painting "Portrait," Ming dynasty, XVth century. Barnes Foundation No. 80. Page 62.

334. Chinese Painting "The Sixth Patriarch of the Zen Sect," by Liang Kai (Ryō Kai), Southern Sung dynasty, "Masterpieces Selected from the Fine Arts of the Far East," edited by Shiichi Tajima, plates LXVII and LXVIII, volume IX. British Museum. Page 65.

335. Chinese Painting "Zen-Zai Do-Ji," artist unknown, Southern Sung dynasty, "Masterpieces Selected from the Fine Arts of the Far East," edited by Shiichi Tajima, plates LXXVII and LXXVIII, volume IX. British Museum. Page 65.

335a. Chinese Painting "Interior Scene," Ming dynasty, XVIth century. Barnes Foundation No. 1087. Page 145.

336. Chinese Painting (fan) "Landscape," XVIIIth century. Barnes Foundation No. 310. Page 65. Illustration, page 346.

337. Persian Drawing. British Museum No. 1930–11–12–01. Page 67.

338. Persian Miniature, XVth century. Barnes Foundation No. 753. Page 56.

339. Persian Miniature, XVIth century. Barnes Foundation No. 752. Pages 55, 56.

340. Persian Miniature, XVIth century. Barnes Foundation No. 756. Page 56.

341. Persian Textile, XVIth century. Bourse Museum, Lyons, No. 564. Page 67.

342. Persian Textiles. Bourse Museum, Lyons. Page 56.

343. Persian, Syrian and Turkish Tiles, XVth, XVIth and XVIIth centuries. Metropolitan Museum of Art, New York; and Louvre. Page 67.

344. Syrian Tile, early XVIIth century. Metropolitan Museum of Art, New York, No. 22.185.13 (51666G). Illustration, page 282.

345. **Turkish Asia-Minor Tile,** beginning of XVIIth century. Metropolitan Museum of Art, New York, No. 02.5.91 (51286G). Illustration, page 258.

346. **Hindu-Persian Miniature** "Interior Scene," XVIth century. Barnes Foundation No. 755. Pages 56, 396. Illustration, page 270.

347. **Hindu-Persian Miniature** "Princes of the House of Tīmūr," circa 1550, by Mīr Sayyid Alī or Abdus Samad (the portraits of Akbar, Jahānjīr and Shāh Jahān—in the pavilion opposite Humāyūn—were added by an Indian artist circa 1622). British Museum. Pages 56, 62.

348. **Hindu-Persian Miniature** "Sultan Mohammad and Mīrān Shād," detail of "Princes of the House of Tīmūr," circa 1550, by Mīr Sayyid Alī or Abdus Samad. British Museum. Illustration, page 324.

349. **Indian Drawing.** British Museum No. 1925–4–30–04 in book 31 of "Indian Drawings." Page 72.

350. **Indian Drawing.** British Museum No. 1926–3–16–01. Page 72.

351. **Indian Painting** (Mughal school of miniaturists) "Portrait of Ja'far Beg (Āsaf Khān), Minister of Shāh Jahān," by Hūnhār, XVIIth century. British Museum. (See also numerous other similar types of Mughal portraiture in British Museum and Louvre.) Pages 72, 145, 404.

352. **Armenian Miniatures.** Collection Gachet, Auvers, France. Page 72.

353. **Tintoretto** (1518–1594) "Origin of the Milky Way." National Gallery, London, No. 1313. Page 155.

354. **Tintoretto** "Portrait of a Man." Barnes Foundation No. 836. Page 157.

355. **Velásquez** (1599–1660) "Infanta Doña Margareta." Prado No. 1192. Page 38.

356. **Velásquez** "Menippus." Prado No. 1207. Pages 145, 157.

357. **New Mexican Santo** "Madonna of the Guadalupe," XVIIIth century. Barnes Foundation No. 1017. Page 157.

358. **Japanese Early Prints,** several examples in Guimet Museum, Paris. Page 60.

358a. **Japanese Print** "A Pleasure-Party Landing from a Boat" by Kiyonaga. British Museum. Page 403.

359. **Japanese Print** "Autumn," by Kunisada (1810–1865). British Museum No. 1921–2–17–03. Page 63.

DATA ON WORKS OF ART MENTIONED 455

NO.
380. Japanese Print by Yoshi Tsuya. Barnes Foundation No. 1115. Pages 61, 62, 63. Illustration, page 328.
381. Japanese Print by Yoshi Tsuya. Barnes Foundation No. 1116. Page 62. Illustration, page 282.
382. Japanese Print by Yoshi Tsuya. Barnes Foundation No. 1117. Page 38.
383. Japanese Print by Yoshi Tsuya. Barnes Foundation No. 1118. Page 62.
384. Delacroix (1798–1863) "Triumph of St. Michael." Barnes Foundation No. 32. Page 128.
385. Daumier (1810–1879) "The Ribalds." Barnes Foundation No. 22. Page 128.
386. Daumier "Water Carrier." Barnes Foundation No. 127. Page 128.
387. Manet (1832–1883) "Boy with Fife." Louvre No. 173. Pages 88, 145, 157.
388. Manet "Dead Toreador." Collection Widener, Elkins Park, Pa., U. S. A. Pages 145, 157.
389. Manet "Head of Boy." Barnes Foundation No. 162. Illustration, page 273.
390. Manet "Men Tarring Boat." Barnes Foundation No. 166. Page 88.
391. Manet "Portrait of Emile Zola." Louvre. Pages 58, 59.
392. Manet "Woman in Landscape." Barnes Foundation No. 820. Page 59.
393. Manet "Woman with Fans (Nina de Callias)." Louvre. Pages 58, 59, 88.
394. Whistler (1834–1903) "In the Studio." Art Institute, Chicago, No. 433. Page 58.
395. Whistler "Symphony in White, No. 2." National Gallery, London, No. 3418. Page 58.
396. Degas (1834–1917) "After the Bath." Barnes Foundation No. 290. Page 56.
397. Degas "Dancers with Hair in Braids." Barnes Foundation No. 143. Page 58.
398. Degas "Four Dancers on Stage." Barnes Foundation No. 307. Page 56.
399. Degas "Group of Dancers." Barnes Foundation No. 213. Page 58.
400. Degas "Women Combing their Hair." Collection Madame H. Lerolle, Paris. Page 58.

458 DATA ON WORKS OF ART MENTIONED

INDEX*

Academicism
  in black-and-white work, 186
  in composition, drawing, modeling,
    208
  in plastic form (general), 8–9, 11–13
Æsthetic experience
  in art, 1–3
  in ordinary life, 1
Arabesque, 39, 61, 65, 132–133, 171, 186
  variation upon, 170
Area-line, 70, 90–91, 132–133, 135
Armenian miniatures, influence of, 72
Art in Painting, The, A. C. Barnes, 45,
  214
Art, roots of, 1–2

Bach, 219, 221
Background
  as sheetlike setting, 48, 157–158
  in composition, 25–26, 56, 156–158,
    181–182
  stripes and bands in, 38–40
Bands and stripes
  see Stripes and bands
Banner (flag), effect of, 37, 39
Bare canvas
  as light, 93–94, 129
  as space, 147
  in drawing, 81, 82, 93–94
  in modeling, 129
  mechanical use of, 209
  thematic variation on, 164
Barnes, A. C., *The Art in Painting*, 45,
  214
Beethoven, 162, 219, 221
Binyon, Laurence, 55 (footnote)
Biographical sketch, 365–368
Black-and-white work, 185–187
Black, use of, 60–61, 104
Blue Still-Life (*33*), analysis, 373–379
Blue Villa (*72*), analysis, 404–407
Brahms, 162
Brush strokes, 45–46, 47, 50, 64, 92,
  132, 147

Byzantine tradition, influence of, 68–71
  in color-pattern, 107
  in drawing, 48, 68–70
  in line, 68, 132, 180
  in portraiture, 179
  in stripes and bands, 69
  see also Oriental tradition (general)

Cartouche (Oriental), effect of, 57
Cézanne
  compared with Matisse, 81, 128–129,
    157, 190, 206
  influence of, 44, 51–54, 81–82, 127,
    128, 144–145, 179, 180, 181, 191,
    192, 193–194
Chardin
  compared with Matisse, 205
  influence of, 44, 144, 191
Chinese tradition, influence of, 64–66
  in color, 65–66
  in decorative design, 56
  in light, 65, 138
  in line, 57, 65
  in space, 144
  in technique, 64
  see also Oriental tradition (general)
Color
  -areas, 101, 106–107
  black, use of, 60–61, 104
  chapter on, 100–121
  Chinese influence in, 65–66
  -chords, 25, 106
  -compartments, 55, 81, 101, 108–109
  compositional function of, 25–26, 108–
    109, 116–121, and *passim*
  -contrast, 25–26, 102–105, 166–167
  decorative function of, *see* chapters
    *Color, Decoration and Decorative
    Design, passim*
  Egyptian influence in, 112
  experiments in, 109–111, 114
  expressive function of, 112, 114–116
  impressionistic influence in, 46–47
  in drawing, 88–89

* The arrangement of the preceding section—Data on Works of Art Mentioned—makes it
serve as a supplementary index.

459